THE BOOK BEAUTIFUL

ALSO BY THE AUTHOR

The Groaning Shelf and Other Instances of Book Love

The Book Hunters of Katpadi: A Bibliomystery

PRADEEP SEBASTIAN

The Book Beautiful

A Memoir of Collecting
Rare and Fine Books

hachette
INDIA

First published in 2023 by Hachette India
(Registered name: Hachette Book Publishing India Pvt. Ltd)
An Hachette UK company
www.hachetteindia.com

1

Hardback ISBN 978-93-93701-42-8
Ebook ISBN 978-93-93701-43-5
Limited edition ISBN 978-93-93701-54-1

Hachette Book Publishing India Pvt. Ltd
4th & 5th Floors, Corporate Centre,
Plot No. 94, Sector 44, Gurugram 122003, India

Typeset in ITC Galliard Pro 11/15
by R. Ajith Kumar, New Delhi

Printed and bound in India
by Manipal Technologies Limited

MIX
Paper from responsible sources
FSC™ C043100
FSC
www.fsc.org

To Thomas Abraham,
who knows books, loves bookshops, embraces readers
and is the bibliophile-publisher every writer wishes for.

I wandered by chance into the enchanted garden of fine printing and have remained captive ever since. The mysterious beauty that confronts the beholder has so insinuated itself into my imagination that I find no avenue of escape – and, to be sure, would not wish one.

– **Norman H. Strouse**, *The Lengthened Shadow*

Sometimes I have to confess that I feel like Sir Thomas when I see a beautifully illuminated manuscript and I am driven after sleepless nights to pay a silly price. Oh bibliomania!

– **H.P. Kraus**, *A Rare Book Saga*

My books are the great joy of my life.

– **Sir William Boothby**, 17th-century bibliophile

CONTENTS

PART ONE

COLLECTING
A Memoir

THE ONLINE ANTIQUARIAN

How (and Where) It All Began

It was, I think, in 2015 that I began collecting rare and fine books in a serious way. Though a bibliophile all my life, I'd never felt the temptation to become a book collector; rather, I was content to look fondly on, and indulgently cheer, the bibliomania of others while safely remaining in the wings. That changed when I began to come across books the likes of which I had never seen or handled before: books printed on a handpress from beautiful metal type immaculately pressed into dampened handmade paper, books where the illustrations were hand-coloured or wood-engraved, manuscripts that were calligraphically written out (not printed) in an exquisite scribal hand and finally, most ravishing of all, illuminated manuscripts – medieval and modern – that were hand-painted in burnished gold and colours.

And, improbably enough, for a bibliophile who had venerated bookshops all his life, the full flowering of my bibliophilia unfolded on the internet through the multiple online listings of rare book dealers and auction houses every day – sometimes two or three times a day, chasing my Want List of private press books and illuminated manuscripts. As soon as one want was fulfilled, I would obsessively chase the next, so that I could go book hunting again – online. This was, fascinatingly enough as I discovered, a more efficient, sophisticated, and rewarding way of collecting books than hunting in physical bookshops.

At just a tap or a click of any one of your digital devices, the inventory (and the attention) of nearly every rare book dealer, auction saleroom, and antiquarian book fair in the world lay open before you. And when you're in India, a place with few antiquarian bookshops and auction houses, this is not just the best way to collect, it's the *only* way to collect.

On a sultry morning in March 2019 I woke up early, unable to sleep from the Bengaluru heat, and turned on my laptop to check my email. Almost at once an email from AbeBooks floated into my inbox – it was one of those familiar AbeBooks alerts for a Want-Match notification: 'AbeBooks has found the books you want'. Advanced Book Exchange, or ABE, is a widely used online marketplace for second-hand and rare books, listing the inventory of thousands of antiquarian dealers around the world.

I was already prepared to quickly dismiss or even delete the email since these come in several times daily alerting you to the possibility that a new listing from an antiquarian seller could contain a book you have been searching for. Often, though, while the new listing is related to the Want List you've created on ABE, it isn't exactly the thing you had hoped it would be.

That humid morning, it was perhaps 5 a.m., a shiver ran through me as I opened the alert: a book I had been hunting for over ten years had just been listed – *Gossip About Book Collecting* by William Loring Andrews. This copy was one of the twenty-nine printed on Imperial Japan paper with the plates extra hand-coloured and gilded. While the edition on Holland paper is also scarce, this one on a finer paper had all but disappeared from the market.

I had come to admire Andrews as a collector, a bibliophile-writer, and a connoisseur of fine bookmaking. He had been one of the founders in 1884 of the Grolier Club, a society of scholar-collectors, and the author of several finely printed books on bibliophily. His books, done in small editions, are sought after for their charming, infectious views on collecting, their deep bibliophilic knowledge of rare and fine books, and the beautiful illustrations that accompany the text – etchings, engravings, and colour plates (some heightened in gold).

I felt an immediate kinship with him when he wrote the following in *Gossip About Book Collecting*: 'I am so tender hearted towards anything that bears the semblance of a fine or rare book that I have yielded to the blandishments of all sorts and kinds.'

I had, over the years, managed to find some of his scarcer productions: *Jean Grolier: Some Account of His*

Life (1892), *Among My Books* (1894, privately printed in an edition of just fifty copies), and *A Choice Collection of Books from the Aldine Presses* (1885). But *Gossip About Book Collecting* (1900), a memoir of collecting and collectors done in two volumes, had continued to elude me in its smaller limitation on Japan paper. The only other time I had seen a copy of it in the market had been in 2010, and I had foolishly let it go, feeling it had been priced too dearly. My hankering for a copy in this very limited edition wasn't for snobbish, oneupmanship reasons – rarity for rarity's sake has never interested me; it was because Andrews had the plates in these Japan paper copies further embellished in gold leaf, and that was irresistible to me.

I hadn't a minute to waste now – if I didn't put the order through in the next couple of seconds, it could get away from me for a second time. The listing is open to millions of ABE browsers around the world, and anyone anywhere could have chanced upon it. More to the point, other collectors who have also had this title on their ABE Want List would have been similarly alerted.

With my hands a little unsteady from the strained excitement of a find, I put the order through as fast as I could. Instantly, an automated email from ABE flew into my inbox: 'Order received'. While that's true for most books you order, it can become wishful thinking for scarce titles, because there's always the possibility that the copy may have already sold since booksellers and bookshops list the same copy on multiple online platforms. For instance, this copy could have already been sold on Biblio (the other frequently used online booksite) and not taken off the ABE listing by the seller. Also, many physical, open bookstores list their stock online, and someone could have just bought that same copy in the bookshop and walked off, while it would still show as available on ABE!

In this case, I was sure I would soon get an email from either the bookseller directly or from ABE saying, 'Sorry this book is no longer available, search AbeBooks for other copies'.

Good luck finding another copy of *Gossip About Book Collecting* in its deluxe issue anytime soon! Ten years is all I wanted to wait. I waited impatiently for some word of confirmation as I set about doing other things that morning and, a couple of hours later, was elated to see an email from the bookseller not only confirming my order but also informing me that the book had been shipped to me, with a tracking number for the shipment. I've described this acquisition in some detail to illustrate what a fantastic tool Want-Match alerts are to collecting online, whether it is from ABE, or from *via*Libri or Rare Book Hub, the two other widely used rare book search engines.

However, I soon discovered that a taste of quick success in the rare book chase doesn't quench your thirst for collecting but only fuels it. Petrarch, the venerable fourteenth-century collector, said that the search for rare books is like other searches: 'success only sharpens the edge of desire'.

It all began when I chanced on a heart-stopping private press book listed on the website of the antiquarian bookseller Phillip J. Pirages Fine Books and Manuscripts that aroused in me a desire to collect assiduously. It was the *Ashendene Press Bibliography*, and though I could only look at it and not examine it in my hand, I felt ready to buy it remotely, online. The price was in four figures and yet I was eager to acquire it. What had led to this? Prior to this, there had been some false starts, when I'd tried my hand at collecting modern first editions – some even signed or inscribed – of my favourite books or authors, but it just hadn't taken.

Once the signed first edition you ordered arrives, and you take in with satisfaction that it is indeed a first impression, you note that it has a fine (if not pristine) original dust jacket, and feel that little frisson at seeing the manuscript hand of a favourite writer on the flyleaf of a copy you now own, you put it away with a contented sigh. And that was that – there didn't seem to be much more to collecting first editions than rarity, chronological priority, and condition, and it soon lost its charm for me. It wasn't that I didn't get the mystique of first editions, it's just that they were never able to engage me with any intensity – an intensity and depth that I finally found with fine press books. Fine press books (also called private press books) are printed with letterpress, that is, from metal type impressed into handmade paper.

It was at the Oak Knoll Fest, a fine press book fair (yes, private press books have their own fair!), in 2012 that I first had a taste of the tactile beauty and craft of finely printed letterpress books. Turning the pages of these books, I could feel the bite of metal type incised into the paper – what a difference it made! I was experiencing for the first time what finely printed books looked and felt like.

The experience was satisfyingly tactile, sensuous, and pleasurable even before I'd started to read the text they held.

If the presswork is sharp, a fine typeface pleasingly proportioned on the page with wide margins, it doubles the pleasure of the text. To touch those creamy, textured papers, feel the bite of type as you run your finger gently over the page, and to gaze on the handsomeness of it all is thrilling.

By the time I spotted the *Ashendene Press Bibliography* – that gorgeous fine press book in the inventory of a rare book dealer a couple of years later – I had already begun buying some choice fine press books that had deepened my desire for them, and had persuaded me to take my collecting up a notch. The *Ashendene* copy on sale seemed tailor-made to be that high spot to kickstart my collecting focus of finely printed books on the arts of the book.

A Descriptive Bibliography of the Books Printed at the Ashendene Press, completed in 1935, is considered to be one of the ten great treasures among private press books, and the model for all fine press bibliographies that came after it. It is printed from hand-set metal type on dampened handmade paper on a handpress, with several wood engravings impressed directly from the woodblock, and the calligraphic initials hand-coloured in red, blue, and green. A beautiful book, a stunning book, a book I couldn't resist even at its perilous four figure price.

I recall clearly that after I bought it (without dithering in the slightest) I had felt no buyer's remorse, no sinking feeling that I may have made a costly mistake. Rather, I was elated, even thrilled, that I had had the good sense to buy it, cost be damned. After the book arrived – an impressive folio in russet morocco – I found myself poring over the *Ashendene*. It confirmed all my first feelings for it – the *Ashendene* was just the book I had been longing for. Here, at last, I could see and *feel* the craftsmanship in fine bookmaking. And what's more, my pleasure was not all just in its craft: I had enjoyed the text – a commentary by its printer, St. John Hornby, on how he'd printed each book – to the hilt. Hornby, the owner of this hobby press, had printed this book all by himself, with the assistance of a pressman, and the lettering artist Graily Hewitt who had hand-embellished the calligraphic initials in each copy.

What I can, or would like to tell you is this: until you've known the sensual, typographic beauty of a finely printed letterpress book, you've never really handled or owned a *real* book.

'Put simply', said typographer Robert Bringhurst, 'the difference between the two technologies is this: letterpress is printing, offset is a picture of printing.'

A year into collecting fine press books it hit me one day why I'd found them so beautiful, so arresting. Apart from their palpable pleasures, one other element, subtle and graceful, casts the first spell – the letterforms, the typographic shape of alphabets. Until fine press books came into my life, I had never realized the extent to which I had cared for, and had been moved by, the beauty, legibility, and elegance of letterforms.

If the idea of a private or fine press is unfamiliar to you – as it had been to me for many years – it would be useful to look briefly at how it all started. Modern fine printing begins with William Morris and his Kelmscott

Press in 1891. More precisely, Morris *revived* the craft of fine bookmaking when he set out to print books at the close of the nineteenth century exactly in the way the master printers of the fifteenth and sixteenth centuries had. What exactly did Morris bring back to books with the way they were printed at the Kelmscott Press?

In a nutshell, he revived printing on a handpress, on dampened handmade paper, using types cut to his own design. Apart from designing the types for his press, he designed and hand drew initials, borders and ornaments to decorate the text. 'I began printing books,' wrote Morris, 'with the hope of producing some which would have a definite claim to beauty.'

Morris, inspired by the example of the beautiful presswork of the early printers and typographers, as well as the calligraphic and decorative work in medieval manuscripts, dreamt of printing books privately where he could bring back the glorious craft and beauty he beheld in the fine incunabula and illuminated manuscripts he owned. Morris was so many things – designer, architect, socialist, novelist, poet – but he was also a collector, a calligrapher, and a manuscript illuminator. Before he began the Kelmscott Press, he calligraphed and illuminated manuscripts by hand.

The books from the Kelmscott Press galvanized the making of fine books again, inspiring other private presses – Doves Press, Vale Press, Essex House Press, Gregynog Press, Eragny Press, and of course the aforementioned Ashendene Press – to print books this way.

A thrill went through me at the realization that what I was experiencing through these modern fine press books were books as they had been first printed in the second half of the fifteenth century – pages printed on a handpress from finely designed letters made from movable metal type, the words incised into a laid paper that had been dampened to absorb the impression and ink from the type more satisfactorily. Private press books and the tradition of fine bookmaking they revived should be recognized, said bookdealer Colin Franklin, 'as a glory of modern art'.

It didn't take me long, then, to realize that I needed to go further back, to the very beginning of fine bookmaking – to manuscript making. It was when my collecting focus shifted from private press books to manuscript illumination that I turned into a proper antiquary. My interest went further back from the birth of the printed book in the fifteenth century to manuscript making from the sixth to the fourteenth century.

Nothing in the history of fine bookmaking compares to the beauty of illuminated and calligraphic manuscripts – not just those from the middle ages that were hand-painted in burnished gold, silver and colours, but even modern manuscripts done in the style of those medieval manuscripts, written out in a beautiful calligraphic hand, and illumined by hand in gold leaf and watercolours.

My highest pleasure came from seeking beautiful examples of Mughal and Persian manuscript leaves with decorations and miniatures. In *A Handbook of the Art of Illumination as Practised During the Middle Ages* (Bell and Daldy, 1866) the celebrated nineteenth-century draughtsman and illuminator Henry Shaw noted that eastern illuminated manuscripts 'display an amount of beauty and minuteness so truly wonderful as to surpass the effort of any European artist'. I was astonished at first to learn this, and subsequently when I began pursuing Indian,

Persian, and Ottoman manuscript leaves, I discovered – to my joy – that in the best examples of Islamic miniatures in gold and silver, this was indeed true.

Two of the finest leaves in my tiny collection of Islamic manuscripts contain four beautiful miniatures from the *Iskandernama*, an incomplete Persian manuscript from 1812. The text of the manuscript is divided vertically by a flowered strip, the effect is lovely, especially in those leaves containing miniatures done in colours and gold.

I acquired both leaves from an eBay auction where, surprisingly, I won them easily. Considering how alluring they were, I'd expected a long, stiff bidding war, but the auction went my way easily. I realized then that eastern manuscripts, however fine or beautiful, don't command the interest and prices western manuscripts do. As regrettable as this is, it meant collectors like me had a chance of acquiring at least a few of the more desirable Indo-Persian manuscript leaves. With my limited funds, I was the classic impecunious collector, so where western manuscripts and early printed books were concerned, acquiring an important incunabulum or an entire Book of Hours was out of the question. What I could afford to collect, then, were fragments and leaves from medieval and Renaissance manuscripts – I did better, however, with modern illuminated and calligraphed manuscripts. Though the price for each of these was no laughing matter, I found some fine examples of modern illumination and calligraphy, and was able to collect them in depth.

Modern fine printing is a large and diverse field, and to collect in depth the books from the great private presses – Kelmscott, Doves, Ashendene, Eragny,

Gregynog, Cranach, and Officina Bodoni – was not going to be possible for me, given my middle-class salary. Luckily, it didn't take me long to find my collecting focus; a line of collecting that didn't need deep pockets and which gave me pleasure and joy – finely printed books on the arts of the book, like papermaking, marbling, type and typography, bookbinding, wood engraving, press bibliographies, bookplates, memoirs, and accounts of fine press printers, bookdealers and collectors (you may recall that Colin Franklin once made a case for book collecting to be considered as one of the fine arts).

While collecting fine press books, paper is the first thing you look for. Or at least I did. I know for a lot of fine press collectors, those smooth Zerkall wove papers are acceptable as letterpress printing surfaces, but I prefer a laid or textured paper, whether handmade or mould-made. I began doggedly pursuing books, prospectuses, specimen pages, and keepsakes printed on these fine handmade and mould-made papers: Amalfi, Barcham Green, Arches, Twinrocker, Tovil, Fabriano, Rives, Umbria, Roma, Magnani, Ingress, Kelmscott handmade, Millbourn Lexpar, Johannot, Hahnemühle, Natsume, Goyu, Kochi and Hosho. When these papers are dampened for printing, they are particularly lovely to the touch.

Fine press books became the gateway for me to collect other forms of books and manuscripts – the extra illustrated book, the leaf book, emblem books, bookplate books, colour plate books, large paper copies, fore-edge painted books, original hand-drawn calligraphic manuscripts, and the one I ended up becoming the most besotted with, illuminated manuscripts.

This book, then, is about collecting fine books and manuscripts, with a particular focus on the book arts, as experienced by an impecunious collector who mainly book-hunts online – browsing, negotiating, and buying from rare book sellers on the internet. It's also about the thrill of the chase, the pursuit of the juiciest rare book bargain, the camaraderie of fellow collectors and the friendship of bookdealers. There are profiles of antiquarian dealers, fine press collectors, fine press printers, favourite writers on bibliophily, favourite books about collecting and dealing, and other 'taller' tales of my adventures in collecting. I try to recount or describe the two kinds of pleasures I found in all this – the pleasure of collecting and the pleasure fine books gave me. And I have to confess, like every collector before me has, that some of the most enjoyable moments are when you make a great find or locate a fabulous bargain.

Becoming a serious book collector involved a deep dive into the antiquarian world of bookdealers, auction houses, collectors, and bibliophile societies. My reading became consumed with press bibliographies, memoirs of dealers and collectors, and the history of book collecting and the antiquarian trade. What a thrill it was for a small-time collector like me from India to 'drop in' and buy – even if only virtually, and even if only something modest – from Quaritch, Maggs, Sotheran's, Francis Edwards and Bertram Rota. All antiquarian dealers who had only been names to me until then. Now, I was one of their customers in a long line of collectors through book collecting history, browsing their stock, speaking with bookshops over the phone or email, and getting a whiff of their bespoke service.

I learnt about book collecting by collecting, not having a mentor or fellow collector to direct me. And I took pleasure in such self-taught connoisseurship, as I waded deeper into the meadows of bibliophily. However, I would not have figured out things as quickly as I did without constantly looking up dealer descriptions and catalogues, which became critical in getting a hang of the rare book market. Finally, the rare book dealers themselves who shared with me their experience of how these fine books transacted through their hands, and the antiquarian book fairs I attended where I could compare notes. 'The dealer is at the heart of book collecting,' as rightly noted by Robert H. Taylor in his essay 'Of Dealers and Collectors' in *A Miscellany for Bibliophiles* (1979).

I became quite adept at playing the book-collecting game. I learnt the rules, and figured out soon enough what rules or codes you could bend or break and what you should stick by in order to collect ethically (just as dealers have to deal ethically). I picked up the skills necessary to ferret out bargains, and knew where and how to hunt for rare and fine books, particularly within my collecting focus.

This is what I suppose John Carter meant by 'connoisseurship' in his *Taste and Technique in Book-Collecting* (1948). 'Book collecting', he wrote rather mysteriously, 'is the orchid in the hothouse of connoisseurship.' Carter describes how connoisseurship flowers with experience. A fairly recent episode from my own collecting experience illustrates this. On an August afternoon in 2022, I spotted by sheer chance a new listing online – from a bookdealer entirely unknown to me – of an attractive Ethiopian manuscript leaf on parchment from a Coptic Bible with a large miniature painting depicting a scene from one of the gospels. The leaf was 14 x 11 inches, with the miniature itself measuring 11 x 9 inches painted in orange, gold, green, blue, and purple. On the other side of the leaf was the text, in Ge'ez script, written in red and black with minimal decoration.

It was a stunning leaf but it had one flaw – a corner of the leaf had darkened and shrunk, almost like it had been singed, though luckily not affecting the painted area. The asking price was $500 – I bought it straightaway, without deliberation. I knew enough by then to realize it would have – even with its flaws – sold for a much higher price had this come up for auction, probably in the range of $1,500 to $2,000, if not more. Also, what usually comes on the market – either in dealer catalogues or in auction listings – are smaller leaves, about 8 x 6 or 6 x 4 inches, usually written out and illuminated sometime in the late nineteenth or early twentieth century. The hammer prices these fall for are between $700 and $900. A large and lavish Coptic leaf like this one, on the other hand, usually indicated an earlier manuscript, possibly eighteenth century – a true rarity on the market, making what I paid an unbeatable price.

Connoisseurship in collecting is also about recognizing that what looks or feels like a high price (for something you are interested in from a dealer's listing) could well be a fair price. If I had not realized this right off, when I spotted the Coptic leaf listing, I would have passed on it, reasoning with myself that I could get it for less at some future auction. There have been and will continue to be several instances where a dealer's price will be more than fair, more competitively priced than the hammer price at an auction sale, and it is connoisseurship that pulls the trigger on such swift, sweet purchases.

My connoisseurship continued to deepen in other ways: in those areas, for instance, where I had collected widely and in depth, I even had a few opportunities to correct or supplement the catalogue descriptions of experienced dealers for some of their listings. It was quite a kick to see the description for a book revised and relisted with the bibliographical information I had passed on to a rare book dealer.

When accomplished and wealthy book collectors are asked to give a talk on collecting or write an introduction to a catalogue of their collection, they invariably begin on this condescending, disingenuous note: 'you don't need a lot of money to become a collector,' even though they've spent a fortune putting together their collection. I started out as an impecunious collector with every intention of remaining one, but after a certain point, you have to spend – if not a fortune, at least a sizeable sum plucked out of your savings.

What I can say, though, is that even collecting on a modest scale, you can put together an attractive and focused collection. I've been able to, for instance, bring into my collection all the fine press books dealing with the arts of book that I wanted to own, that I desired to have, and that I thought were important. Though a small scaled collection, it still reflects the craft of the book from its early beginnings to the present.

There are just a few things, maybe about a dozen books, that still continue to elude me, but that's a tantalizing, welcome feeling too – that the hunt goes on!

After my immersion into online antiquarian book collecting and dealing, I now feel very differently about physical bookshops, which no longer draw me like they once did. When you have at your fingertips, and just a few clicks away, access to the stock of thousands of antiquarian bookshops from every corner of the globe, the brick-and-mortar bookshop – whether just one very fine rare bookshop or even a city full of them – can feel severely limited in scope.

The hunt for rare, fine, and beautiful books so famously and variously recounted in the classic accounts of book collectors that have assembled their collection from visiting and buying from actual bookshops is decidedly more charming, hands-on, and immediate, but what I discovered to my surprise and joy is that book hunting online as you explore rare bookshops flung across the world can be just as immersive, stimulating, and perhaps more rewarding.

Getting online is only the start – the key that opens up the rare book world of collecting and dealing. Once you've begun speaking directly to the bookseller via email or phone, you can negotiate a deal, especially if the book is expensive. You – or the dealer – can propose a direct purchase.

There's always more hope that what you're looking

for will surface online. Though I hasten to add that this doesn't mean what's online is virtually infinite or boundless – if you browse long enough and hard enough, you'll discover that the truly rare, scarce, and desirable books are still hard to come by, or that they're beyond the price you are willing to pay. And that as endless as the listings seem, it's really only the inventory of those rare book dealers that stock your collecting focus that will concern you, the rest you can (mostly) ignore. Each collector can only know the market in their own collecting field or fields.

The best book search engine is *via*Libri, which combs through multiple online listings to match your search. Rare Book Hub, another search engine, specializes in bringing you auction listings, both upcoming as well as from past auctions. You don't make a purchase directly on these websites (as you do on ABE) but use them to search through the online second-hand and rare book market around the world. This is especially true of *via*Libri, which is 'the world's largest search engine for old, rare and secondhand books'. You can list your wants in the Wants Manager tab, and 'Libribot' will search the internet for listings that match your Wants, and issue similar email alerts.

Jim Hinck, founder and developer of *via*Libri, once pointed out how being able to collect online has ushered in another golden age of book collecting – or more radically, how book collecting 'has only just recently entered its golden age'. On his *via*Libri blog, he lists six factors that unequivocally demonstrates this:

Never have there been greater opportunities to find and purchase genuinely rare books from anywhere in the world.

Never have there been more powerful tools for researching and evaluating them.

Never were truly rare books so abundant and so easily identifiable in the market place.

Never again will they be so cheap.

Never have true bibliophiles had more possibilities for assembling unique and important collections, guided only by their own genius and passion.

Many such collections are already being formed.

I concur completely. My own experience bears this out. Though my collection is far from being important or unique, it has got to where it is now – a decent and interesting collection of fine books and manuscripts – because I could go book hunting anywhere in the world digitally.

Only late in the collecting game did I figure out that auctions are the collector's best chance to get the rare book you want at half its market or catalogue price. This hit me hard when a copy I had bought from a bookseller for $450 turned out to be the same copy that had sold at an auction only a few weeks earlier at $200. The dealer had bid for this book at the auction, won it, and marked it up. That's how the rare book business works. Auctions are not always the cheapest places to buy, but often the hammer price for a lot tends to be considerably less than how the same lot gets priced in the market. Since most auctions are online now, you can participate from wherever you are through your laptop or phone, and place bids; or you can simply enter a 'Max bid', and check how you fared after your lot has sold or once the auction is over.

Take, for instance, a fairly recent auction I placed a bid on in July 2022: Lot 391 from a small auction house in the UK that had come up as a Matchmaker alert from Rare Book Hub. Lot 391 was J.O. Westwood's *Palaeographia Sacra Pictoria* (William Smith, 1843) with fifty chromolithograph illuminated plates copied from medieval manuscripts. It was the first nineteenth-century book to successfully pull off plates in gold and colours that had been entirely printed without hand-embellishment, predating Henry Noel Humphreys' more famous work, *The Illuminated Books of the Middle Ages* (Longman, 1846–49). Before them, Henry Shaw, J.B. Silvestre, and Comte August de Bastard d'Estang had only partially used lithography for their illuminated plates, relying instead on hand-colouring and gilding *by hand* – particularly in the large paper copies – a far more beautiful and authentic way to show colour and illumination in facsimiles. But chromolithography being cheaper had fully taken over by the 1840s and Westwood had been the first to use this to beautiful effect in *Palaeographia Sacra Pictoria*. The book, especially in its 1843 first edition, had become scarce and expensive. The 1849 Henry Bohn edition is also becoming scarce, but it is not as pricey as the first where the plates are far more brilliant and pleasing, with bright colours and the gilt nicely burnished.

At the time of this auction listing the only copy of the 1843 edition with a bookdealer was $1,700. And the last auctioned copy that had come up on eBay, where I had been the underbidder, sold for $850. Though the Rare Book Hub alert must have been in my Matchmaker tab for a week or so, I only saw it on the morning of the auction. I scrambled to get myself registered via Invaluable, an online live auction platform, and place my bid. The auction was already underway by the time my registration was approved and the bid was accepted. I was willing to go up to £430, not including the 29 per cent buyer's premium fee plus the international shipping cost (which I was bracing for to be high since this volume is a heavy quarto) which would come on top of the hammer price. Lot 391 was knocked down to me for £130 – the only other bid for it had come from the auction floor, and my internet bid on Invaluable secured it for me easily.

I was left feeling quite chuffed at how lucky I had gotten – something many collectors will echo as their experience, too. The collectors and dealers who might have had an interest in this book had somehow missed seeing the listing and the only other interested bidder for it hadn't been very keen on it. If he or she had been as eager to have it as I had been, who knows what the price would have been driven up to? But though the hammer price does not reflect the additional buyer's premium fee and high shipping cost for this transaction, you can still see how much lower it is than what a bookdealer would have wanted or asked for it.

Earlier, sometime in 2020, I had had similar luck at auctions for large paper copies of Henry Shaw's *Illuminated*

Ornaments Selected from Manuscripts of the Middle Ages (1833) and *Dresses and Decorations of the Middle Ages* (1843) in which the plates are extra hand-finished and heightened in gold. Either collectors with an interest in nineteenth-century illuminated books missed spotting the lot or did not realize the copies were the scarce, coveted large paper issues.

But be prepared for some disappointment as well. Bidding at an auction makes you more vulnerable to losing, unlike a purchase from the stock of a bookseller or a dealer's catalogue, which – after a little negotiating – can still be yours. The prize at an auction has a way of slipping away from you. Sometimes you shrug it off, but more often the loss lingers. (Several emails in my inbox from auction houses have this subject line: 'You did not win this time'.) There's a way to beat this of course, like my friend who takes no chances by placing the highest possible bid and winning most of the time.

I didn't have funds like that at my disposal, so I would instead trawl through the listings of dealers daily, spending several hours in a day going through dozens of newly listed acquisitions on *via*Libri, using sharply honed keyword searches. This might strike you as a chore, but it was always engaging and addictive. I had to often tear myself away from such tenacious browsing to attend to real chores.

Gratifyingly, I discovered that being a book collector was far from the stereotypical, satirical picture of a fusty antiquarian or a foaming bibliomaniac (they were really the exceptions in book collecting history), rather the serious collector leans more towards being scholarly about their pursuits, deepening their knowledge of their collecting field, and emerging as an amateur bibliographer. The same goes for the dealer who, though a business person, is steeped in scholarship and bibliography. There is no other way out if you need to bibliographically recognize the books you want, the books your collectors want, and to write your catalogues.

All through the history of the antiquarian book trade, dealers, collectors, and rare book librarians have contributed vastly to the scholarship of rare and fine books.

As for ungovernable bibliomania, and the uncontrolled spending that erupts from it – well, those days are mostly gone. Though I suppose every collector at some point in their life will find themselves in the grip of a brief spell of what can feel like bibliomania – what this really is, is a collector at the height of their book hunt, a point in one's collecting life that peaks, suddenly finding things from your Want List that you never thought you'd ever find are now surfacing in the market – at higher prices than you ever wanted to pay, but never mind damn it! You can't let it get away again. It's not uncommon for collectors reflecting on this period of feverish collecting to say, 'You know, the only books I regret are the books I didn't buy.'

A BIBLIOGRAPHIC FIND

My first bargain coup, so sweet and satisfying, was itself a little primer on collecting because it revealed to me the mechanics of the rare book chase, and how to navigate the antiquarian book trade. The first lesson was that you can't do without a checklist or bibliography if you hope to make a find. As a bibliophile who'd only just turned into a typophile, I was naturally eager to learn all I could about modern fine printing and private press books, and one of the first fine presses I found myself drawn to was the Allen Press in California. From 1939 to 1984, Lewis and Dorothy Allen printed some of the best fine press books on a handpress.

I forked out $50 for a copy of their handsome bibliography – I rush to add that this was the 1985 facsimile edition put out by the Book Club of California, not the ravishing 1981 original printed by the Allens in a small edition of 140 copies on handmade paper, with original specimen leaves from the press. (That one is usually priced between $1,200 and $1,500, and is becoming increasingly scarce in the market.)

That July afternoon in 2013, gorging myself on the

book, I perked up at the end of Carey Bliss's essay 'An Appreciation of the Allen Press', where he mentions, almost in passing, that of all the lovely ephemera Lewis and Dorothy Allen had printed over the years, none was superior to the 1968 broadside keepsake titled 'In Bookbinding Then' that they had designed and printed for The Roxburghe Club, the San Francisco (not London) bibliophile society. It was particularly special for the use of a striking hand-coloured woodcut initial, the letter 'I,' engraved by Mallette Dean, and hand-coloured by Dorothy Lewis, that begins the text and runs all the way down to the bottom of the page.

While the bibliography at the end lists all the broadsides and keepsakes and prospectuses the Allen Press had printed including this keepsake, I was lucky to have chanced on Bliss singling this piece of ephemera out, or I would surely have missed noting that it was exceptional. In fact, the moment I read this, I put the bibliography down and checked AbeBooks. No copies listed. Naturally, it had become scarce. Desirable as it was, and printed in a small number, it's the kind of thing that gets snapped up the moment it is listed.

Scores of fine press collectors must have become familiar with Bliss's remarks since the publication of the bibliography in 1985, and yet here I was foolishly hopeful of finding it in 2013. Plus, the broadside was printed in 1968 by the Allens. What chance in hell did I have? I looked for old listings, auction records, and bookseller catalogues (often available to view years later as a PDF file on the internet) and after flicking past several Google pages, pulled up an auction copy, long sold, reaching a hammer price of $300.

[ALLEN PRESS]. Cobden-Sanderson, Thomas J. In Bookbinding Then. (1968). Folio broadside for the Roxburghe Club, with the initial 'I' engraved by Mallette Dean, reprinting the essay originally published at the Doves Press in 1900. A fine copy tipped in to a brown folder, as issued for the members.

Even if it had been available, I could not have paid such prices, as much I yearned to possess it. Then a thought struck me: why not search with more inclusive keywords, such as 'Roxburghe Club keepsake + Mallette Dean'? A single listing came up – on Alibris – and the description simply said, 'Loose Leaf, Mallette Dean woodcut, in wrappers', priced at $14.

I was sceptical right away, but still checked out the listing. There was no image of the item, or further description. I could write and ask the bookdealer for photos and more information, but that could easily backfire if it was indeed the real thing – the seller could realize how scarce and valuable it was, and relist it at a higher price.

I decided it was worth the gamble, and put the order through. And waited. Not very patiently. The parcel arrived some three weeks later. The size of the package – a long, narrow, flat cardboard parcel – made me hopeful. It at least seemed to fit what a folio-sized broadside might need. It was securely packed, and it took me a while to get one end of the long cardboard open, so that I could slide or coax whatever was inside rather than ripping open the parcel completely.

Peering through the slit, I could make out a long brown folder, and as soon as I managed to gently tug the thing out, and caught a glimpse of what was laid into those wrappers, I knew it was the *very thing*, because part of the long, yellow/orange hand-coloured woodcut initial was already visible. Once I had the Roxburghe folder out, I had to sit down to take in this piece of collector's luck properly. It was indeed handsome with its long initial that runs along the entire broadside size of 12 x 8 inches. The accompanying text was a note on bookbinding by master binder and printer T.J. Cobden-Sanderson of Doves Press. The long initial in the broadside was a tribute to the original page-length red calligraphic initial hand-drawn by Edward Johnston in the famous Bible from Doves Press.

How long had this thing been sitting in this bookseller's stock, tucked in somewhere in a pile of other ephemera? It was almost as if it was waiting for me – but that of course is just my collector's vanity and wishful thinking. But finding a scarce, sought-after ephemeron like this in the market that had been printed all those years ago was surprising and delightful.

I began to get a clearer picture of how the antiquarian world of collecting and dealing seemed to be set up – something that must be familiar and obvious to collectors abroad, but was new to me in India. This early find emboldened me to continue the hunt more vigorously, spurring me on to look for more rarities at bargain prices.

A collector can safely and boldly assume that many things that are rare or scarce or fine in the market will always come and go – and then come again! It's endlessly recycled, thank god. But, of course, not at throwaway prices like the keepsake – that was luck on my side, and the bookseller's mistake on his. The scarce items only get priced higher each time they return. Collectors sell their collection at an auction or in a private sale, dealers buy the items and relist each one. And then another collector comes along and buys it, and for a time this item disappears from the market. Until another copy becomes suddenly available, listed by another dealer, and there is a collector waiting for it.

So, the second lesson learnt was that I could put my faith in the antiquarian market, and that it would keep bringing the goods. You just need to have the funds – at least at the right time – so that when something from your Want List appears suddenly in the market, you can swoop down on it.

The third lesson was that booksellers make mistakes, and it's through those cracks that bargains, some juicy, some just satisfying, slip through and fall into your lap.

As I write this, there is still not a single copy of 'In Bookbinding Then' listed in the market – though I am acutely aware how this could change in a flash. Another copy could come up for sale, the only question is what would it be priced at?

Coming back to the Allen Press – the printing aesthetic of Lewis and Dorothy Allen would define for me what the 'Ideal Book, the Book Beautiful', should look and feel like; their obsession for fine bookmaking by hand deeply influenced what my favourite kind of fine press book would be to collect: printed on a handpress, on dampened handmade paper. Heavenly Monkey, the press of Rollin

Milroy in Vancouver, is probably the finest contemporary private press that designs and prints beautiful books this way, which is why it is my favourite fine press at work today.

Before I end, one more quick example of a small Allen Press coup where I have to once again credit the bibliography. Since the time of my first find I have gone on to buy several books from the Allen Press over the years, not at bargain prices, alas, but by paying the high prices their books command. I was lucky to find most of the prospectuses they printed, which are exceptional for being printed on the same beautiful handmade papers and fine metal faces used in the book it was announcing. I was particularly pleased with finding two of their scarcest prospectuses – for the *Allen Press Bibliography* and their celebrated book on how to print on a handpress.

One day a most unusual Allen Press item surfaced at John Windle Antiquarian Bookseller. It was neither a book nor a piece of ephemera – it resembled a little booklet, and was priced at $100. Printed on the handpress of Lewis and Dorothy Allen in 1951, it was P.B. Shelley's *Ode to the West Wind*, set in Jan van Krimpen's Romanée typeface, and printed damp on an English handmade paper with orange Fabriano wrappers.

In my many years of browsing I'd never come across this item – it looked to be scarcer than their books, and going by the images the dealer had provided, utterly beautiful. Each page of the poem was decorated around the borders with autumn leaves falling in bright and deep colours – flaming orange, red, green, and purple. Once again, the border engraving had been done by Mallette Dean, and Dorothy Allen had hand-coloured the leaves in each copy.

I needed no further encouragement to get it, but nevertheless I quickly dipped into the bibliography, turning to the checklist section of all the important and desirable Allen Press ephemera compiled by D. Steven Corey towards the end. It was listed under their Christmas keepsakes. And what I read there made me rush and put the order through before someone else got hold of it: 'Perhaps the most charming edition of the *Ode* ever printed. One of the supreme achievements of The Allen Press.'

I must hasten to add here that the accounts of rare book bargains I narrate in the book do not mean that's the only kind of buying I was interested in, or always pursued – that's not solely how I built my collection. More often I paid the high prices these fine press books usually commanded. Bargains are always welcome, and fun, and you always hope to clinch more of them, but it also feels good to pay a stiff price for a book that you keenly desire.

The market can also get even with you – there are times when I have overpaid, too. Or paid what I thought was the only price to be paid, only to see a lower priced copy of the same thing turn up a week later.

H.P. Kraus, the revered manuscript dealer, said in his autobiography that if he thought a book was worth $500, then that's what he would price it at – it did not make a difference to him if he had paid $40 to obtain it or $400. 'Customers sometimes want me to pass on the discount I got when buying the book,' he wrote in *A Rare Book Saga* (Putnam, 1978) 'but why should my fortune or my lack of it be a factor? If I find a one-dollar bill on the roadside, I'm not going to sell it for fifty cents.'

That's how the antiquarian trade works for not just dealers but collectors too. The stock of the dealer and the collection of the collector are fuelled by the substantial bargains that come their way. It's just that the dealer finds more bargains than the collector – that's how a living is made in the rare book trade. And one of the ways a dealer is able to make many or large finds is by going after several lots in an auction or buying up an entire collection, while collectors – at least modest buyers like me – buy one rare book at a time. As a collector you pay the high (though usually fair) prices the market demands for the books you want. And if you are fortunate enough to work closely with a few dealers, they'll try and give you as many breaks as they can in pricing, generously lowering their margins to make it possible for you to buy that stiffly priced book you have your heart set on.

'THE TWO LUCKIEST PEOPLE ON EARTH'

Bookman's Holiday

The first book that gave me a taste for private press books and created a desire in me to collect them is a little-known, underrated beauty called *Bookman's Holiday* (1971). It was also, at $85, the first expensive book I bought – up until then I had not paid more than $40 for a book. (I don't have to tell you that in Indian rupees this was already a lot.) It was printed in a small edition of eighty copies, and I felt thrilled and lucky to own a copy. *Bookman's Holiday* isn't, as the title might suggest, about a bibliophile's pleasure in holiday reading, or the bibliophilic indulgences of a holidaying collector. It is a rapturous account of two young fine press printers on a pilgrimage to visit the widow of a private press printer they admire, and examine the beautiful books he had printed.

The 'famed' books that this couple, Foster and Ruth Johnson, had come to see all the way from America to England were the books from the Ashendene Press. The widow was Cecily Hornby, the wife of St. John Hornby, once proprietor and printer of the Ashendene Press. The Johnsons had made this journey on the invitation of Michael Hornby, their son.

Written, designed, and printed by Ruth and Foster Johnson of the Bayberry Hill Press, everything about *Bookman's Holiday* delighted me: the handmade Tovil paper dampened for printing, the use of two admired typefaces in fine printing, Centaur and Arrighi, with the metal type nicely impressed into this lovely English paper, the text printed in red and black, and most beautiful of all, the hand-flourished calligraphic initials in bright blue, in the fashion of an Ashendene Press book itself!

The size of the book was an impressive 15 1/8 x 10 1/2 inches, a folio, with marbled boards for its covers and decorated endpapers. The first thing you physically feel is the crisp paper, pleasantly cockled from damping. You can see right away, even before you've touched it, that the colour in those long, elegant calligraphic capital letters that begin a chapter or a paragraph has been applied by hand, because you see it is slightly raised on the paper – and sure enough when you move your fingers over it, you can feel the thickness of the hand-applied watercolour.

It was an absorbing experience much before I'd even gotten to the text! And when I finally got to it, I relished it to the hilt. From the first page I found myself caught up in the couple's wonderment and pleasure at everything they beheld (or were about to behold) on this printer's pilgrimage. Their admiration and love for the Ashendene Press and its books – the very reason for this long trip they'd made – comes through joyfully in their narration:

> *If Ruth and I aren't the two luckiest people on earth, then surely we are right next to it! Loving beautiful books as we do, & particularly the books we consider personally to be among the most beautiful books ever printed, those of the Ashendene Press, what greater luck could we possibly have than that which befell us on June 22nd & 23rd, 1970.*

A word about the Ashendene Press and its printer, St. John Hornby, would be useful here. The Ashendene Press remains one of the most sought-after private presses by collectors for the beauty of its impeccably printed books. Hornby began the press in 1895 as a hobby press, printing on a handpress from a garden shed, using the finest handmade papers and a proprietary typeface designed for him. At first, he printed for friends and family and gave the books away. But as his reputation as a truly gifted fine printer grew with each new book, they were hotly pursued by collectors and all copies were subscribed for even before the printing had begun.

The books were distinctive for the use of hand-flourished calligraphic initials in red, green, blue, and gold. (You can tell now that *Bookman's Holiday* is modelled after an Ashendene folio.) Many of them were done in elaborately tooled bindings by the finest bookbinders of the day, and most books had a small run printed on pure vellum. This fits into a long tradition in the private press movement of printing some copies on vellum; apparently because nothing can rival the perfection of a page printed, illustrated, and illuminated on vellum. Hornby closed the press in 1935, and died in 1946.

Now, back to the Johnsons and their bookman's holiday to visit the home of Mrs Hornby in Worcestershire and view copies of the entire output of the Ashendene Press – all of them Hornby's personal copies, either specially bound for him or copies inscribed by him.

That June morning the couple bundle into a train from London to Oxford, where they are met by Michael Hornby, the printer's son, who picks them up in his car, and they drive through the beautiful countryside of the Cotswolds, and arrive at Cecily Hornby's house not long after. Ruth and Foster take to the old lady right away, and they walk through a pretty garden tended by Mrs Hornby herself. After a delicious lunch topped with a dessert of big, juicy strawberries, the moment they are looking forward to arrives, the very reason for which they crossed the Atlantic – Mrs Hornby opens a huge bookcase, and 'if ever there was a treasure chest disguised as a bookcase this was it,' remark the besotted couple.

Cecily Hornby shows them all the copies of the Ashendene Press printed on vellum, as well as several special copies with fine bindings, the work of Douglas Cockerell and Katharine Adams, two of England's most admired bookbinders. Then follow several pages of mouth-watering descriptions of what they see, including the manuscripts that Hornby commissioned to lettering artists Graily Hewitt and A.J. Fairbanks, with illumination in gold by Louise Powell. As they take leave of Cecily

Hornby, she gives them a few vellum sheets from *Daphnis and Chloe*, admired for the Gwen Raverat wood engravings in them.

In the evening it is supper at Michael and Nicolette's house with surprise dinner guests Charlotte and Colin Franklin, the collector-dealers. More Ashendene books and ephemera are brought out by Michael, and they ooh and ahh over the sublime beauty of the books. One of the books that Foster and Ruth printed from their Bayberry Hill Press is brought out by Michael – it is a paper St. John Hornby had read at the Double Crown Club, a dining club for printers and bibliophiles, that had gone unpublished. Taking the Hornbys' permission, the couple printed the *Ashendene Press, A Paper Read at the Double Crown Club* in 1970.

Like *Bookman's Holiday*, it echoes an Ashendene Press book, with its lovely, large, and bright coloured initials. Colin Franklin remarks that they should have perhaps used a greyer, subtler blue than the dark blue in the book, and the couple say that this is exactly what they were told at Bernard Quartich, the antiquarian firm, when they brought copies to show the bookshop. (I disagree, and think the blue is striking and enchanting, even if a little overdone.)

The next morning, before they are dropped off to the station at Oxford, Michael and his wife present the printer couple with a copy of *Hymns and Prayers for Use at the Marriage of Michael Hornby and Nicolette Ward at St. Margaret's Church Westminster* (1928), one of the more elusive minor pieces from the Ashendene Press. Michael has inscribed it to them. They are thrilled, but protest saying it's an expensive book – and then laughingly add that they had just seen a copy at Maggs (the other famous London rare book shop) for a hefty £50. But Michael insists, and they take it away happily. (Today this scarce Ashendene booklet when found can fetch £700.)

What is a copy of *Bookman's Holiday* priced currently? Curious, I check on AbeBooks, and there's just one copy available at $650! It looks like it has steadily grown in reputation. I am doubly glad, then, of the copies I own – yes, *copies*. A couple of years after I bought my first copy of *Bookman's Holiday*, I spotted another modestly priced copy, and I could not resist getting it because it had two rich associations attached to it – the copy belonged to Michael Hornby with his ownership signature, and laid in was an old bookseller's invoice to hint which bookseller had bought it from Hornby for stock. It was the celebrated and beloved manuscripts dealer, Alan G. Thomas, one of my bibliophile heroes.

A few years later I was to have more luck with the two other beauties from the Bayberry Hill Press, both of which are association copies that I bought for a satisfactorily low price: a copy of the *Ashendene Press, A Paper Read by Hornby* and a copy of *C.H. Hornby, Gentleman*. Inscribed in pencil on the flyleaves of both books are presentations from Michael Hornby to Decherd Turner, a widely admired rare book librarian who was responsible for acquiring a large archive of the Ashendene Press (with the assistance of Colin Franklin) to the special collections library he had been curator of. Turner has written inside each of these copies the following: '*Michael Hornby, March 1st, 1975, Decherd Turner: Signed for me by Mr Michael Hornby when I had lunch with Mr and Mrs Hornby at Pusey House, Easter Monday, 1975*'.

Bayberry Hill Press was a true private press, a bona fide hobby press – the Fosters never priced or sold any of the books they printed. They either gave them away or swapped them for other books. Printing for pleasure was their printer's credo.

Though I would not know it then, my deep fulfilment with *Bookman's Holiday* for the subject of its narrative account, and the way it had been printed, would give me my focus as a collector: fine press books dealing with the book arts. That is, the various arts of the book I was becoming so in thrall to: papermaking, marbling, type and typography, fine printing, private presses, wood engraving, calligraphy, the lettering arts, hand-colouring, and manuscript illumination.

A FINE (PRESS) BARGAIN COUP

As a typophile who had only recently discovered the pleasure and joy of a finely printed letterpress book, I was naturally in a hurry to pursue (if not always successfully acquire) beautiful examples of contemporary fine press books that appealed to me deeply. Book hunting assiduously, I would often still end up arriving a little too late – the fine press party would be over, and the lights turned out. The edition had been so small – not more than 50 copies printed! – that the book had been snapped up, or sold out almost before publication. But sometimes my luck would hold, I'd get my timing right, and the bibliophile goddess would smile down on me.

One such fine bargain coup I managed – a true fine press rarity – was a book done in a tiny edition of just thirty-one copies, none for sale – yet I acquired it, and that too (in retrospect!) at a magical price.

Titled *Henry &*, it was a fine press book no one had probably seen in the market until then, since it was privately printed for just four people. The subject of the book was Henry Morris, the accomplished and (sometimes) satirical printer of the Bird and Bull (B&B) Press. Four people who had worked or collaborated with Morris offer affectionate reminisces about working with him. The copies were divided between them, while Morris was presented with a finely bound copy. A little note on Henry Morris and his press would be relevant here before I say more about how I came to acquire this scarce private press book – not just to embellish my find, but to also illustrate the large part they played in shaping my collecting focus.

I was lucky to stumble on Henry Morris's Bird and Bull Press early in my initiation into fine press books – here was a prolific, ambitious private press printer who was completely focused on making fine press productions with book arts as the sole theme of the press. Because Morris chose subjects that are close to a collector's heart, you could immerse yourself in the text as well as its myriad fine press qualities.

I stumbled on my first B&B book by chance. One day, using a university's Interlibrary Loan service, I requested a copy of *Dr. Rosenbach and Mr. Lilly*, an enjoyable true tale by Joel Silver of the transactions between a rare book dealer and a rich collector. Instead of sending me the trade edition, they sent me the finely printed letterpress Bird and Bull edition! I relished everything about it, and if I recall correctly, I held on to it as long as I could, using up my two renewals. I returned it reluctantly. I felt as if an exotic, strange and exciting creature had flown away from me. Could I get one for myself? No. Even the lowest priced copy on the antiquarian market was well beyond me at $450. I now own a copy of that B&B title, but the purchase would come after nearly two years of dreaming and saving up for it.

I can't think of a single other fine press who has published so many finely printed books on bibliophily and the book arts. Morris covered them all – papermaking, marbling, wood engraving, book collecting, bookselling, booksellers trade tokens, emblem books, bookbinding, intaglio printing, biblio spoofs, bibliography as well as a vast deal of commentary on fine press printers and fine printing. And then there was the attractiveness of his books: the early titles from the press were printed on handmade paper (in many cases, paper he had made himself), the text printed from a fine metal type with satisfying impression, appropriately or beautifully bound (often quarter leather and marbled boards) and – this is perhaps the most remarked upon element in his luxurious productions – including tipped in or mounted samples of whatever the book at hand was dealing with. If on paper marbling or a paper marbler, then several original samples of beautiful marbled paper mounted on a full page were included, if on a famous hand papermaker like Dard Hunter, then specimens of various papers made by Hunter over the years.

Morris and his books kept me happily preoccupied in my early collecting years, negotiating with dealers on prices, hunting for bargains, and chasing after scarcer titles. And that's how I found myself one day contemplating having to make a fairly expensive purchase of a book *about* this printer, and not one printed by him.

When the scintillating collection of fine press books and material related to the book arts belonging to the noted bookbinder Gregor R. Campbell came into the market, there were about a dozen things in there that were highly desirable, scarce, and even singular. While the dealer who bought the collection priced them according to their value and scarcity in the market, there was one item that (at least temporarily) slipped through the cracks and was underpriced at $275.

Though *Henry &* was a book I desired, I felt for a slim book of some twenty odd pages printed in just black and white, it was priced rather high. But after only hesitating a little I bought it, not fully realizing the price was more than fair. I – as well as the bookseller – recognized its real value perhaps a week or so later when he listed a second copy at the more marked up price of $850. Even at that price this second copy was bought up quickly. No third copy has turned up so far.

Campbell had been one of the four people associated with the book and had got his share of the copies, and in making a move to sell his collection, had given up a few copies (probably just the two which sold out) of this book. The other three contributors here on Morris were: Sidney E. Berger, scholar-collector and bibliographer, the late Robert D. Fleck, bookdealer, and Wesley Bates, the wood engraver; all had personal reflections to offer combined with some juicy details about what it was like to work with Morris over the years.

When I bought *Henry &*, I had recognized that it was an unusual item as a book on Henry Morris had never been done before. And given the very limited edition and my own desire to collect all things related to fine press printers, and in particular, Henry Morris – an interesting, ingenious, and funny character – I found I could not resist the temptation to get it. So, a week later when a second copy of this book showed up at a higher price, I had to learn why.

And I was able to find out directly from the source. Coincidentally, around the time Campbell's books got listed at Rulon-Miller Books, I had been corresponding with Sidney Berger. I had been a fan of Mr Berger for all his bibliophilic writing, as well as for his ardent book collecting over decades, resulting in a vast collection of book arts material, notable for its famed collection of decorative papers. Just a few weeks before I ended up buying *Henry &*, I had written a fan mail to him, and he had responded warmly.

Imagine then my excitement at seeing this in the colophon for *Henry &*: 'This book was initiated by Sid Berger'. Rather than sending him one more email, I called him up and told him I had just bought *Henry &*. He began in surprise with 'Where the devil did you find–' and stopped himself short, laughed, and finished with, 'oh, okay, I know...'

He then went on to share with me how the price of that second copy was raised significantly after he had provided the dealer with the background to the origins of the book, as well as how those thirty-one copies were distributed. Berger had worked closely with Morris on several B&B books, including that magnum opus, *The Handmade Papers of Japan*. (My own favourite Berger-Morris book is *The Anatomy of a Literary Hoax*.)

They would keep in touch often, even when not working on a project, but after Morris closed his press, Sidney found him often (and quite naturally) in low spirits. That's when he decided he had to do something to cheer his old friend up, the kind of bibliophilic project Henry Morris himself might think up of, and hit upon *Henry &*. The background to the making of this book was eventually added to the description of the second copy by the bookshop as a note from Sidney.

It read:

> After Henry sold all his type and printing equipment, I called him and he was in the dumps. I felt bad for him and I wanted to raise his spirits. So, I called Tim Hawley, who has his Contre Coup Press. I told Tim I would write an essay about Henry if he would print it. We decided to do it with others who had worked with Henry (Greg Campbell, Bob Fleck, and Wesley Bates) and each author (and Henry) got 6 copies. The colophon says '30 copies', but in fact there were 31, since a special deluxe copy in full leather was done for Henry. Bob and I drove out to see Henry and present his copy to him. Also, since this is not a book that Tim did from inception to completion (since it was my idea and all of us wrote for it), he didn't want the imprint to be Contre Coup, so he has it as being printed in Garamondo by the Contre Kook Press. If you put it on the market, it is not a B&B title, but it is a Henry

> Morris book in its own way, so it should appeal to the B&B collectors. They are, after all, essays about Henry, and they add to the information and lore about the B&B Press.

I waited with bated breath for my copy to arrive safely in Bengaluru, and when I finally had *Henry &* in hand, I was well pleased: the fine, judicious printing by Tim Hawley of the Contre Coup Press was indeed enlivened by a bit of biblio foolery in the book by him. The printing was attributed to the Contre Kook Press. He had handset the type, and luckily, had chosen a paper with texture and character to it, rather than a smooth or wove paper that contemporary printers seem so puzzlingly eager to use.

The private press books from Henry Morris that I've enjoyed the most are not so much what B&B is most known for – those important and luxurious books on papermaking and marbling – but the more personal things from Morris, in particular his three bibliographies and the two private journals he turned into books. After these, what draws me most are those biblio spoofs and hoaxes from Morris's bibliophilic mischief-making that has delighted me (as well as scores of B&B collectors).

'BEAUTIFULLY SET JEWELS'

John S. Fass and the Hammer Creek Press

I came under the spell of John Fass and his Hammer Creek Press almost as soon as I had begun collecting fine press books. His exquisite presswork was one thing, the legend of his life as a private press printer was something else. In the 1950s, Fass lived in a one-room apartment at a YMCA in the Bronx, his small Albion handpress tucked under his bed, which, when the mood struck him, he would pull out to print all those beautiful things. I could never get over this, that this was the Hammer Creek Press, this little bachelor pad studded with an assortment of type and ornaments neatly and compactly stored in typecases, a small iron handpress, and a stock of fine European and Japanese papers to print on.

I am so glad I had the good sense to pursue and buy five Christmas and holiday greetings done by Fass from James Cummins Booksellers in 2014 for $200. I knew even then, though I took a few days to consider making the purchase, that this was very fairly priced; that anything from Fass and his Hammer Creek Press was scarce, and highly desired for his exquisite arrangement of type, ornament, and colour on fine papers. But what I didn't know then was how positively rare it was – and is – to find Fass ephemera in the market.

And among the most coveted things from the Hammer Creek Press are the holiday greetings Fass did for friends. The fine press collector Kenneth Auchincloss, who had a great deal of Fass material in his collection, called these greetings 'beautifully set jewels, which sparkle with their designer's shy originality' , as mentioned in *Fine Printing in the Twentieth Century: Selections from the Collection of Kenneth Auchincloss* (2005). Fass made delicate and ingenious use of type ornaments to construct his greetings. In those initial days of collecting, I would take my time about making a purchase. This is good strategy when you've just started collecting, except when rarities in your collecting field appear in the market – that's not the time to dither.

I took a full three days before putting the order through for these Fass greetings – three of which were even more uncommon for being signed by the printer. I called the bookshop, had them describe each greeting to me, send me photos, and just before saying 'yes, I'll take it', I negotiated for a small discount, and got it! I realize now that this small but lovely offering from Fass ought to have been priced higher even back then. It was probably priced the way it was because there's no standard way to price Fass ephemera. Since they seldom come on the market (collectors never let go of them), there are no previously listed prices or auction records to consult or compare with.

Depending on how highly a dealer thinks of his work,

or how attractive or special they look to a dealer, a price emerges. A collector gets lucky when it is mispriced. Not long ago, about midway through 2019, a dealer listed a wood engraved illustration of a turtle done by John DePol for Fass. The turtle was the Hammer Creek Press mark, and wood engraver DePol did many turtles for Fass (not for money but in exchange for Fass's beautiful books). It was priced at $15, and I bought it of course, but even I didn't realize what it was exactly until it arrived.

It was a large, original trial proof engraving (9 x 6 inches) of a Hammer Creek Turtle by DePol printed by Fass on an exquisite-looking (and feeling) tissue-like handmade Japanese paper. Given how unusual and striking this item was with the rich association of DePol and Fass, it could have easily been priced between $150 and $200. All the dealer saw was a black and white illustration of a large turtle on a thin, tracing sheet-like paper, and assigned a 'suitable' price.

In that one-room apartment Fass stayed in, he kept a row of miniature wooden presses he had built himself. To visitors they looked toy-like, but they were perfectly workable. In fact, among the first things he printed had been done on a tiny wooden handpress he had built. It was so small that he had to use his fingers to ink the type! He called the books and ephemera he printed on this tiny press as coming from the Hell-Box Press. When he moved to printing on another press, it was still a small handpress that he used with such skill and delicacy to print his books that now carried the imprint of Hammer Creek Press, with the turtle as its press mark.

The beautiful little book that tells the story of this printer is a treasure in itself: *John S. Fass & the Hammer Creek Press*, first published in a charming private press edition limited to one hundred copies and then in an equally charming trade edition by David Godine. (Godine's edition, which is as good as the original, is available in the market for so little that you should rush to get a copy.) 'John Fass avowedly prints for pleasure,' wrote Eugene Ettenberg in the book. 'There are mighty few who, upon seeing his books, booklets, bookplates, and other printed pieces, do not in turn get a sense of pleasure from his work.'

It is this aspect of Fass, a hobby printer quietly printing for his own pleasure, that draws you so deeply to his work. By day John Fass was a designer and typographer in the publishing and advertising industry, and in his off hours and weekends he turned private printer in his 'snug bachelor quarters' at the YMCA. Out would come the little Albion and using various fine papers from Europe and Japan, Fass would print little broadsides, bookplates, and greetings making judicious and pleasing use of printers' flowers and ornaments. It was his custom to give away the little things he printed to friends.

Fass had got the idea to become a hobby printer when he turned his skill at making cabinets and bookshelves into building little wooden presses modelled on the early presses from the fifteenth century. He learned to print expertly and beautifully on small surfaces. In 1950, he acquired a small iron handpress that had once belonged to the typographer Bruce Rogers and then to the illustrator

Valenti Angelo, and with this he was able to print booklets and books of ten to forty pages in a tiny print run. Three gifted artists drew or wood engraved the turtle pressmarks for him – Burton Carnes, Valenti Angelo, and John DePol. Many were finely illustrated with wood engravings, especially with the turtles printed for Fass by John DePol. He printed them with 'different inks on a variety of paper stock'. Some booklets were just a display of Hammer Creek turtle pressmarks.

In the late '40s, Fass would drop in often at the Chiswick Bookshop to buy fine press books and invariably stay to talk with Herman and Viv Cohen, the owners of this Aladdin's Cave–like bookshop devoted to fine bookmaking. Here sometimes he would run into friends from the Typophiles – an adventurous group of printers, illustrators, and graphic artists who spent all their days thinking and talking fine bookmaking – and then they would have lunch. Aveve Cohen in *Reminiscences & Remembrances of Herman and Aveve Cohen and the Chiswick Bookshop* says, 'It was John's endearing custom, after lunch, to pull out of his pocket one or two of his latest printed items and present them to those at the table. All were noticeably beaming on their return to the shop.'

The Cohens admired Fass's printing, and felt it was high time he began selling his work rather than just handing it away. They urged him to bring every little thing he had printed in his apartment to them, so they could catalogue and introduce it to collectors. One day not long after, Aveve Cohen goes on to say, Fass turned up with a shoe box full of his printing. No two copies that Fass printed were ever alike even of the same thing, nor would he keep a record of how many copies he printed of each thing. His work began to be immediately collected. Those few lucky collectors probably got them all at very modest prices; but even in his own time the Hammer Creek pieces grew scarce since they were often limited to five or ten copies. Fass's reputation quickly grew, leading to a Grolier Club exhibition of his work, where on opening day, Aveve says, 'one could almost hear the oohs and ahs of admiration' from visitors at such immaculate, pretty presswork from an unknown printer.

After Fass's health began to fail in the late '60s, he returned to his hometown of Lititz, Pennsylvania, to live with his sister. When he died in July 1973, Herman and Aveve Cohen, according to his wishes, took charge of his belongings – his various small presses, the type, and all printing ephemera and samples of his work. Bruce Rogers, whom Fass had been deeply influenced by, too was a fan of his work. He once wrote this to Fass, as mentioned in *John S. Fass and the Hammer Creek Press*: 'Thank you very much for your gift of the charming little book showing your varieties of type. It is done with your usual exquisite taste. I shall always be glad to subscribe for anything you do (if not too expensive). Ever yours, B.R.'

Alas, for all my knowledge of Fass and his work as legendary in fine printing, I did not chase after a big book from the Hammer Creek Press that came up on eBay many years later. It was, I think, in 2017, that I spotted this listing and even today I kick myself for losing it. (Since then, it has never come on the market.) It was *The Hammer Creek Type Specimen Book*, and included a handwritten letter from Fass to a customer. I had not seen Fass's holograph letters in the market. The opening bid was $275 (some people would have paid that just for the letter).

When I looked at the listing, there was already a bid signalling competition. I could make out straightaway that this bidder was serious, that they wanted it desperately. I could have been a real contender, too, but I had just overspent on a slew of fine press material and had told myself that I wasn't going to buy anything for a while. I put in my max bid, which I already knew was not high enough. Who knew who else was waiting to bid, not showing their hand?

Within minutes of the auction ending, I was overbid by the same bidder, who, I realized now, was the only other eBayer interested in it. I let the auction run out, and watched this bidder walk off with the Fass item for an impressive sum. I tracked *via*Libri for a while after that to see if this was a dealer who would then relist it, but it never showed. It's been this way with Fass items – they have all been swallowed up into a collector's collection. No wonder Fass material does not recycle.

I had had a lucky break earlier when I acquired a substantial Hammer Creek book with a delicious bonus thrown in – only the seller I bought it from didn't intend it to be one! At a dealer on ABE, I saw *The Work of the Hammer Creek Press* listed for $250. The price was reasonable – I had seen Hammer Creek items listed in the $350 to $500 range. But this was sometime in 2014, and in those fledgeling days of collecting I had to weigh every purchase, however desirable or attractively priced, carefully. What decided it for me was the bookseller's description for this item, noting that laid into this copy was a promotional item from the printer. So, I let a couple of weeks go by before I decided to approach the dealer to ask if it could be discounted for a direct purchase.

In retrospect, I am amazed that this much sought-after Fass item was still sitting there, unclaimed. The bookseller agreed to lower the price slightly, and I didn't waste another second in putting the order through on the phone. The seller said he would have it in the mail the same day. Half hour later, it dawned on me that I had forgotten to remind him to make sure that little piece of promotional material from Fass laid into this copy of *The Work of the Hammer Creek Press* was included. He might just forget to do it, so I called the bookseller back hastily, and when he came on the line, he said curtly, 'I've shipped it, and yes, the ephemeron has been included.' Wonderful.

Well, I didn't know just how wonderful it would be until the parcel arrived. The ephemeron was not some Fass scrap but a much sought-after early Fass item, with the long, playful title, *The Hammer Creek Press Has Engulfed the Hell-Box Press.* It was, as many Fass things are, a stitched pamphlet with three John DePol wood engravings of the handpress with a first showing of the turtle press mark. This notice in booklet form was Fass announcing the beginning of his most endearing private press in 1952 – the Hammer Creek – and the closing of his brief, experimental Hell-Box Press.

DECORATED AND HAND-ILLUMINATED BY VALENTI ANGELO

The secret to collecting Valenti Angelo is to look for those very personal books he designed, hand-lettered, illuminated, printed, and bound. Beautiful books that he did all by himself on a small handpress (and yes, that very same handpress used once by Bruce Rogers and later by John Fass) in an edition of just fifty copies. They are, of course, harder to find, and cost more than the books he illustrated and decorated for other publishers and presses, but much more satisfying to collect. And much more fun to chase after, since they can be elusive, and more rewarding to behold.

The hand-lettering, decoration, and illumination he did himself was under his own private presses, the first called Golden Cross Press and the other, simply, the Press of Valenti Angelo. For the little books from these private imprints, he chose a brief text, usually a kind of religious or book artsy fable that ran ten to twenty pages, handset the text using two of his favourite types (Goudy

Tory and Koch Jessenschrift) from his own collection of metal typefaces, and then, for each individual copy, hand-lettered the initials. Then came the final Angelo touch: hand-colouring and illuminating the initials and the illustrations in blue, green, red, and gold.

Towards the end of collecting all the Angelos I wanted, I managed a collecting coup of sorts to get three lovely and very lavish fine press books on his work that had been, price-wise, beyond my reach. These accounts I'll keep for the end of the chapter. I got lucky with not just the big books, but on the way to collecting Angelo, I would come upon many small, attractive bargains of ephemeral things from his hand that were under-priced, or simply lost in a pile of ABE listings.

Before I get into how I collected his most sparkling work, in particular those illuminated jewels from his handpress, I must tell you more about Valenti Angelo, what turned him into an illuminator, and the widely admired work he did for the Grabhorn Press and the Limited Editions Club. As a boy in Italy, Valenti went to a school run by monks. One day he chanced on his favourite teacher, an old, bald monk with a ragged beard, reading a book in the morning sun in the monastery's courtyard. He had often seen the teacher do this, but this time he saw there was light sparkling from the book, and the monk's face seemed to be lit in a kind of golden light.

When he drew near, it was unlike any book he had seen – a medieval Book of Hours, handwritten and decorated in many colours and burnished in gold. The sun had caught the gold and glinted afar. Valenti thought it was the most beautiful book he had seen. This 'golden book' would go on to markedly influence his style of bookmaking and decoration.

When he came to America in 1905, he took up many odd jobs, mostly working in factories, and at night going to school. He wanted to paint, but was also deeply drawn to beautiful books. Later he would say, 'Who could have thought then of a career just decorating books?' (This line is from his autobiographical essay and has been repeated in many of his books.) In 1926, a friend took him to the Grabhorn Press, a fine press in San Francisco run by two brothers, Edwin and Robert Grabhorn, who had already made a name for themselves as fabulous designers of fine books.

Angelo showed the Grabhorns some of his work, and they immediately invited him to collaborate with the press. In his autobiographical essay from the beautifully produced 1976 checklist of his work put out by the Book Club of California, he recalls one of the Grabhorns telling him that they may not be able to pay much, and then adding these magical words, 'but you'll have a chance to do fine books'. That year he worked on *The Letters of Amerigo Vespucci,* doing initials, illustrations, and a hand-coloured map. Overjoyed at the fine quality of the book, he felt he had done the right thing leaving a lucrative commercial job to work at a fine press. Each day at the press he was learning more about fine bookmaking.

Before Angelo's arrival at the press, the Grabhorns had done books where the initials were printed and hand-coloured, but with Angelo this became more prominent, and he added a new dimension to the Grabhorn books – illumination in gold. His most spectacular work in this direction was *The Voiage and Travaile of Sir John Maundevile* in 1928 where Angelo drew for each copy thirty-four large decorative initials, each illuminated in two colours and gold, thus making in an edition of 150 copies, a grand total of 5,300 initials, all different! Plus, numerous rubricated paragraph marks. The book itself was meant to look like a medieval manuscript, and succeeded brilliantly. (It is now a $2,500 book, and though I once got a chance to acquire it for $550, I foolishly passed on it.)

During the Depression, the fine and rare book market took a hit, and the Grabhorns did not have many fine books to offer the artist. Angelo then decided to try his luck in New York (selling his hard-won collection of fine press books to raise money and passage), and moved there with his family in 1933. He straightaway became part of the Typophiles, the convivial band of typographers, printers, calligraphers, wood engravers, papermakers, collectors, and lovers of fine printing who would meet over an informal lunch to drink, eat, and talk to their hearts content about fine bookmaking.

But there wasn't much work, and initially he struggled until he met George Macy, founder of the Limited Editions Club (LEC), who welcomed him with open arms and gave him many sumptuous commissions, keeping him busy and happy, and his family fed. (There were other printing houses he was illustrating for as well, such as the Peter Pauper Press and the Overbrook Press, but his most charming work is to be found in the Hammer Creek

Press books of John S. Fass, all of which are difficult to find today.)

The LEC books were done in an edition of 1,500 copies (the number of subscribers) and for at least four of these books Angelo painstakingly hand-coloured and illuminated either initials or borders or illustrations. *The Book of Psalms*, *Rubaiyat of Omar Khayyam*, *Song of Ronald*, the Koran and the *Sonnets from the Portuguese* features elaborate flourished initials from the hand of Angelo. These books today are found abundantly on the market, and in varying condition, thus they can range from $25 to $300, depending on condition and special attributes (or the lack of it) for each copy.

All the LEC books done by him contain at the colophon a lovely bonus: his manuscript signature, usually in pencil. For the Heritage Press books, done in a larger print run by Macy, the most beautiful was *Song of Songs* (1935) with several initials in pure gold by Angelo. This can be had for as little as $10. One day I stumbled on a beautiful variant copy of this book: the frontispiece illustration of two lovers in a garden printed in black and white was here pleasingly and carefully hand-coloured by Angelo. No doubt he had done this for an admirer or friend, as he often had. To my utter shock and delight, after I opened the book on its arrival, I found every linocut illustration in the book had been hand-coloured by the artist, not just the frontispiece. Such extra hand-coloured or illuminated copies by him have become next to impossible to find in the market, and coming across this so casually was such a lucky, lucky find.

Around 1935, he began his own adventure in designing

and publishing with the Golden Cross Press. He brought out a series of titles for collectors of fine books under the Golden Cross Press imprint, all of which he designed and illuminated, though he had them printed by several fine printers of the day like Hawthorn House, Walpole Office, and Timothy Press. For instance, *The Book of Esther*, my first Golden Cross purchase, with its many large, flourished initials in colour and line drawings filled in gold, was printed at Hawthorn House. As pretty as it was, it still lacked the personal, hand-illumined touch of the later books printed by Angelo on his handpress.

There is, though, one exception to this Golden Cross period: *Quattrocentisteria*, 1937. This folio-sized book is enchanting for its gold illumination, hand-colours and the charming line drawings. I was fortunate to find a pleasing association copy, inscribed by Angelo to George and Helen Macy.

In 1949, he began his second private press, the Press of Valenti Angelo, and printed first on a Washington handpress, and then switched to a smaller press – the famous Hughes and Kimber that he bought from Bruce Rogers, which then went to Fass, who then sold it back to Angelo ten years later for the books Angelo would print and illuminate in San Francisco in the 1970s and '80s.

The book that got me immersed in Angelo's ouevre was a lavishly illustrated bibliographical checklist of his work put out by the Book Club of California in 1976 as a tribute to this master decorator. It reproduced illustrations from his best work, several in full page (and the book is an impressive folio, 14 5/8 x 10 1/4 inches) with some illustrations, initials, and decorations hand-coloured by Angelo himself. Done in an edition of 400 copies, *Valenti Angelo: Author, Illustrator, Printer* was finely printed by Andrew Hoyem, and contains 43 specimens of Angelo's printing of which 35 are in colour.

Here finally was the bibliographical information I had been so eager for: checklists of the various books and ephemera Angelo had done under his private imprints, illustrated from specimen pages from his prolific output. Here also was Valenti's story, told by him in an autobiographical essay, as well as essays on him by those who had closely worked with him, including a charming little preface by Robert Grabhorn.

The book is printed letterpress on a mould-made paper that has a nice texture to it, and most, if not all, copies are signed by Angelo. (The first 30 or 50 copies were even extra hand-coloured by Angelo.) It's printed in a really satisfying way, the metal typeface sharp and crisp in the paper, the decorations, initials, and illustrations nicely impressed into the paper.

Press of Valenti Angelo would have two phases, in Bronxville, New York, from the mid-1940s to the early 1970s, and in San Francisco from the early to the late 1970s. *The Court of the Printer's Guild* and *The Book of Ruth and Boaz* are fine examples of the hand-finished work of Angelo for colour and illumination. They contain lovely, hand-lettered initials showing colours and gold. Angelo also frequently used linoleum cuts to make illustrations and prints, which he would then colour by hand.

Before winding up in New York, and heading back to San Francisco (a move that came after the death of his wife, when he ached to go back to his roots) he printed a fabulous checklist of his work on his handpress in a small edition of 55 copies, with several illustrations and illuminations. *Valenti Angelo: Author, Illustrator, Printer: A Checklist of His Work from 1926 to 1970* is not a scarce book, though it is (deservedly) pricey – in the range of $850 to $1,200.

Once back in San Francisco in 1977 at the age of 77, he took a fifth-floor apartment on Nob Hill, which had a spectacular view of the city, even though the space itself was tiny. He revived the 'Press of Valenti Angelo', having brought along with him the little handpress and cases of his favourite type. (He had to leave about 200 pounds of type ornaments in Bronxville, NY.) He brought four with him: De Roos, Goudy Tory, Perpetua, and Koch Jessenschrift. (The Goudy face, he says, was cut specially for him by Frederic Goudy, who personally handed it to him just before the 1950 fire that destroyed Goudy's printing and foundry shop.)

I particularly like the books and broadsides he made in this period more than any other. I have always felt that like the wood engraver, John DePol, Angelo produced his best work towards the end of his life. His daughter, Valdine, recalled it this way in a reminiscence she contributed to *Con Amore*, a 1992 bibliography of Angelo: 'His small apartment on Nob Hill became a treasure trove of beautiful things, his tiny press room and sure hands produced some of his loveliest works, diminutive in size, but alive and gem-like in beauty.'

The books he made at the Press of Valenti Angelo were limited to 25 to 65 copies. The smaller the number, the more beautiful the edition. Since it was entirely handmade, he could embellish each copy with five and seven line initials (about two inches) rather than the usual three line (half-inch) initials, and use three to four colours and burnish them in gold.

I found three lovely examples of the same title he had done over the years for a nice price. Each was printed on a different paper with different styles of initials, varied colours and gilding, and different bindings. It was, I think, sometime in 2016, when I was looking for something unusual from the hand of Angelo that I came across three variant printings of a charming little book from him titled *True Charity*, from Houle Rare Books. The text of *True Charity* was a short, famous parable – something I couldn't be less interested in: I was after Angelo's decoration and illumination here. I knew by now that he often did various versions of the same title, varying the decorative work inside. The three copies from this rare bookseller were priced $75 each. In my cautious, cheapskate collecting style I thought I would buy just one, but wanted the more attractive edition. But I had no idea which one would be more to my taste, so I called the bookseller and asked him to describe each copy to me.

But the bookshop owner wasn't interested in describing the copies to me – his response was: 'They are just 75 bucks each, why do you need to think so much?' I was taken aback, but though he had snapped at me, it was just the goading I needed, and I got all three, thank goodness. When the copies arrived, I was pleased – all three were special, something the bookseller had not bothered to note. One was on Japanese handmade paper, where the gold and hand-painted colours stood out on this beautiful paper as though they were from an actual medieval manuscript, and the other had a little card inserted at the back with a note from the Cohens of the Chiswick Bookshop – something I had been hankering to have! The last was on another fine paper, and hardbound, rather than in wrappers. Only 50 copies of each had been printed by Angelo on a handpress and signed at the colophon.

Just to give you a sense of how scarce *True Charity* is, since those listings in 2016 I have never seen a single copy of it, in any edition, come on the market. But luckily, the way the antiquarian and rare book market works, such rarities always come around. It's possible – and I hope this is the case – that when you look for a copy, you'll find one. I have seen things I have absolutely given up on ever seeing come back miraculously to the market.

The most lavish bibliography of Angelo is *Con Amore: Valenti Angelo* (1992) compiled by James Linden, and published by him in folio as a very limited deluxe edition in 100 copies of which 85 were for sale. It is also one of the most ravishing fine press bibliographies I've seen. (Sadly, though, it came out after Angelo's death.) While chronologically it picks up where the Book Club of California checklist (BCC checklist) leaves off, this has seven essays by friends and colleagues, and Linden packs the book with examples of Angelo's hand-colouring and illumination. And it is printed letterpress on a lovely mould-made French paper, Rives Heavyweight.

Some examples of Angelo's work are even tipped in. My favourite is an original bookplate he made for

Linden on Barcham Green handmade paper that Linden generously spared for each copy: the bookplate is tipped into each copy. The essays are mostly personal reflections from Valenti's family, friends, and admirers. Linden's own story of how he met Valenti in his last days, just before the artist had stopped working, and then began collecting his work furiously, is an enjoyable entry.

The copy I acquired was one of the specials: a 'Subscriber's Copy'. While there is no difference in the printed book for this and the regular Publisher's Copy, the Subscriber's Copy comes with a little folder of extra material that Linden put together. And in each folder are at least five to seven sheets that show Angelo's work in hand-painted gold and colours!

Biographically and anecdotally, the best book on Angelo's life, work, relationships, and friendships and more wide-ranging essays on his hand-colouring and illumination can be found in the last book about this exceptional modern illuminator: *Valenti Angelo: The Man and the Artist* by Heron Books published in 2010. It took the editors 10 years to put this book out, with 32 contributions from collectors, librarians, dealers, friends, colleagues, collaborators, and printers. It is also extensively illustrated. My good fortune was finding one of the 25 special copies in which most of the contributors had signed.

My last delightful and unexpected Valenti Angelo find has to do with a special copy of a book I have already mentioned, *Valenti Angelo: Author, Illustrator, Printer,* the Book Club of California checklist, of which there are usually a dozen copies on ABE. I knew of course of the slight variation in the copies, namely, some copies have a handwritten note in pencil by Angelo saying 'this copy has been hand colored by me for...' and mentions the name of the collector.

As soon as copies of this BCC checklist were available for sale, Angelo let it be known that he would be happy to hand-colour copies for a small token fee, and for some collectors he knew intimately for no charge at all. He took much pleasure in this. I found a copy of one of these specials on eBay – when I bid for it and won, I didn't know that's what it was – and it was such sweet surprise to open the book and see so many initials and illustrations not coloured in the regular copy, here brightly coloured with a few even featuring gold illumination!

This is how Angelo had wanted to decorate and colour the BCC checklist, but had been thwarted. In this copy, one can feel the raised hand-colouring for many images, especially the stunning full-page one of Job, the strong colours shaded differently. And the most beautiful illumination here is for the title page of one of his famous broadside keepsakes – 'The World's Justice' – with four deep and bright colours with gold in the background for the opening initial and decorated letter.

It did feel to me as if Valenti Angelo himself had led me to this copy.

MASTER OF THE BURIN

The Bibliophilic Wood Engravings of John DePol

In 2014, a fine press book I never dreamt I would own suddenly became mine when I chanced on a copy usually listed at $750, for $175. The dealer had a little note in his description that the leather spine label with the title tooled in gilt had slightly faded. But for this, the copy was near fine. *John DePol: A Celebration of His Work* is an 80th birthday festschrift from various private press printers to a master wood engraver.

It is one of the most beautiful books I own, and it is also, I feel, the fine press book where the beauty of relief printing – the text is printed from letterpress and the illustrations printed from engraved wooden blocks on dampened paper – is at its most gorgeous. In particular, I have to single out the work of printers Neil Shaver at Yellow Barn Press and Michael Tarachow at Pentagram Press for printing the text and the wood-engraved illustrations here with masterful impression – the words and images feel chiselled into the fine mould-made papers they used.

John DePol is the wood engraver I like best, and collect the most. I am not a completist, so to collect everything with a DePol engraving in them hasn't had the appeal for me that it would have for the completist collector. Instead, I have looked for those books, keepsakes, broadsides, bookplates, and original prints made directly from the blocks where DePol's illustrations have had an immediate fascination for me. I began first with the material that was (and is) easily available at prices that suited me.

The work DePol did for Yellow Barn Press, Pickering Press, and Pentagram Press – for the reasons I have already cited – came first. The deep impression and the perfect register with which his wood engravings were printed by these presses is simply thrilling. Later, I moved up a bit, paying higher prices for the slightly scarcer DePol work found in John Fass's Hammer Creek Press, the Allen Press, and the very limited editions (only 50 copies) of the Zauberberg Press. The most fun was had chasing original prints DePol himself made of his engravings as a separate issue, each copy signed and dated in pencil.

Whenever he would become fond of an engraving he had done for a press, he ran off a few more impressions from the blocks on a handmade or some finely laid paper, and sold it directly himself.

DePol's engraving style and his deep bibliophilic feeling for private press books enabled him to come up with just the perfect illustration for a text. His style was to use a contrast between dark and light in a boxwood engraving to make a fine, subtle, and accurate wood-engraved illustration, whether of a person, a thing, a landscape, a building, a bird, or a book. Over and over again, the printers and presses he made engravings for have remarked on his uncanny ability to imagine and judge exactly the illustrations a book needed without any of them spelling out what they wanted or required.

Above all else, for me DePol's work is such a joy because much of his engraving work was bibliophilic in nature: wood-engraved illustrations of handpresses, libraries, bookshelves, books, bookplates, and portraits of craftsmen in the book arts (such as Dard Hunter, Bruce Rogers, William Morris, Gutenberg). DePol was a serious book collector, so he knew how much a bibliophile enjoys seeing bibliophilically themed illustrations that are accurately, evocatively, and pleasingly done.

No one was better than him in strewing a fine press book with little bookish vignettes. Engravings of beautifully bound books on a table, a private library with a fireplace and a stuffed chair for the collector, a book collector snugly ensconced among his rare books, bookplates for collectors and printers (the most beautiful, and certainly the most difficult to do, had been the bookplate for Michael Tarachow and Merce Dostale showing a couple sharing the joys of a book under a tree), a monk at the lectern table, a monastic library, the Kelmscott-Goudy Press, Kelmscott House, iron handpresses, Victor Hammer's wooden handpress, John S. Fass's press, Valenti Angelo's press, and the portrait of 'A Happy Book Collector', the frontispiece engraving in the miniature book *You Can Judge a Book by Its Cover* – which now, to my utter delight, graces the cover of this book.

Of course, by the time I began collecting DePol, he was no more, and whatever I got hold of was from rare book dealers. One substantial purchase stands out for me – some 15 wood-engraved broadsides, all signed and dated by the artist, that were both lovely and hard to find. This was from Peter Keisogloff Rare & Fine Books. I would keep coming across their listings for some 30 DePol signed impressions, each listed separately at varying prices. I think I saw it for several months before I finally did something about it. I don't know why I had not gotten around to calling the bookshop and asking for more details sooner – but the moment I realized several impressions in this listing were scarce and highly desirable (long having sold out in the market), I rushed to make a deal.

I made a list of the keepsakes I wanted, and asked the bookshop if they could do something about the price for a purchase of 20 or more of the engravings. They were happy to take 30 per cent off the total price since they had had it listed for a while now without anyone showing great interest. The 20 I carefully picked were, by the way, all bibliophilic in theme as well as printed on fine papers with a nice bite to the impressions. For this, I had the bookshop go over with me on the phone, piece by piece, what the texture in the paper felt like, if the impression had good bite to it, and an oral description of the image or illustrations in each keepsake or broadside.

I'm tickled to say I took all the best stuff. I had gotten lucky, really, that some of DePol's finest and proudest work had stayed in the market unnoticed all these years. The next set of delicious DePol ephemera I stumbled on was the last thing Neil Shaver did at the Yellow Barn Press – a folder of the best ephemera from the press, numbering more than 50 pieces, that included some exquisite DePol engravings in them, all on fine papers with a laid finish.

The loveliest, rarest (yes, rare not just scarce) thing related to John DePol that I have in my collection is a large clamshell box full of greetings and wishes from fine press printers and book arts luminaries from around the world to Thelma and John DePol on their 50th wedding anniversary. It was titled *Thelma and John, May 31st, 1996.* This tribute portfolio was conceived and put together by Michael Tarachow and Merce Dostale of the Pentagram Press.

DePol did his best and most prolific work after he retired, in his 60s, and was engraving until his 80s. He was a master of the burin, and he taught himself to engrave on boxwood. While he worked for several commercial firms, his heart was so much in being an engraver, and the pleasure and enjoyment he got in making illustrations for the various private presses that surrounded him, that he would take work after hours, on weekends, during his vacation. He could not wait to retire and do this full time. From the '50s to the late '70s, DePol made engravings for several commercial and financial institutions, earning his daily bread.

In the book, *From Dark to Light*, a commentary on his work by Joan Digby, she observes that typically he would begin early in the morning and work straight for four to six hours, taking a break in his garden. For a surface he used the end grain of the boxwood tree, which is hardest.

Gradually, though, boxwood became difficult to acquire, and he, like many in this field, had to settle for maple. His tool was the burin, a sharp cutter.

Watching him work, Digby describes how a wood-block illustration would emerge under his burin. First, he would make a sketch in graphite pencil on tracing paper, and this he would work on for as many hours as it took to get it perfect. Next, he would coat the surface of the end grain with a rich black ink carefully chosen for this, and allow this to dry overnight. On the next day, if the end grain was completely dry, he would take the stub of a candle and rub it on the surface, and smooth it out with his hand.

Then he would carefully lay the tracing paper with its sketch on the waxed end grain until the lines of the sketch from the paper faced down to be impressed on the wax with a burnisher or spoon. Against the black, the lines would take on a pewter colour. Now would come the actual engraving with the burin. He would hold the boxwood in his left hand firmly, and begin engraving with his right, precisely, steadily, and expertly cutting away into the lines. At first you could only see a blur and then the beginning of some pattern, in all this time the wood flakes would curl up from the wood and fly away.

Finally, you would see the sketch emerge on the surface of the wood. Once observing his work, Digby noticed it was raining in his landscape on the end grain, and his burin was cutting the stipples that fine rain makes as it falls. He had to be incredibly careful not to miss with the burin – that happened once and six hours were wasted.

It was a portrait of Pushkin for the Allen Press, and the burin had slashed Pushkin's eye!

During these decades, DePol contributed to the work of several fine presses, most significantly the work he did for John Anderson's Pickering Press. This forty-year collaboration sparked off many substantial books, such as *Words of the Masters*, *A Commonplace Book*, and the very scarce and highly desirable *A Victor Hammer Manifesto*, containing a finely accomplished wood engraving of Hammer's wooden handpress. After Anderson had printed DePol's block of the handpress (40 on dampened Magnani paper, 10 on handmade paper), he wrote this to DePol: 'Over the years I have seen more of your work than most, but this time, as I told Carolyn Hammer when I sent her proofs, you surpassed yourself. If you never do another block, you can rest comfortably on its laurels' (*John Anderson and the Pickering Press*, Yellow Barn Press, 1994). A copy of *Manifesto* still eludes me, but to my joy this sweet engraving turned up in the DePol festschrift, printed directly from the block on a full page in that gratifyingly tactile way Shaver has such mastery over when printing wood engravings.

Between Anderson and DePol it was a long-standing relationship of friendship and work, with Shaver and his Yellow Barn Press it was a glorious collaboration that grew into a deep friendship. It's difficult to pick out just a few favourites from the engravings DePol did for Yellow Barn – almost every one of them is a keeper. The full-page black and white engraved portrait of William Morris in *The Kelmscott Press Golden Legend*, the smaller two-colour portrait of Morris in *William Morris, Master Printer,* as well as his engraving of Kelmscott House here, a whole book of engraved illustrations of iron handpresses in *American Iron Handpresses*, and a particular favourite for me are the engravings of monks and scriptoriums in *Our Debt to Monkish Men*.

DePol's engravings for the Pentagram Press are some of my most favourite illustrations: they are so indelible and ravishing for the craftmanship and taste with which Pentagram's printer, Michal Tarachow, transfers DePol's woodblocks directly onto dampened paper.

There is a Pentagram Press poster done for the Oak Knoll Fest (a fine press book fair) showing a large engraving of an unlit, closed bookshop, and a bibliophile waiting outside that is so charming. The man in waiting, DePol has said, is himself – a devoted book collector who roams the premises of antiquarian bookshops. An image or illustration of this sort – bookshop storefronts, a browser, and more – are common enough; what lifts this engraving by DePol to greater heights is the depth and beauty Tarachow is able to bring to it by finely impressing the woodblock into paper, making this bibliophilic image leap out of the poster. It is warm and alive and immediate, something you will never get in a woodblock printed flat and dry.

COLLECTING STANBROOK ABBEY PRESS

A Tale of Two Admirers

From the first time I heard of the Stanbrook Abbey Press, I was smitten. The fact that a small band of cloistered Benedictine English nuns had once printed books as beautifully and impeccably as the best fine press printers of their day had me rejoicing. Sister Hildelith Cumming, Stanbrook's Master Printer, and the other sisters who worked the press used the elegant, flourished metal types of Jan van Krimpen, fine English handmade papers, hand-coloured or gilded calligraphic initials, and sumptuous bindings to make their books and keepsakes.

The motto of Dame Hildelith and her fellow nuns at the press was: 'Fine Printing for the Glory of God'. Or so I'd like to think! 'Most of its texts had a devotional theme but the printing itself was an act of praise, using fine types and paper and hand-illumination for "the glory of God"', noted the press's bibliographer David Butcher in *The Stanbrook Abbey Press 1956–1990* (1992). In particular, the press was famous for its 'Illuminated Folders' – a poem or a prayer printed from fine metal type on handmade paper in two or three colours, with calligraphic hand-drawn initials in colours and gold, while a few even carried a miniature watercolour to accompany the text. This handsomely printed leaf with gold burnishing was then tipped into a folder made of handmade paper, with the title of the prayer printed on the cover.

It was in 2015 that I first discovered the existence of this glorious private press, but where, I wondered, would I find the things they had printed? The press had done most of its fine printing between the late 1950s and the mid-1980s, and I already sensed the nicest things from this press would be scarce and pricey. When I looked at what the online rare book market had to offer, I found only one dealer in the UK on ABE listing a few items from Stanbrook. I was so glad to have come upon Woodbridge Rare Books – the bibliographical description for the Stanbrook items here sounded knowledgeable, accurate, and enthusiastically written. I began tentatively buying a few things from Bill Woodbridge, its owner, and from here on ensued a correspondence – on Stanbrook and other fine presses – that continues to this day between us.

What follows for the most part is my year-long email exchange with Woodbridge Rare Books. I've reproduced our correspondence (with some minor edits for clarity and brevity) in the hope that it might be of interest to a collector to get a glimpse of my transactions as a fledgling collector with a specialist rare book dealer (who also happens to be an accomplished collector). Anyone with a particular interest in this monastic press will certainly find it useful and entertaining – not, I hurry to add, so much for what I say here but for what Bill writes about the press, his collection, and his experience and perspective as a rare book dealer in fine press material, which is informed, thoughtful, and enjoyable.

I discovered that Bill was – *is* – the foremost collector of Stanbrook today (he would brush this off) with a complete run of the press (minus one or two of the scarcest – even near mythical – things from the press that probably no SAP [Stanbrook Abbey Press] collector can hope to unearth today), as well as being currently the top dealer in SAP material.

A brief introduction, before I get to our email exchanges, to Stanbrook Abbey Press. How did a humble monastic press transform itself into a highly accomplished fine press? A press doing functional printing for the Benedictine community had been in existence since 1876 at the Abbey, but it was only in 1956 when Sister Hildelith took charge of the Abbey's printing shop did it strive to be a fine press. The same sense of skill, beauty, order, perfection, devotion, and craftsmanship that Dame Hildelith had brought to her earlier life as a gifted pianist and her present life as a contemplative nun, she now brought to printing and bookmaking. She decided from the start that if the old press at the Abbey was to be revived, it would be worthwhile only if the printing was of the highest order.

But neither she nor the nuns that made up the printing

office at the Abbey knew very much about fine printing. They had seen examples of finely printed books, but had little experience in fine bookmaking. Dame Hildelith then turned to the private press community to guide Stanbrook in all matters typographical. At the heart of this initiation was rising to sound craftmanship. And the press took counsel and instruction from printers, typographic scholars and designers such as Robert Gibbings of the Golden Cockerel Press, John Peters of the Vine Press, type scholar John Dreyfus, and most importantly, Jan van Krimpen, the Dutch type designer.

The work of Stanbrook Abbey Press would go on to become a showcase for the lovely types of van Krimpen: Cancellaresca Bastarda, Romanée, Spectrum, and Lutetia. In particular, Sister Hildelith's favourite type to use in the Illuminated/Greetings Folders was the elegant chancery type, Cancellaresca Bastarda.

The first book from the press, *Christmas Lyrics*, is a beauty. Sister Hildelith had indeed set a high bar for herself and had met it. It had several hand-drawn initials in colour and one burnished gold initial, the collaborative work of illuminator Margaret Adams and the scribes at Stanbrook. From here the press just went from strength to strength, producing superbly printed books and ephemera. We have to remember that the nuns accomplished all this while going about their duties and fulfilling their vows at the Abbey. All the dampening of handmade paper, the hand setting, pulling the press, and distributing the type had to be done between prayer, contemplation, and domestic chores.

The work of this monastic press was the equal of the great and classic private presses. In due time though, during the 1980s, collectors didn't pay as much attention to the work from Stanbrook as they do now. In 1992, all that changed. David Butcher, a collector and a scholar of fine printing, produced the first bibliography of the press, sumptuously printed by the Whittington Press, with tipped-in specimen leaves. Once the bibliography was out, describing the various achievements of the press, pointing out their more notable books and ephemera, and how beautiful and brilliant they were, collectors woke up. They were now suddenly interested in this neglected press, and began assiduously searching for these items, with the result that the market was not only picked clean, but in due course, any listing of SAP items began showing higher and higher prices.

The scarce things from the press, done in just 25 to 50 copies, became scarcer – the deluxe editions in their full leather bindings were snapped up quickly, and even the books and keepsakes in their regular edition became quite sought after.

When I first began emailing Bill Woodbridge, he had a full-time job, and was trading on ABE part-time, and in the course of our email exchanges I have seen him turn into a full-time fine press dealer. Something I am especially chuffed about is having been a spectator to his Stanbrook collecting journey, particularly at a watershed moment: his unearthing, after a decade-long hunt, of two ultra-rare Stanbrook items that he had given up hope of ever finding. When he had first introduced me to his personal

Stanbrook collection, he had apprised me of his desiderata, and just a year later, in the thick of our correspondence, he wrote to say he had found them!

Outside of Woodbridge Rare Books, I would occasionally spot promising Stanbrook pieces from other dealers that felt underpriced to me, and I tried not to miss getting those. Or there would be the odd, out-of-scope Stanbrook item that Bill didn't have in stock, and I'd have to buy it elsewhere. One such rather attractive edition was the *Stanbrook Abbey Press History* (written by Dame Hildelith) that had been specially bound by the papermaker John Mason in quarter leather and decorative sides, with endpapers made from his very pleasurably coarse Silurian paper.

It was only halfway into my collecting of Stanbrook that I finally bought the bibliography (*The Stanbrook Abbey Press: 1956–90*), but until I got hold of this (it had felt expensive to me when I was just starting out as a collector) Bill had been my 'Butcher' passing on details from his copy, as well as adding his own considerable bibliographical knowledge of productions from the press. I've found him to be a principled, meticulous dealer, and though I haven't been one of his top customers, he has never been anything but generous, warm, and friendly.

There came a point when both of us, without realizing it, had chased after the same scarce Stanbrook pamphlet, making the same enquiries of the dealer who was taken aback that two customers had wanted to know the answer to the same question concerning this pamphlet: did it have a green or blue cover?

On 29/01/2015 03.42, AbeBooks <inquiries@abebooks.com> wrote:

>AbeBooks has received the following inquiry.

Dear Woodbridge Rare Books, I am writing to ask if the shipping cost or the price for the two Stanbrook Abbey Press prospectuses ('Christmas List of Publications' and 'Path to Peace') could be reduced? I am keen to buy these prospectuses as I am a fan of private press work, especially of Stanbrook Abbey, but I am also, alas, an impecunious collector.

Thank you.

Sincerely,

Pradeep

Dear Pradeep,

Thanks for your query. Yes, I could certainly do something on the shipping. As they are both small, I could do both items in a single package for a shipping cost of £5.00 (pounds sterling) on the Royal Mail International Standard service (5–7 days delivery aim, not tracked).

So putting everything together that would be:

W0227 Christmas List of Publications	£15.00
W0226 Prospectus for The Path to Peace	£20.00
Total	£35.00
Shipping	£5.00
GRAND TOTAL	£40.00

Please let me know if this is acceptable to you. Stanbrook is also my absolute favourite amongst the presses – these are two of the best ephemera in my opinion and they're duplicates from my own personal collection.

With best regards,
Bill Woodbridge

Bill,

Thanks very much. I've just placed the order.

I was drawn to these items because of your bibliographically rich descriptions.

Pradeep,

I do enjoy writing the descriptions; it's a bit of a labour of love especially for the Stanbrooks'. I am relatively new to the trade, and only have an online presence. I know a fair amount about Stanbrook, and could bore for England on that subject. I've taken the liberty of attaching a 'short form' catalogue of all my stock, much of which isn't yet listed on ABE. No more Stanbrook ephemera unfortunately, but plenty of small Whittington Press pieces. No pressure, but if anything else from here was of interest I could send a photo/description and also, if you wanted it, include it in the same package hopefully at no extra shipping charge for any small items.

Finally, I have dug out a duplicate Stanbrook ephemeron lurking in my own collection – a specimen leaf from 'The Path to Peace' – so I'll slip that inside the Prospectus with my compliments.

Best regards, I look forward to hearing from you again.

Bill,

One Whittington Press item in your short form catalogue that straightaway interests me is One Rainy Day. *I adore the large Miriam MacGregor wood engraved (historiated?!) initial of the letter O that opens this little essay showing young student printers at work.*

Pradeep,

No problem, I'll hold off on posting the package – no hurry!

Here's a photo of the 'O', magnificent as you say. This variant has a handmade brown paper wrapper with a red flower device on the front cover, and comes in maroon paper sleeve. All in fine condition.

One Rainy Day and the Typophiles postcard look like this:

W0147 'One Rainy Day' 1/150 ordinary	£30.00
W0189 Typophiles postcard invitation	£5.00
Total	£35.00
Shipping	f.o.c.
GRAND TOTAL	£35.00

The postage cost has crept up a bit with 'One Rainy Day' but I'm happy to keep to the £5.00 I originally quoted. Hope this is OK with you and if so, I'll send a PayPal invoice for the extras.

Typophiles photo attached.

Bill,

Thanks. Invoice paid. I'd be keen to know more about you as a collector, especially of Stanbrook Abbey Press. (I'm guessing you have a fairly complete run of the press.) Also, something more about you as a dealer in SAP.

Pradeep,

So sorry I didn't manage to get back to you yesterday (Monday) – however I did ship your package as promised so hopefully this will be with you in 5–7 working days.

My journey, briefly, was along the lines of:

- Unfocussed collecting without having a clue what I was doing apart from buying random nice-looking books
- Awareness of private press books, and realisation that these embodied just about all I wanted in books
- Unfocussed collecting of semi-random private press books
- Realisation that Stanbrook Abbey Press embodied just about all I wanted in private press (and were relatively affordable, and could potentially form a 'complete' collection one day)

- Focus on SAP, increasingly to the exclusion of all others
- Increasing completeness of SAP collection necessitating tracking down and buying large parcels at auction to acquire the few remaining 'wants'
- Disposal of surplus and duplicates arising from these parcels, usually ad-hoc and often via eBay
- Setting up as a professional (although part time) through ABE in order to move the above onto a sounder footing, and to properly manage the ever-increasing volumes of stock, and with the aim of making a profit

I've thoroughly enjoyed every step of the journey so far, and have been lucky to have had some great support and mentoring as a collector and, more recently, as a trader. I'm sure many people must make similar journeys, and of course the barriers to entry are so much lower as an online trader compared to trying to do the same thing twenty, or even ten years ago.

Bill,

Thanks very much for your engaging notes on how you got started. Can I follow up with a few more queries on collecting SAP?

Pradeep,

I did have it in mind to write back to you as things have developed somewhat, culminating in me resigning from my 'day job' at the end of March to concentrate full-time on the book trade. A fantastic development from my point of view! So many apologies for having to stall you for so long during a bit of a delicate stage, but I'd now be happy to answer your questions if you'd like to send them through, and in time develop my 'essay' on collecting SAP a bit more.

Bill,

That is a fantastic development, the software industry's loss is surely the antiquarian book trade's gain. Congratulations. I'm sure the transition must have its difficulties, but also brings with it, I am equally sure, great rewards. Please do keep me posted on your experiences as a full-time rare book dealer as they unfold.

P.S. Have you ever done one of those courses or seminars on rare book dealing? Do you think now that you are full time, you would want to?

Pradeep,

I am afraid of sounding rather arrogant but I've never really considered one of these seminars/courses would be value for money in my case. Nearly all of my 'tradecraft' (as opposed to knowledge about the books themselves, more of that in a minute) has come from observing and dealing with rare book dealers in the UK for over 20 years, and one mentor in particular has been extremely generous and open (both before and after I moved from purely collecting into dealing) with tips, advice and especially guidance in matters of etiquette, not just for buying but also for selling. I've found that his standards and behaviours are pretty much duplicated in all the serious (small and large) dealers I have encountered, so I'm reasonably confident that I've tapped into the accepted ethos of book dealing (by which I mean: terms of trading and knowing when to flex them, credit, returns, pricing, inter-trading with other dealers, relationship with the auction trade, talking about customers to other dealers [or not], margin, sourcing, descriptions and other topics which should be easy in themselves but if mishandled can turn sensitive or toxic pretty quickly).

Here are a couple of quick examples of what I'm talking about – I've never seen them written down anywhere but they're vital to know as I nearly came a cropper in the early days:

- If dealer A is lucky and buys at auction very cheaply, and dealer B then 'wants' that book and knows all about the auction and perhaps had even considered bidding himself but didn't, dealer B should be prepared to pay dealer A's full price less any trade discount that A is willing to offer. Appealing to the fact that dealer A is making a huge margin on the auction price, that dealer B could well have competed with him but didn't, and should therefore pass some more of the margin onto dealer B is just not done!
- Conversely, if dealer C has a customer wanting a book not in his stock, it is perfectly acceptable

for him to source the book from dealer D at D's price less any offered trade discount and then sell it to his customer at whatever margin he can make. He doesn't even have to be coy with dealer D about having a customer, it's just accepted practice that *it's the books that are traded, not the customers*!

It's not a big problem, but I do sometimes feel rather a 'junior' when talking to other very well-connected booksellers (and sometimes customers!) who can often reminisce about the previous three owners of any particular item that comes up, and also recall what wine was served at some lavish Press lunch 20 years ago (I exaggerate, but you get the idea). I also think I could probably do a bit better in my descriptions in that I haven't achieved 100 per cent accuracy when using the more technical terms – the London Rare Book School have a course on bibliography so I may well do that at some stage.

Where I have a huge gap of course, and probably always will having started at this late stage, is in knowledge, especially anything approaching 'scholarly' knowledge, of the books themselves. I can hold my own on Stanbrook I think, and hopefully Whittington, but outside those two narrow areas and a more superficial knowledge of English Private Press I'm pretty much blind, and am likely to know far less than my customers! I'd feel quite embarrassed about trying to sell anything remotely desirable or valuable simply to make a profit, if I literally had to first Google it to find out what on earth it was! Not to mention the more down-to-earth concern that without expertise a profit would be unlikely anyway. That's mainly why I think I will stick to Private Press/Fine Printing and hopefully improve my breadth of knowledge a bit within that field. It does help that pretty much every other major division of the book trade (antiquarian, First Editions, illustrated etc.) doesn't appeal to me personally anyway.

Finally, have you read John Carter's 'Taste and Technique in Book Collecting'? It looks old, fusty, and irrelevant at first sight, but it has many very penetrating observations on the mind of a collector (which hasn't changed much over three centuries it seems) and the relationship between this and the trade. Well worth a read.

Bill,

That was a mini-seminar in itself, and a valuable lesson in tradecraft. Thank you!

Pradeep,

As promised, here's a very abbreviated list of the Stanbrook Abbey pieces that have come in. Bibliographically they're quite intricate to describe so this is only a summary flavour (with Butcher numbers) before I do the full descriptions for ABE. If you are interested in any, it's probably best if I sent you photos first, so you can get a more accurate idea of what they are before deciding. All fine unless otherwise noted, and they're mostly in the earlier and more desirable handmade paper folders – C2 and C3 in particular are in Millbourn Lexpar folders, the highest quality paper used by SAP (apart from the Japanese ones perhaps) which later ran out even for printing, let alone folders.

A38 Youth and Age, 1/160 on machine-made paper with red printed initial, quite scarce £50

C2 Prayer of King Henry VI, gold initial with additional hand-drawn decoration in colour £50

C2 Prayer of King Henry VI, blue initial with additional hand-drawn decoration in colour and gold £40

C3 Christmas Card (Giles Fletcher), hand-drawn initial in colour and gold decoration, scarce £50

C10 The Stars (verses by D.M.M.), hand-drawn gold and colour decoration, handmade paper cover £50

C10 The Stars (verses by D.M.M.), hand-drawn gold and colour decoration, machine-made paper cover £40

C14 He Abideth. (From a XIV Century Manuscript), hand-drawn colour initial and gold decoration £50

C19 The Seekers, 1/10 with calligraphic title, hand-drawn gold and blue decoration, very scarce £100 (sheet Fine, cover Very Good)

C22 Rune of Hospitality, C22c variant without hand-decoration £30

I guess of these I'd recommend C2 in either version, which is a beautiful jewel-like classic; the gold initial in it lights up spectacularly.

Do let me know what you think sometime next week – no hurry.

Bill,
While I look at your list to see what I'd like, I'd like your thoughts on a couple of SAP items (Leo the Great, Christmas Lyrics) *listed with bookseller Andre Swertz in Switzerland. I've attached the titles in a Word doc with his prices.*

Pradeep,

That's a very good price for *Leo the Great*, which isn't that common; yes, you should definitely grab it if it's available. I dealt with Mr Swertz several years ago, he was very reliable and had some nice items. *Christmas Lyrics* 2nd Edition: that's good value if the condition is OK; the prices for this book have risen quite considerably as I recall, even though it's always readily available. It's really attractive and absolutely classic Stanbrook, also its status as the first book of the press makes it a must-have (don't worry about it not being the incredibly scarce and pricey 1956 1st edition, the 1957 is practically the same book). It does have a slightly more primitive feel than some of the later productions, understandably as Dame Hildelith set the bar very high for a first effort and not every element achieved perfection, but you'd have to be a real fine printing snob to worry about that (which I'm sure you're not!). It would be a good pair with 'Leo' (SAP's subsequent book) – you can see some of the evolution in technique.

Bill,
Thanks for your informed notes on these two early SAP books. From your list I'm just picking two for the moment: Prayer of King Henry VI in the gold and blue initial.

Pradeep,
That's great – I know how tempting it is to go for every single variant of these pieces, of which there appear to be an infinite number!

I make that:

C2, gold initial	£50.00
C2, blue initial	£40.00
Total	£90.00
Less 10% discount	£81.00
Shipping Royal Mail International tracked & signed	£12.15
TOTAL	£93.15

PS: You really must, if you can, try to make provision to buy a copy of 'Butcher' (*Stanbrook Abbey Press Bibliography*) at some stage! I'm completely unbiased here as I don't have one to sell, but I'm happy to let you know if I see a bargain. Cheapest at the moment seems to be £200 unfortunately, a shame there was never a trade edition.

Bill,

I'll start looking out for an affordable copy of the Butcher SAP bibliography, now that I am getting deeper into the press. One more collecting question if you'll indulge me again: I hear this from quite a few collectors turned booksellers – that after turning dealer, they don't feel a need to collect for themselves because the stock itself gives them that pleasure. It is enough that the book passed through their hands, that it was with them for a time, that they turned it over, handled it, examined it, and then let it go to a customer, making room for more stock. Do you think you might eventually feel that way too, or have you already begun to feel that way?

Pradeep,

Very easy to answer this one: emphatically not! I know plenty of other dealers do feel this way. I do rather like being surrounded by more fine books than I would ever have in my personal collection, but if I really do 'want' something myself then I've got to have it (permanently), not have it merely pass through my hands. This is probably a bad reflection of my materialist and acquisitive nature – perhaps if I give myself the benefit of the doubt it's more to do with the ideal of 'completion'. With 'completeness' as one of my major objectives in collecting, the idea that I might hang on to books for a while, enjoy them, and then let them go is anathema to me. I have had to make a couple of 'forced sales' in my time purely for financial reasons (my Gwasg Gregynogs being one) and have hated it each time! How I would feel about letting a personal collection go once it was complete remains to be seen I guess.

On another note, I'm very chuffed as I've just collected a longstanding project from a bindery in London. Can't remember if I mentioned it – it's a custom-made drop back box to house my two Stanbrook miniatures, 'The Addresses of Queen Elizabeth'. They did a very good job.

One of them is in an Elizabeth Greenhill binding – my only excursion into the realms of designer bindings (thank the Lord, considering the price!). The 'ordinary' is always on the market for very modest prices, although to be honest it's not very interesting inside. The bindery also made me some leather spine labels for the binders I keep the smaller Stanbrook items in – I could bore you with a photo of these if you're interested...

I think the Greenhill binding (a miniature mind you!) was £850 at auction about five years ago, and everyone I showed it to since thought that was a bargain. There's a Bernard Middleton binding of 'Patriarch Tree' on ABE at the moment for a huge price but thank heavens it's out of scope.

Bill,

What about those fabled Illuminated Folders I'm now finding out more about? I don't see them on the market at all – you must have them I am sure and it will be interesting to hear you on how you acquired them? Were they once upon a time more visible in the market?

Pradeep,

Another very good question. The more I go on, the more I turn to these rather than the books themselves if I just want an evening immersing myself in the beauty of SAP. You're right that they rarely come on the market but I think it's more a question of booksellers either not realising what they are, or not bothering to catalogue them properly because they are just 'ephemera'. I haven't noticed any particular deterioration in availability over the years – they've always been hard to find and relatively expensive, but prices are certainly becoming steeper. They were of course at one time easily available new from Stanbrook and they all appeared in various Price Lists over the years, but those days were long gone before I started collecting. I guess it's most accurate to say I acquired them 'slowly'. I then got a bit of a kick-start with a small parcel of thirteen very high-quality C and D list items from New York. A few years later a large and diffuse Stanbrook collection came up at auction in London. There were about thirty books and two bulging box files overflowing with smaller items in completely random order – a bit like opening Tutankhamen's tomb!

Some of the remaining C and D 'wants' are the toughest nuts of all to crack. In particular, if you ever see one of these: C5 'A Meditation on the Crucifixion' – please run, don't walk, to your computer and email me immediately to name your price and I would be completely at your mercy! This is one of the scarcest things from the press, and one of the two or three things I don't have from the press, though I have been looking for years now.

Bill,

The C list items sound most desirable – to fuse illumination, decoration, and fine presswork is everything I would desire in fine printing. Even though I am just staring out, I, too, feel I would like to focus more on C than A list from Stanbrook – so, if you ever acquire them for stock, please let me know right away. On another note, did you feel, as collectors often say they do, a kind of low, an emptiness on completing the collection?

Pradeep,

I have contradictory feelings: as the collection is only 'nearly complete' and the wants become fewer and more difficult, the thrill of the chase gets more enjoyable, and the satisfaction is definitely more intense when I get a success. But that's balanced by very long periods of drought during which nothing comes up and I have no leads to go on at all. But just when I think I've finally reached the point where nothing else will ever be obtainable, something tends to turn up. I think if I ever did truly complete the collection, I would certainly feel the 'emptiness'!

Bill,

It has been a while since I last wrote. I'm writing just to say hello and ask how things at Woodbridge are going? Hope it's okay to keep in touch with you even if I'm not ordering anything?

Pradeep,

Good to hear from you – don't worry about having to write back with an order, it's nice to hear from you in any event! Sales are still going well, but personal collecting is where the real excitement is at the moment. After months of inactivity, suddenly two Stanbrook pieces from my list of 15 remaining 'wants' came up on ABE last week which I managed to secure. It's very odd though – my automatic alert on 'Stanbrook' didn't seem to pick them up, although they were correctly described, which is a bit worrying. These two are quite modest 'D' list pieces, but much more excitingly I am (I hope) about to purchase an extremely scarce major 'C' list illuminated folder. Negotiations aren't yet finalized so I don't want to say more yet.

Bill,

Exciting to know you are on the chase again – I focus so much on you as book dealer I forget to ask about your collecting as it happens now in the present. Thank you for sharing this with me. Well, I can't wait to hear about the scarce C list Illuminated folder, after you have it in hand of course – though, I can take a good guess at what it could be!

Pradeep,

Now that the major Stanbrook is purchased, I can say more – it's C4 'A Meditation for the Crucifixion'. A huge, magnificent, and excruciatingly scarce item – Butcher only says 'very few copies were printed' and my own guess is less than 20. I'd never seen one on the market in 21 years. I had to make a pretty steep offer to acquire it but I consider it money well spent – I'm sure I'll never encounter another.

It may not be quite the rarest of the remaining 'wants' (that honour probably goes to 'Two Lytell Prayers', just 12 copies on vellum) but it is certainly the most spectacular and top of the list for desirability.

Bill,

C4! I wondered if it could be 'A Meditation'... not too long ago you wrote saying if I ever saw one, I should run, not walk, to my phone to tell you... Thank you for including photos of C4. How beautiful it is! I wish Dame Hildelith had decorated/illuminated more for SAP. It is I guess styled after those historiated initials from medieval illuminated manuscripts.

Are you allowed to reveal more details of the transaction? I would be most curious, though I would understand if you couldn't.

On then to 'Two Lytell Prayers'! on vellum. And best of luck on the chase.

Thanks for sharing your great find with me. It must give you quite a buzz, which I am sure will stay with you for quite some time to come. 21 years of looking and hoping, and it is now in hand.

Pradeep,

Yes, that's the one. Sorry I can't say too much more about how I got it unfortunately, other than it was a private sale. You're right in that it is precisely a 'historiated initial' as seen in medieval manuscripts – although this one is accompanied by printing rather than manuscript of course. Dame Werberg Welch painted the illustration, and Dame Hildelith herself did the gilt initial, according to Butcher.

P.S.: I've acquired a few copies of an interesting SAP rarity for stock – a poster done for an exhibition of Stanbrook Abbey Press material. It shows a sketch of a nun at work in the press. It is, unusually enough for a poster, printed on handmade paper and both the lettering and the image are printed letterpress as far as I can tell. If you are interested let me know, I'll be listing these at £30 each.

Bill,

I think I would be most interested in the SAP poster. Can you tell me what the size/measurements are?

Pradeep,

It's 76 x 51 cm. Condition Near Fine – a tiny nick in the bottom right corner, you can just see it in the photo, and obviously the curl from rolling which is easily corrected with a bit of reverse rolling. No creases, unlike the first Whittington poster.

Let me know your thoughts! I didn't know these SAP posters even existed until very recently.

Bill,

That's big. Somehow, I had expected a smaller poster, more like a large broadside. Would you have to ship it rolled then at extra cost, or do you think the regular postage would apply?

It is a rather nice, one-off item as things related to SAP go. I'm assuming you yourself don't want it because it is not printed by SAP, and so out of scope?

I have been getting deeper into SAP, reading as much as I can about the press, as well as making some progress with collecting the press. Some attractive ephemeral items mainly, which I could not resist when the bookseller offered me 30 per cent off the total price! I think I may have completely forgotten to mention I bought a copy of the Butcher bibliography a while ago when it came up for $300, the lowest I have seen that at, and so even though it would considerably dent my funds, I went for it. Enjoying it immensely.

Pradeep,

Yes – the poster is quite substantial! It would look great framed on a wall I think (that's what I'm going to do with my own – don't worry, I made sure I kept another one for myself before deciding to sell this one!).

I'd be happy to do the shipping for £11.25, although the actual cost would come in a shade above that, I think.

I meant to ask whether you had a copy of Butcher yet – it's great news that you do. It's an absolute essential for SAP collecting and has brought me huge enjoyment over the years. I still have to regularly return to it and each time I find there is some piece of information I've missed, often of some significance and relevant to the 'search'. In fact, without it I don't think I would be collecting SAP at all. I must send you my list of items which I think he missed. The only frustration I have with the book is that it says so little about the dynamics of collecting SAP, relative scarcity, etc., (apart from a few passing comments) although he spoke with some major collectors (mostly sadly dead now, I believe) to compile the entries – and he is a collector himself.

What are the pieces you have bought? Have you got a 'Question the Beauty' (C1) yet – you'll be blown away when you see one, if you haven't already!

Let me know about the poster in due course, I'm not planning to advertise it any time soon.

Bill,

The poster is perfect for your room with the SAP collection – after all, what could be a better exhibition of SAP fine printing than your near-complete collection of the press?

Question the Beauty – I wish! What I got was On the Centenary of the Press, Ubi Caritas, Path to Peace *folder,* Ten Rules, *and* Stanbrook Abbey Press: A Tibute. Ten Rules *is very nice indeed. I went in with a mind to buy only two out of this lot, but when the bookseller volunteered a substantial discount and threw in shipping, I extended the list to include all these.*

I'll take the poster.

Do please send me the list of 'Not in Butcher'. I think you've mentioned the Merton book, and some variants.

Pradeep,

That's great, I'm sure you'll like the poster – and it's rare (honest, despite my having more than one copy!).

That sounds like a super little SAP parcel to me. *Ten Rules* is very nice but often not in great condition – I assume you got a good one? *Stanbrook Abbey Press: A Tibute*, in my experience, is a scarce item so you may well have got a bargain! It was a spoof of SAP printing (with typos and spelling errors and awkward presswork!) prepared secretly by the nuns and presented to Dame Hildelith for her silver jubilee at Stanbrook Abbey. A very modest production indeed, but genuinely amusing and very well thought out. Originally distributed amongst 'friends of the Press' but now extremely scarce on the market – even in its second issue which was hastily produced after the first was suppressed.

If you've pulled off a real coup and have managed to get the first suppressed issue (look for 'Willie

Skinflint' instead of 'William Rustleflint' as the author of *The Limping Goddess*) then we can forget all about that invoice and I will pester you until you invoice *me* instead for a rather larger amount!

David Butcher's article on Stanbrook for *The Private Library* journal (Autumn 1993 issue) tells us why the first issue of *Tibute* was scorched: 'One hundred copies were printed for private circulation, but before they could be distributed Dame Hildelith spotted an unintentionally offensive reference to a good friend of the Press and the whole edition had to be corrected and reprinted. Almost all the copies of the first printing were destroyed and even the second printing is rare as it was distributed only to the Community and friends.' Only a true Stanbrook enthusiast recognizes its real value.

P.S.: If by any chance you got the SAP parcel from Plurabelle Books in Cambridge (pardon me for asking, but it sounds very much like a set I was sniffing around recently myself), I already know the answer to the *Tibute* question!

Bill,

Plurabelle it is. Which means you already know what I have is the second issue of the Tibute *– I'm guessing you must have spotted this copy on ABE and queried Plurabelle on this, just as I did. It was, of course, the Butcher SAP bibliography that set me off on this wild goose chase (and I suspect it won't be the last) for that first issue. Their* *description for the* Tibute *said 'blue paper covers' which the bibliography notes was the colour of the first issue, the second being green. And even though I didn't particularly want the* Tibute *(scarcity alone has never appealed to me, even scarce private press books – unless of course they are also lovely) since it was so deliberately plain, I was aroused by the possibility that this could be that elusive first issue. The surest way to verify I realized was to check if the name 'Skinflint' was present, rather than just verifying the colour of the wrappers. So, I rang up the bookshop and within a minute it was all settled – no Skinflint. And they had mistaken the green covers (from toning?) for blue! I suppose somewhere a first issue copy exists?*

I'm so glad I bought the spoof – apart from its rarity in the market, it is such a joy!

Pradeep,

How fascinating – thanks very much indeed for sharing the story with me, my hunch was right. This proves it's a very small world, as you'll see from my side of the story...

Plurabelle were the dealers from whom I recently bought two scarce SAP ephemerons – *Blake Trilogy* and *Holy Night* – and whose big parcel of SAP items didn't come up against my automatic search, worryingly. But another item they were listing was the *Tibute*, so I ordered that as well on the basis (as you point out) that the description was 'blue covers' which immediately set my heart racing as this pointed to the first issue. And if there had been any error, I could easily sell it on again as a second issue.

Next day the orders for the first two were accepted, but Plurabelle cancelled the *Tibute* order! When I contacted them, they were extremely apologetic, but explained that the *Tibute* was amongst a subset of their SAP items being reserved for another customer 'while he made up his mind'. These things happen, but I was in some agony thinking that a first issue might have got away, so I pleaded with them to give me the details even if it was headed towards somebody else. Much to my relief, they came back after a short while and confirmed it was Rustleflint – second issue, and again were very apologetic that their description was a bit misleading (the cover is actually dirty bluey-green, as you know!). They also said – 'funny, another customer asked exactly the same point about this book...'

So – all's well that ends well I guess! You're delighted with your parcel, and I'm delighted with the *Trilogy* and *Holy Night*, and no-one missed out on a first issue *Tibute*. I have seen one copy of the first issue, I can't recall the exact cover colour but it's now at the John Rylands library in Manchester and not likely to emerge from there.

So – I'll invoice you $58 for the SAP poster. Thanks for your order! I'll only be able to post Wednesday or Thursday I'm afraid as I'm off to stay with my dad in London for a couple of days.

Magnificent though the *Bibliography* (and Butcher's many other bibliographic works to an equally high standard) is, the mind-boggling scale of the task he faced was only brought home to me when I went to the Bodleian. After spending a couple of hours with six box files of Stanbrook ephemera – everything from junk mail, 'Dear Dame Hildelith, you may have won the holiday of a lifetime...' through to *Two Lytell Prayers* on vellum – my head was reeling with the effort of mentally collating it and working out what was what, even with the knowledge from 'Butcher'. Even though I sort of knew it, I was completely unprepared for the scale of the vast and varied SAP output (unfiltered by dealers or 'Butcher' scope) of small pieces, ephemera, jobbing printing, Benedictine 'official' printing, pre-SHC printing... It was only then I finally realised just how much judgment and scholarship DB had to exercise in knowing what to include in the *Bibliography* and what to leave out. Put yourself in his shoes of being faced with this lot, and potentially unlimited and unknown further sources of SAP 'stuff', and out of the chaos creating the well-ordered A, B, C, and D lists which (despite my list!) aren't missing any items as far as we know 25 years later. And all in the pre-internet age!

Anyway, that's enough rambling on for now! I'll let you know when the poster is on its way.

Bill,

Nothing from you on Stanbrook will feel rambling to me, so never hesitate to say more.

I must say Plurabelle have been very decent about this whole thing; they never pressured me the whole time I was making up my mind which took about a week, and never shot off an email to me in the middle to say they have had another sale for Tibute. *I would have never known if you hadn't just told me.*

Bill, I can't agree with you more when you say that 'only a true Stanbrook enthusiast recognizes the Tibute's *real value'. For me, too, apart from its rarity and charm, each time I look at or even think about it, it makes me imagine that special time in the Abbey when the 'minions of the press' were secretly preparing this right under their Printing Mistress's very nose, and then the moment of revelation, and Dame's Hildelith's total delight. So, of course, if one is a fan of SAP, one couldn't not have it in the end: the telling camaraderie of it all, the fellowship SHC and her fellow sisters enjoyed and shared over fine printing! One has to be a damn good printer to confidently produce something plain, even faulty, and show it off with such mirth.*

Butcher's achievement in compiling the bibliography is staggering indeed (as he briefly explains in Matrix 12 with 'The Impossible Takes Longer'), and one is eternally grateful to him and the Whittington Press for having pulled this off.

Please take your time about mailing the poster, no rush.

Pradeep,

Thanks very much for letting me know you got the poster, always reassuring! Glad you're pleased with it.

Just thought I'd give you a quick update as another SAP development has recently arisen which may be of interest...

I was chugging along quite nicely with the 'scope increase' items. Twelve pieces are either already with me, or in the post to me, leaving another ten or so to get, some of which should also be relatively easy.

However, in a classic story of how one thing leads to another, not to mention being in the right place at the right time, in the process of innocently browsing through a couple of these items at a dealer prior to buying them, I was offered the chance to look through 'two big boxes of Stanbrook which have only just come in'. You can imagine my response to that! Suffice to say that after 30 minutes of rummaging through the first box and getting less than half way through, I was sufficiently convinced to put in an offer for the whole lot – which was accepted.

As always with these treasure-troves (not that I've seen more than a couple over the years) it consists of everything from the odd absolute gem to piles of (duplicated) less interesting stuff, down to the absolutely worthless (in my opinion anyway, you may have a different view!).

I of course, as the new owner, have the privilege of cherry-picking for my personal collection, which is rather a delightful exercise. The star item for me is – you've guessed it – *Two Lytell Prayers* on vellum. Slightly variant to Butcher (manuscript cover in a calligraphic hand, and no copy number) but I'm not complaining! Plus, plenty of SHC ALS (Autograph Letter Signed), very timely given our recent correspondence.

However, even having done that, there are a lot of interesting pieces remaining that I will be putting on the market. I thought I'd share the short-form list of these with you in advance (I've shared it with just one other SAP enthusiast customer, so if there's any competition it will be first-come first-served, but I don't anticipate there will be a problem).

You may want to get out your 'Butcher' and have a browse, but here are a few that might be of interest for starters:

Question the Beauty – stunning, with gold initial and a miniature of a duck below the text. It has the later blue card covers but the Margaret/Harry Adams quality is as high as it ever was. This was Stanbrook's first illuminated folder, and perhaps the best for the overall balance between text, layout, calligraphy, and illumination – an exquisite piece which epitomises the SAP style. Dame Hildelith did several reissues of *Question the Beauty* subsequent to its first publication in 1957, which are identifiable by coloured card wrappers as here – the quality and beauty of the original issue was entirely maintained. Haven't seen one on the market for a few years now...

St Aelred's Prayer – quite modest but lovely and early colour printing. I can offer a quantity discount on this one. (!)

The Unicorn (sheets) – a great way of getting a taste of a very scarce and expensive book, this is a 'coherent' gathering of leaves starting with the title page, and a hand-done initial.

Mary's Spinning – on two different Japanese papers (cover and body) so soft and fibrous that they feel like cloth.

As always, more details/photos on request, I won't be putting them on ABE until the New Year...

All the best, I guess it's also time to wish you compliments of the season!

Bill,

Wow, splendid. And congratulations on nabbing Two Lytell Prayers. *Your want list is quickly filling up, not to mention the scope increase items you've been quick to pick up.*

Right off I can say I'd like Question the Beauty. *Please reserve it for me.*

Also, is there anything in the ALS (from SHC) that you feel you can part with? Even just a short note or tiny letter – and not even of any consequence content wise – just a personal note etc. Or some peripheral SAP related matter. If so, I'd like to buy it.

Pradeep,

Many thanks for the fast reply!

I have just realised *Question the Beauty* isn't even on the list, but don't worry, it is for sale. The reason is that I was dithering about keeping it for myself, and it was in the 'keep' category on the spreadsheet until a very recent change I made after I pasted to the Word file. Fine condition, and retail price is £100, so £90 to you. Consider it reserved.

Here also are photos of all the items you mention, apologies for the shadows – three versions of the *Chester Processional*, two with and one without gold. The *Michelangelo* is quite difficult to get.

Retail prices should all be in the right-most column of the table? But just in case,

Chester Processional (gold/colour)	£40
Chester Processional (colour only)	£30
Unicorn sheets	£25
Michelangelo	£60

I think I can do something on the ALS. The item in the photo would fit your description pretty much perfectly – it is tiny but it isn't entirely peripheral, being addressed to a Stanbrook–published person, Phillida Gili (illustrator of *A Remaining Christmas*). In the spirit of Christmas, and SHC herself, I can't charge for this one – I know you treasure her manuscript.

Enjoy the decisions!

Bill

P.S.: *Question the Beauty* miniature is NOT a duck after all, as you can see. Ornithology was never my strong point!

P.P.S.: *Michelangelo* now reserved elsewhere – sorry!

P.P.P.S.: *Michelangelo*, *Sonnet CXVI*, *Dialogue with the Madonna* and *Sussex Songs* all now sold – hopefully that won't cramp your selection too much!

Bill,

It's only Question the Beauty *I will be ordering – at least for now. I hope making only a single order doesn't*

disappoint – Michelangelo *and the* Shakespeare Sonnet *are the other two I would have liked. It turns out that I did already have* Chester Processional *(but without the gold).*

I am very delighted to see the quick sales: it's nice to see such buying buzz around SAP printing suddenly. If early next year some of this stock is still available, I hope to be able to get more.

Thank you very, very much for including an ALS from Sister Hildelith. Something I'll treasure greatly as you've noted. I like Gili's work very much – in other private press items I have seen. And I think she's Reynolds Stone's daughter, no?

Pradeep,

That's great, I think you probably (rarity apart, where the *Sonnet* claims the prize) have the best of the bunch. No disappointment at all, great to see you get something good (and to see some cash coming my way so quickly to offset my purchase of course!).

I don't think there will be any more sales now prior to my putting them up on ABE, which will be a gradual process commencing early Jan, so no pressure on you to come back quickly I hope. You're very welcome to the SHC item, it's the least I can do! Yes, Phillida Gili is Reynold Stone's daughter.

With *Two Lytell Prayers*, I think I now have all the pieces that Butcher lists as being done on vellum – apart from the single copy of *Question the Beauty* that SHC gave to Jan van Krimpen on his only visit to Stanbrook. That one may be a little challenging to acquire...

All the best, and compliments of the season if we don't talk again before Christmas.

Bill,

Thanks very much.

Reflecting a little more on your spectacular discovery of this SAP lot – weren't you simply stunned that it contained Two Lytell Prayers? *I would imagine that you – like many serious SAP collectors – must have fantasized about stumbling on some such SAP bundle and further embellishing the fantasy by imagining that – lo and behold! – it would also contain this elusive item in the lot. (I imagine some such thing happening with the C4 Hildelith illuminated historiated initial in the Crucifixion folder.) It feels like your discovery of this is one instance of a collector's fantasy coming true. Plus, there's the other fantastic aspect to it: a SAP dealer like you stumbling on a such a packet for sale with its many desirable items for stock!*

One question about this transaction, and once again without you having to go into any details of price, name of dealer, etc. – did the source/party you acquired it from know Two Lytell Prayers *was in there? That is, know its rarity and value, and so the bundle had accordingly gone up in price? Or did it simply come as one SAP bundle, with the* Prayers *simply included or thrown in? (I'm just wondering how much of a greater bargain this was!).*

Compliments of the season to you and your family too.

Pradeep,

Yes, I was extremely stunned (if one can be) by discovering *Two Lytell Prayers*! So often these big bundles (well I say so often, there have been very few over the years) are full of only very predictable stuff – either another collector/dealer has rifled through them already, or they were someone's 'ephemera' pile in the first place with the better items being held elsewhere (those are my theories anyway). From the examination of about 25% of the contents I knew that things were better than this – for the record the other 'must haves' that emerged were *Dialogue with the Madonna*, *A Thanksgiving*, and *Evening Prayer*. These aren't SAP jewels by any stretch of the imagination – none are particularly small limitations, and physically they are all very modest – but they are (were) worth a great deal to me as I had never seen any examples in 21 years (apart from at the Bodleian).

But then at the very end of our long day I was sitting in a café waiting for my wife to do some final Christmas shopping, and I couldn't resist poking about in one of the boxes once more. Near the bottom, and difficult to get to (imagine balancing the box on one knee, and lifting up a large and wobbly pile of small SAP items with one hand while trying to rummage below them with the other), just below a newspaper clipping of SHC's obituary, and other scraps, there was a plain white envelope which I assumed contained similar items. On a whim I removed it, with difficulty, and saw a handwritten title 'Two Lytell Prayers/One of 12 copies presented to Pope John XXIII' (slightly misleading of course as he only got one copy, and I doubted that he happened to have left it in my box). A true Howard Carter moment, but like him I could only believe the envelope had long since been robbed. But no! There it was. All in all, a great feeling. I hope you get the chance one day to come across and 'have a go' with one of these giant bundles – if it's of SAP, please be merciful if you find something in it that I need!

The honour of the remaining 'want' least likely to be found now passes to the Rebecca Bestall *Meditation* (C13). Butcher says 50 copies I think (or some other encouragingly large number) but the Bodleian don't have one, and neither do any of the four serious private collections I have seen over the years, whether for sale or not. And I have been personally warned, by someone who should know, to resign myself to never getting a copy! Ominous or what?

Bill,

Going back to your earlier email about finding the SAP lot: even more remarkable to learn that when you bought it, you didn't even know Two Lytell Prayers *was tucked away inside. What a moment that must have been in the cafe, as you opened the envelope to see them.*

Thanks very much for giving me the story in some detail: as usual I relished every bit of it. Such brilliant bibliophilic finds probably happen once a decade in the annals of collecting, and certainly only one or two times in a collector's lifetime.

Though I hope this won't be your last.
best,
Pradeep

P.S. The parcel is here! Very lovely the Question the Beauty *folder. Thanks again for the gift of the SHC manuscript note. A rich addition to my autograph collection.*

Pradeep,

Excellent, very glad you liked them both. My pleasure with the manuscript note!

Thanks very much for your kind wishes, same to you for 2016.

I'll get on to putting some of the new SAP items on ABE next week, hopefully.

All the best,
Bill

Postscript: Years later, just as it had happened with the *Tibute*, Bill and I ended up bidding on another rare Stanbrook item on eBay without quite realizing we were bidding against each other – though at some point during the close of the bidding, I began to feel one of the bidders had to be Bill. This was one of the 50 specials of the Stanbrook Abbey Press History in two volumes, the first volume is the history of the press in a fine full leather binding, and the second volume is full of tipped in specimen leaves from the work of the press, including a leaf from the extremely rare *Rituale Abatum*. Bill himself says he has seen only a couple of copies of these specials, and he was bidding for stock, not for himself since he of course already had a copy of it (including variant productions of the *History*).

There were only three bidders in the end, and I dropped out as the auction was drawing to a close; the current bid had already crossed my Max Bid. It then came down to those two bidders who kept the battle going until the last few seconds when a snipe bid settled it. After the auction was over, I asked Bill if he had perhaps been one of the bidders, and he shot back an email almost immediately saying yes, and he had been the winner as well! What's more, he had even guessed the identity of the underbidder! What a small world after all is the rare book world, concluded both of us.

MY FINE PRESS HEROES

Victor and Carolyn Hammer

My greatest private press heroes are Victor and Carolyn Hammer. The first time I saw a book they had printed, I gasped in pleasure. The metal type felt not just deeply pressed into the dampened handmade paper, but looked *carved* into the paper. While I have seen some fine press printers use less ink and more pressure than others to achieve impression (pressman Harold McGrath, notably for Gehenna Press), nobody in the history of modern fine printing went as far as the Hammers did with their deep impression in the books from the various fine presses they operated over the years.

In the typographic journal *Matrix* (vol. 7, 1987) Sebastian Carter, the scholar-printer of the Rampant Lions Press, describes the ways Victor Hammer went further than any modern printer (excepting perhaps Dard Hunter) in how he made a book:

> But Victor Hammer went further than William Morris: it was not enough to use handpresses, but they must ideally be reconstructions of the wooden presses

> in use before the beginning of the 19th century. The model for the design of his types was found not in early printed books but in manuscripts of the period between the fall of the Roman Empire and the rise of the Carolingian, on whose uncial script he based first his own handwriting (his calligraphy) and then his types.
>
> And he was not content as Morris was, to draw over photographic enlargements of his models and hand the sketches to a professional punchcutter, but after his first unhappy experience of this process, he gradually taught himself the craft of punchcutting and cut his own letters.

The reason to take note of Hammer's work, Carter goes on to say, is the sheer quality of it. His books,

> printed sometimes in an edition of only hundred, are strange but self-evident masterpieces. On their Magnani and Hosho papers, with their intricately cut and printed two-colour initials, and their dense and rhythmical pages of type, they are magnificent achievements. The quality of their presswork is little short of miraculous. The *Samson Agonistes* and his edition of Holderlin's poems must rank among the most beautiful books printed this century.

Victor Hammer, Carter reminds us, came back to the most simple and essential in printing so that he could have control or mastery over his craft. It was not a stunt to call attention to his printing, but for 'its own virtue'. Neither did he want his uncial type to come off as an effect, to startle you, but felt strongly that it was a letterform that brought grace and strength to the text.

Victor Hammer's first press was the Stamperia del Santuccio (The Press of the Little Saint, or The Press of the Lesser Saint) begun in Florence in 1931. A true private press, the vision and work and labour of one extraordinary craftsman printer. The first book from the press was *Samson Agonistes.* This is a scarce book, and appropriately expensive when found. (Presently I see a copy for $5,720.) In 1939, Victor Hammer relocated to America, and set up his press there with his son. He married Carolyn Reading, a rare books curator who had become his pupil, teaching her to print alongside him in the same manner he had always been printing.

The books from this period, roughly from the 1950s to the 1970s, were printed under two imprints: Stamperia del Santuccio, which Hammer revived again, and the Anvil Press. For most of these books, Victor designed and composed the pages, and either his son, Jacob, or Carolyn physically printed on a wooden handpress, usually from one of his metal uncial types (American or Andromaque) always on dampened handmade paper with a deep and glorious impression.

Such was Victor Hammer's affinity for printing, says his wife, that one time in his early days of retirement 'he "wrote" a book by setting its text directly in type, without benefit of manuscript proper'!

For these reasons I have loved and admired the books

printed by Carolyn Reading Hammer; she's the most underrated fine press printer, I feel. She printed books as finely as Victor did. Neither Carolyn nor Jacob made everything by hand as Victor had, but their craftmanship reached his standard, and they were faithful to his printing aesthetic of impressing metal type deep into the paper. Looking at a book one of them printed, you can't tell whether the presswork was done by Victor, Jacob, or Carolyn.

After Victor died in 1967, Carolyn continued issuing books from the Anvil Press, choosing essays and meditations by her husband, and printed them on his wooden handpress in the same uncompromising way Victor had. She had worked alongside Victor on many books, and knew his ways and methods well: she carefully chose her handmade papers, used various forms of his uncial types, the composition and margins of each page was handsomely set, the presswork sharp and deep, and handbound the books.

I have been lucky in acquiring some of the best books Victor and Carolyn printed, or rather I should say, made. While I don't have *Samson Agonistes* and *Gedichte,* or some of the more deluxe, hard-to-find Anvil Press books, I've managed to get at least half a dozen of the noblest books they printed in terms of text and presswork and paper. My most recent finds, happily, have been the elusive Stamperia Opus broadsides.

There was also one item – a true rarity – concerning Victor Hammer that gave me immense pleasure and satisfaction in finding. It's a very personal, emotional piece of printing that links two important craftsmen in his life:

the calligrapher and type designer Rudolf Koch and his son, Paul Koch, who had been instrumental in teaching Victor how to cut punches for type. They were also the dearest of friends.

When Rudolf Koch died in 1934, Paul printed a beautiful memorial service for his father, with the music printed in red and black – something Paul was renowned for at Haus zum Fürsteneck, his printing shop. Since Rudolf had been so close to Victor, Paul involved Hammer in the production and used an early cutting of his Samson uncial type to print the six-page service. It was titled *In Memoriam, Rudolf Koch/Preface of the Mass for the Dead.* The German bookdealer I bought it from told me that the collector he had acquired it from had been a devotee of the things Paul Koch had done at Haus zum Fürsteneck, and had a large collection of items from the shop in beautiful condition. And indeed, this eight-page sewn memorial tribute was in very fine condition. The six beautiful pages of text and music in red and black are printed on a lovely, laid paper. The music notations were cut in steel by Paul. The size of this memorial was an impressive 13 x 9 inches. Probably only a few copies were printed for friends and family.

My favourite book from the Hammers was printed not by Victor but by Carolyn – *Chapters on Writing and Printing*. It was an expensive book for me to buy – I got the superior edition done on Japanese Hosho paper – and I saved up over a few months to be able to buy it. It happened this way: I had been slowly buying more and more of the higher-end press books from Frederic Shearer of Entropy Books, and he had been letting them go at prices revised for me. Every four to six months when I felt I had saved enough to buy a few press books, I would look at his inventory on ABE carefully, and pick three to four titles and ask him what was the lowest he could go on them if I bought all four. He had long realized the limitations I was working with, and never failed to mention a sum that I found tempting. If not exactly bargains, they were priced well below what other dealers were asking. So, this time around in my list was *Chapters on Writing and Printing*, and I asked him if he thought I would like it. Frederic wrote back to say that in his eyes it 'was a perfect storm of a fine press book for the way text, paper, and presswork come together in it'.

It is indeed a beauty – to see metal type in black and red pressed into those feathery white Japanese handmade papers is more exquisite that I can describe. One of the pages showed a beautiful two-colour initial in blue and red cut in brass by Carolyn. The book, like all the Hammer books, will have to be read and handled. Because to be sure Victor Hammer printed books so that they should be read even as they give pleasure in the way they are printed, and in the way they feel in a bibliophile's hand. The uncial type, it is worth repeating here, does really grow on you, and in this book, I felt hooked to this typeface.

The little rarity from the hands of Victor and Carolyn Hammer I have is *Notes on the Two-Color Initials of Victor Hammer* done in 1966 in an edition of 125 copies. It shows and describes how the Hammers made their glorious initials. The final initial of the letter in lowercase is printed in blue against a scarlet background dotted with white printers' flowers.

PRINTING WITH A HANDPRESS AT HEAVENLY MONKEY

The greatest attraction to me of finely printed letterpress books when I first discovered them – the very reason I had begun to collect them – was to enjoy and relish fine printing done on a laid handmade paper that had been dampened for printing, allowing the metal type to press into paper, and to swoon over the sharp letterpress impression brought about by the 'dwell' of a handpress on a page. But I had become increasingly disappointed and frustrated at coming across example after example of present-day fine press books done on smooth, wove papers, printed dry, with little impression. And then I came across Rollin Milroy and his Heavenly Monkey Press (based in Vancouver, BC) and knew at once that this was exactly the kind of contemporary fine printer I had hoped to come across – his work had gone even beyond my deepest desires of what a private press book ought to look and feel like.

His *Elements in Correlation: Printing with the Handpress at Heavenly Monkey* (2009) for me was a substantial and deeply resonant contemporary press book. This was not only printed in the way I liked, but also the book *itself* was about how and why the most natural, rewarding, and superior method of fine printing is damp printing of handmade paper on a handpress.

Elements in Correlation was the first fine press book I bought on approval – I liked the sound of it, but it would be an expensive purchase for me. Because I had bought a few small things from Vicky and Bill Stewart's Vamp & Tramp bookshop in the past, they very kindly sent it to me with the understanding that I would need to pay for it only if I was going to keep it. When the book arrived, I handled it very carefully, with the possibility of a return hanging over my head; I had to ensure it would be sent back in the same condition. The cost of the book? $1,000.

I needn't have worried. It turned out to be a beautiful and immaculate book. My copy is the regular issue (there was a deluxe, too) done in an edition of just 40 copies, set in Dante roman and italic types and printed by Rollin Milroy in two colours with a Washington press on dampened Heavenly Monkey (HM) text paper. This slim, elegant folio was bound in quarter leather with boards covered in a paste paper created by Claudia Cohen specially for this book.

The presswork is exquisite; the text is a rousing, engaging, personal account of why Milroy prints the way he prints. The epigraphical quotations that begin the chapters are finely done pieces of shaped typography, as is the colophon. Tipped in are leaves from other presses and publishers showing both – printing on paper that was dampened and paper that was not.

Elements in Correlation, explains Milroy in the introduction, started out as something to do between projects and then grew into something larger: 'an exploration of the nature of my own beliefs in how a letterpress page should look'. And this deepening belief left him feeling completely unconnected to so much of contemporary letterpress printing out there. The answer, as it turns out, lies in what Richard Gabriel Rummonds, handpress printer, has called the kinship between the handpress and handmade paper.

'Printing damp', Milroy goes on to note, 'is the most natural way to print letterpress. How is it, then, that it has become the rare exception among contemporary letterpress printers?' He surveyed the books in his collection relating to handpresses and printing, and found there a general consensus that 'dampened handmade paper is the best and truest way for printing letterpress, and the tool best suited for printing this way is the handpress'. And yet many contemporary press books are printed dry with imperceptible impression on smooth, wove mould-made papers or worse, machine-made papers.

In looking at what other handpress printers before him had said on the subject, Milroy found they had much to comment on the spiritual, technical, and practical qualities that separates handpress printing from other presses, but they were less expansive on why handmade paper and why damp? This he had to answer himself because for him 'it all starts with the unique results that can be achieved only when type is printed damp'.

What drew me most to the text was Rollin's own note on 'Why I print how I print'. The book opens with a magnificent epigraph from the guru (and poet) of handpress printing, William Everson, elegantly and strikingly laid out by Rollin.

> When this finely-inked type is pressed into the paper and held there in what is called the 'dwell' of the handpress, to lie at the very bottom of the impression, then when the sheet is removed all about it the light refracts from the crimp the letter made in its strike, and glows there, and the whole page becomes radiant with a suffused, a subdued and upcast light. You see it at its most gracious and most pure in damp printing. For as the sheet, without blemish, truly a holy thing, is lifted from the tympan and held lightly in the hands, seemingly so receptive as to almost show the impress of your breath, then all your labor, all that accumulated endeavour floats there in the soft upgiving of its light, wholly resolved and made proportionate before the awareness of a perfect page. It is the final joy of printing.

Rollin mentions another champion of damp printing on a handpress – Lewis Allen of the Allen Press, who wrote in his manual *Printing with a Handpress*: 'The hand press not only records, but glorifies because the hand printed sheet emanates a unique liveliness and sparkle... an indispensable ingredient in the excellence of hand press printing is the use of damped paper; without it the hand press loses one of its most vital virtues.' Rollin recalls that it was the books of Dorothy and Lewis Allen that first opened 'his eyes (as well as nose and fingertips) to the total experience of the handprinted book'.

As he probes deeper into the reflections of other handpress printers – Harry Duncan, Victor Hammer, Porter Garnett, and Giovanni Mardersteig, he presents a clear case for the best paper to print damp is handmade paper, and that 'the most beautiful letterpress printing is to be achieved by printing damp'. He quotes Giovanni Mardersteig, printer at the Officina Bodoni, on printing damp, '*The image of the type is clearly impressed in flawless black upon the paper as though the characters were engraved*'.

Turning the page, you see on the verso, another quote from Everson, this one printed in red and black, again gracefully done in shaped typography. The quote's a real beauty, one of those things I myself feel very intensely about – paper.

> The most fundamental thing about a book is to find the right paper, because it's the whole ground of the being of a book, and the quality of the paper is in some ways the most elusive... Critics of the book generally focus on the type and when people get into printing, the first thing they get into is type. They learn to recognize the different faces, and become pre-occupied with them. But the paper is more fundamental, because that is where the beauty begins, and in the end, that is all that beauty comes back to – the substance of the paper, the field on which the whole thing can act.

The usual reasons given by fine press printers today for not using handmade papers and not printing damp is that it is expensive and takes too much time. But, argues Rollin, expediency and cost should not be an excuse today for not using dampened handmade paper if printing by letterpress is central to a private press's notion of a fine book. Because when letterpress is seen at its best when printing from dampened handmade paper, why compromise? Bruce Rogers himself, Rollin points out, had felt that the books he had designed and printed damp had been far more successful than the ones that were printed dry.

Rollin quotes a lovely passage by Rogers, where he talks of how printing damp makes the type itself a part of the paper. 'The punching of type into dampened paper raises printing almost from a two- to three-dimensional medium, and the slight halo or highlight created around the individual recessed letters give a sparkle and life to the page which cannot be obtained by dry printing.' Rogers ends by saying that the vigorous pressure of the type into the paper causes the print to become an integral part of the paper, rather than merely to lie on the surface. Milroy ends this section of the book with Everson: 'with damp paper a good piece of printing can be made brilliant'. And, he adds, 'perhaps that alone is my reason for preferring to print damp'. What appeals to him is 'crisp printing in deep black on a damp handmade sheet...'

The more time I spent with *Elements in Correlation*, the more I felt urged to write a small note to the printer, wanting to somehow convey to Rollin the deep affinity I felt with his book. Up until then, I had never written to any of the contemporary printers whose books I had been collecting, but *Elements in Correlation* felt so meshed into my own sensibility of a fine book, I felt compelled to write. And so I did. Weeks went by and I didn't hear back. Just when I had forgotten to look for an email from him, a response arrived.

Fri 18/9/2015 6.20 p.m.

Dear Pradeep -

I can't be formal after such a kind note. Since HM sells books through booksellers (vs direct), I rarely get feedback from the people who ultimately own & read the things. The books by others that you mention are exactly the ones that inspired me, and I get impatient with books about a printing process or technique that don't actually show it!

I'm a big fan of Yellow Barn (tho I think Neil printed the Goudy with a bit too much impression, which is easy to do with a heavier sheet when dampened). If you get the chance, his Kelmscott Golden Legend *is a great book (and I'm not even a Wm Morris fan!).*

Kind regards & thanks for taking the time to write,
Rollin Milroy
Heavenly Monkey

Since then, he and I occasionally exchange emails, and quite apart from sparing his time to read what I write and respond, I owe Rollin a debt of gratitude for other kindnesses...

The more recent books from HM press have been well out of my purchasing range. But the three HM books, apart from *Elements in Correlation*, I own and have relished thoroughly are *A Letter from Carl Dair*, *A Young Printer in San Francisco*, and *An Alphabetical Accumulation*.

THE FOUR TYPOGRAPHIC JEWELS OF GEHENNA PRESS

The typographical and ornamental beauty of four Gehenna Press books feel to me unsurpassed by anything else done in the same vein by any other printer, press, or designer so far. The four books are, in the order they were published: *Cancellaresca Bastarda Displayed* (1965), *Flosculi Sententiarum* (1967) *Romeyn de Hooghe to the Burgermasters of Haarlem* (1971), and *Zapf's Civilité Disclosed* (1995). The delicate, pretty, and masterful arrangement of type, ornaments, and colour by its artist-printer Leonard Baskin and the way his pressmen, Harold McGrath and Arthur Larson, impressed them into beautiful papers in these typographically ornamented books is exquisite beyond telling.

Acquiring these four books, both scarce and expensive, has been one of the highlights of my collecting focus in the arts of the book. Baskin, an artist and sculptor, founded the Gehenna Press in 1942, and some years later was joined by an extraordinarily gifted pressman named Harold McGrath. Together they printed some of the finest typographic and illustrated letterpress books of the twentieth century. In 1965, Baskin had this idea to make a book showing the calligraphic beauty of Cancellaresca Bastarda, a metal typeface designed by the Dutch typographer Jan van Krimpen, modelled on a chancery script, that the Gehenna Press had acquired in three sizes.

Baskin says he was moved to show their 'felicity and subtle beauty' in a book decorated with ornaments in variations of colour. For one setting he even uses seven colours. It is difficult to describe the beauty of these typographic arrangements as they strike the eye – it was a magic only Baskin could achieve over and over again. Commenting on his extensive use of type ornaments, also fondly called printers' flowers or fleurons, Baskin notes in *Flosculi Sententiarum*, 'I have ever been interested in these marvellous flowers that grow in the hidden gardens of printers cases, and their use, both scant and profuse, by early printers.'

For a text he took mottos and printed them in various shaped typographic settings. Baskin was very fond of shaped typography, and used it with a delicacy and restraint that only a few fine press printers have achieved or pulled off in modern fine printing. My copy of *Cancellaresca* is unbound, with six extra leaves and the scarce prospectus. I acquired it by swapping some fine things in my collection with a dealer who didn't, fortunately for me, mind letting it go.

The next typographic gem from the hand of Baskin and McGrath, *Flosculi Sententiarum*, I bought from James Cummins Bookseller. This copy was signed and inscribed by Baskin at the colophon. If in *Cancellaresca* Baskin used bon mots, in *Flosculi* he turned to strange, interesting, and striking moralistic sayings from around the world. In both cases, the text was just a pretext to show type and ornament at their most beautiful and purposeful.

This second entry in the Gehenna Press triumvirate of typographic beauties is the most venerated: *Flosculi Sententiarum*, or 'Printer's Flowers Moralized'. It was done in 1969 as a quarto in a small edition on handmade paper. It uses more colour (and even some gold) and a variety of devices and fleurons, and more dazzling arrangements to pull off a strikingly beautiful specimen book of type ornaments. On *Flosculi*, Baskin himself once admitted to scholar-collector Sidney E. Berger (in his *Parenthesis* journal profile) that, 'The book is a tour de force of typographic play: one page passed through the press nine times to achieve its diversity of colour and gold.'

Colin Franklin, collector and scholar bookseller, was another admirer of the Gehenna Press and spoke highly of Baskin's delicate experiments with fleurons in his essay in the catalogue *The Work of Fifty Years 1942–1992 The Gehenna Press*, noting that these books had been done with a certain amount of 'typographic jeux d'esprit'.

The third book, *Romeyn de Hooghe to the Burgermasters of Haarlem* (1971), does not use ornaments and is a more purely typographic exercise. Its chief glory is its thrilling display of Cancellaresca Bastarda: no book or broadside or keepsake done by any press, including the Stanbrook Abbey Press – which had specialized in the use of this fount – has shown van Krimpen's type to its complete effect and elegance as Baskin and McGrath have in this slender book. Only one hundred copies were printed, and copies of the book, as you may have guessed, are scarce in the market.

Not even Gehenna's own *Cancellaresca* can boast of showing off this type in this masterful a manner. It is all black and white except for a touch of red, done on a delicate handmade paper, a letter written by artist Romeyn de Hooghe in all of just six pages – but what pages! You could swear looking at it that it is a beautifully handwritten calligraphic manuscript bound between boards. What gives it away as a printed book is the fine – no, perfect – register of van Krimpen's graceful metal type into the paper achieved by that master-pressman Harold McGrath. The outstanding feature of this Gehenna book is the presswork.

It is Baskin's unerring design, but this book belongs to McGrath for making the near-impossible possible. It was Baskin's intention this time to not let anything distract from displaying this type – not ornament, not colour. Baskin set out to do this book 'to show every ligature, swash form and connected letter that van Krimpen devised for his beautiful type. It is remarkably calligraphic in feeling as van Krimpen intended'.

When anyone mentions van Krimpen's *Cancellaresca*, it is usually in connection with how adorably the nuns at the Stanbrook Abbey Press used this face for many of their books, keepsakes, and illuminated folders. In fact, no other press has shown it off so attractively as Sister Hildelith and her fellow nuns have done, with the single exception of how Baskin and McGrath designed and printed with this face for *Romeyn*, and *Cancellaresca Bastarda Displayed*.

The fourth type and ornament masterpiece from Gehenna is my absolute favourite of the set: *Zapf's Civilité Disclosed*. I'm sure you've guessed by now from the title that it is Baskin's display of the Civilité type – once an elegant humanistic hand – as designed by Zapf. It came out in 1997 and is typographical ravishment itself. The prospectus introduces the book this way: 'Hermann Zapf, the celebrated type designer and typographer has designed a new Civilité typeface following Granjon's general lineaments, but its twisting and turning permutations are redolent of Zapf's genius.'

Baskin, to me, is without doubt the greatest arranger of type and ornaments in the history of modern fine printing. Each page, each composition, each frame was like a typographical painting. The colour was vivid and thickly laid on, and the ornaments and type correctly pressed into these highly textured European papers. The text was a mix of quotations again, a little more literary this time than moralistic.

Baskin knew exactly how Zapf's beautiful chancery hand should be showcased – I dare say in some arrangements here, not all, he may have surpassed Zapf, who was a master type designer himself. Another pleasure of Baskin's finest typographical book is that here two giants of typography meet, greet, and kiss. I've read somewhere that Zapf had chanced on the book perhaps a year later, and was entirely surprised there was such a book (Baskin hadn't told him or sent him a copy!)

and was utterly charmed by it, and wished to have a copy. He wrote to Baskin and asked if they could swap his recent book on typography for the one from Gehenna. I'm not sure what came of it, but I really think Baskin should have taken a copy and laid it at Zapf's feet, or at the very least inscribed a deluxe copy of it and presented it to the typographer whose graceful typeface inspired him to make a Gehenna specimen book from it.

(There is a discrepancy in the printing details for this book in the prospectus and what is actually in the printed book. The prospectus promises everything on handmade paper: 'One of 100 copies printed upon various handmade Czech and Italian papers', but this later proved to be too expensive, and was dropped, with only the deluxe (I think) on those papers. But dealers go by the prospectus and list the book as being on handmade paper...)

Perhaps Baskin's greatest admirer is Sidney E. Berger, the collector, bibliographer, and author who spent several days with Baskin, watching him work, and wrote of their time together for the book arts journal *Parenthesis*. Talking of these typographic works of art from Baskin, Berger says, 'With equal skill he had produced some of the most beautifully realized typographical books I have ever seen.'

He recounts what wood engraver Barry Moser told him once about Baskin, that there are no absolutely perfect books, but 'Leonard had done two or three of them'. And mentioned *Flosculi* and *Cancellaresca*. What stays and resounds for me in the many things Baskin said to Berger is this: 'I would like to see type handled clearly, ornamentally if necessary, and in a beautiful way if possible.'

THE GRANJON ARABESQUE AND OTHER FLEURONS

The first fine press book I bought showing typographic flowers – *The Granjon Arabesque* – remains a favourite in this field of books displaying decorative fleurons. Elliot Offner, at his Rosemary Press, constructed the ornaments here using Robert Granjon's arabesque patterns. Few books on fleurons, save the ornamented bijous of Leonard Baskin's Gehenna Press, have used as much colour as Offner has to show these type ornaments at work.

What's more, it's a complete winner for me because within these garlands constructed out of Granjon's arabesque ornaments are quotations on type and ornaments by Bruce Rogers, Hermann Zapf, Frederic Warde, and D.B. Updike to name just a few of the most revered typographers and printers quoted here. *The Granjon Arabesque: Thirty Arrangements of the Ornaments with Type* (1969) is printed on undamped Frankfort cream paper and hand set in Centaur and a variety of other typefaces and monotype ornaments.

I was fortunate to get hold of a copy of *the Granjon Arabesque* that was one of only 50 in quarter leather by Arno Werner. The bookseller hadn't quite noticed the difference in the split of copies (the rest in cloth spine) and had priced it much less than even the regular edition. Score!

Apart from this, and the three type-ornamented jewels from the Gehenna Press described in the previous chapter, there are two other gorgeous specimen books of printer's flowers worth noting – Richard J. Hoffman's *When a Printer Plays* (1987), and Mark Arman's *Fleurons: Their Place in History and in Print* (1988) from his Workshop Press. Both are printed in various colours, with Arman's book containing a few fold-outs displaying ornaments in all their glory. My only quibble with Arman is that he prints all his books with zero impression on paper. He uses a kind of strong, archival parchment paper with a calendared finish, and though type and ornament are printed on a handpress, they show no bite on the paper. Some fine press enthusiasts may not mind it, but I think it's a shame there's no texture or tactility to his beautiful and dexterous compositions.

Hoffman's *When a Printer Plays: A showing of Printer's Flowers and Typographic Fleurons Arranged in Arabesque Patterns* contains 260 arrangements of typographic flowers in fourteen colours. Hoffman spent ten years researching ornaments and their place in printing, and even more years collecting these ornamental type-units. Over the years, he produced many books on type and ornament, but this, without doubt, was his masterpiece.

Accompanying the arrangement are quotes from typographers and designers as well as his own scholarly commentary on these fleurons.

The challenge in using these metal decorations is that these type ornaments are not fully formed in a beautiful pattern or shape – that is, they are not readymade decorations to use on a page, but are instead small, partial decorative metal units that the printer or designers will have to arrange in an attractive and meaningful pattern. Apparently, going by what all the designers have told us, they can be played around with endlessly and inventively. No printer or type designer can exhaust the patterns one can make out of these typographic flowers. It is left to the printer to be original, brilliant and fresh in arranging these flowers to decorate a page.

The pattern for these ornaments, such as the arabesque, came to the west from the east. The arabesque design was found repeated on cloth from Persia and Turkey, as well as in their calligraphic manuscripts. In Europe, the arabesque was carved on wood and used mostly as design on the covers of fine leather bindings. A little more than a decade after printing from movable type was invented, these ornaments were cut in metal to form type ornaments. A book printed in 1478, in Verona may be the earliest appearance of printer's flowers in a book. These flowers also appear in the books printed by the famous printer Felice Feliciano.

By the sixteenth century, many metal ornaments in the form of a type unit were cut and recut. The most famous is the arabesque designed and cut by Granjon, in about

1565. In the eighteenth century several type designers, punch cutters and printers emerged, offering a robust set of beautiful ornaments. From the hands of Fournier, Baskerville, and Bodoni came these specimen book of type and ornament.

These decorative materials are available in foundry metal type (cast and cut in a type foundry) and Monotype, which revived many type ornaments from the late fifteenth to the seventeenth century. Fleurons are similarly available in Linotype. These typographic flowers are used to make borders, head and tail pieces, chapter headbands and primarily best and most used to decorate initials.

A great classic of specimens of typographic flowers is Frederic Warde's *Printers Ornaments: Applied to the Composition and Decorative Borders, Panels and Patterns* (1928). Printed in black and white with a small section at the back showing ornaments on coloured paper stock, this was a pioneering attempt by typographic scholar Warde to take these small type units cut by Monotype, and arrange them in nearly endless combinations of ornamentation and pattern. It is a tour de force. Particularly in its deluxe edition printed on handmade paper.

Another little beauty that I found many years ago is a rather obscure, but very charming book on fleurons. *Printers' Flowers: Whimsicalities from the Windsor Press* is a scarce little thing, a jewel, by the Windsor Press done by the Johnson brothers in 1933. There are zero copies of this book in the market at the moment. I've seen it appear every once in a while, and disappear just as quickly. It features many tiny ornaments in colour, all charmingly done.

About 150 copies were printed and bound in decorated boards in a 16mo size book.

Another master of ornaments in colour is Michael Tarachow of the Pentagram Press. Michael's beautiful and lyrical handling of type and ornament can be seen extensively in his famed set of the Pentagram Press Ephemera. They also sparkle in another special book from his press, now rather scarce in the market: *The Glint Ornaments at Work and Play*. He has used various papers for his printing of type and ornament, but luckily for all of us who desire to see such things printed on dampened mould-made papers, the printer at Pentagram has always obliged.

Elsewhere in the book I have emphasized how Michael prints his text and engravings with a deep and fine impression on lovely papers. Another notable exercise from Pentagram Press on fleurons displayed in colour is *An Exploration of the Granjon Arabesques* (1990). The deluxe edition, or rather the first 40 bound in cloth, includes a beautiful tipped in specimen leaf.

Leonard Bahr of the Adagio Press did a lovely book called *Experiments with the Bradley Ornaments* (1967) where he printed ornaments on variously coloured Fabriano paper. If books showing printer's flowers interest or tempt you, and you want to make a cautious purchase, I'd suggest you begin with this book.

Along with these, two contemporary masters of combining type and ornament to great effect and beauty are Robert LoMascolo and Mark Argetsinger. Robert uses ornaments in delicate and surprising ways. He has made a couple of stunning broadsides where the large illustration is entirely constructed out of metal flowers. All his books use them in rich and deeply satisfying ways. One of his books that I have, *The Ocean Wave* (stories by Ambrose Bierce) uses modified *gold-foiled* Bruce Rogers ornaments – frolicking dolphins – to decorate the title page, and other head and tail pieces. It's sheer ingenuity and craft.

Argetsinger's ornamental work can be seen in the many trade and limited editions he has designed for several institutions and publishers. One of my treasures is a limited-edition broadside he designed with Fournier ornaments: the text is Fournier on ornaments, and it is framed in blue Fournier ornaments. It's a scarce thing, and I had the good luck to spot a copy at Honey and Wax Booksellers. I called and got the owner, Heather, to ask if this had been designed by Argetsinger, and she said, 'Yes, yes, it is beautiful'.

There is also a beautiful business card he had done for the Stinehour Press in a blue and red ornamented border that is immensely, *immensely* pleasing. But I *don't* have it, and would love to get hold of it someday.

All the books and broadsides I've discussed showing arrangements of printer's flowers are brilliantly worked out, carry important and useful text on the subject, and the ornaments – dexterously and pleasingly combined by these veteran printers – are a delight to see. If a printer or designer can use type ornaments judiciously and expertly to decorate a text, no other adornment is needed to beautify a book.

B.R.

Why is Bruce Rogers, or B.R., known as 'the greatest artificer of the book who ever lived'? Why isn't this Hermann Zapf or Giovanni Mardersteig or William Morris? Beyond the obvious reasons – the fine press masterpieces he created, the graceful Centaur type he designed, and his playful, joyous use of type and ornament – I think one answer lies in the marvellous response he offered in *Venetian Printers* (privately printed, 1924) to the old question of what books he'd take with him if he was to be marooned at sea. He said:

> When my own time comes to be marooned on a desert island, instead of taking along the favourite volumes that most amateur castaways vote for, I think I shall arrange to be shipwrecked in company with a Monotype caster and a select assortment of ornamental matrices. The fascination and amusement – and the occasional happy result – that can be got out of the almost numberless combinations of a few simple units would enable me to *cast away* for an indefinite period of great contentment.

It was the satisfaction, pleasure and excitement he got – or could get – from just *seeing* how type and ornament could come together in his head or a proof sheet than necessarily needing to see the results on a printed page that marks him out as the endless artificer of the book. When B.R. as he was affectionately known, was just a schoolboy he hand-lettered a single copy of a book, and rather than illustrate it with some drawings or sketches (as others would have done), he made some etchings himself and using a hot iron from his mother's kitchen pressed the plate marks into the paper. (When Hermann Zapf was a young man, he wrote out many calligraphic books in various inks.)

I've never had the funds to buy the best books that Rogers designed. I would dearly like someday to own at least a few of them: *The Odyssey* with the twenty six roundels in black and gold he created just for this Homer translation by T.E. Lawrence (which typographic-scholar Jerry Kelly feels is the greatest book in modern fine printing), the gorgeous *Song of Roland* with hand-coloured illustrations done after the stained glass windows of the Chartres Cathedral, and last but no means least, the book done at the Montague Press in 1915, *The Centaur*, showing the first use of his most famous type that combines 'timeless beauty with utility.'

(What a coup it would be if I were to stumble on one of the 12 very scarce copies of *The Centaur* that B.R. had himself hand ruled in red!)

I have three small things, though, related to Bruce Rogers that I am thrilled to own. Before I get to them, I want to mention some of the very first things by B.R. that I acquired. I am proud that the first autographed book from the hand of this typographer I bought was *The Twelve Moneths & Christmas Day*, with his signature on the note (as called for). I lucked out. It turned out to be – at the price of the regular edition – the deluxe issue, printed on English handmade paper and with this edition alone signed by the designer.

I had particularly gone after it for its mythical status in this designer's canon as the only book for which Rogers himself had hand-set the type. The next lovely B.R. designed book I bought, *Persephone*, remains such a mouthwatering bargain for the way it continues to be underpriced. Here, much before the gold-black roundels in *The Odyssey*, Rogers created a gold roundel for this book; the rest of the book, too, has ornaments and lettering in gold.

To welcome B.R. from his long sojourn in England, after he had completed making the Oxford Lectern Bible, the Typophiles organized a dinner, and printed an invitation to members that showed an illustration by W.A. Dwiggins of B.R.'s device, but mischievously altered by this distinguished lettering artist. It's certainly a scarce thing, since not many members would have preserved this invitation – this was listed for just $10 (by an ABAA dealer who I thought might have known better) and I was happy to grab it.

I managed to get an ex-library copy of his Grolier Club bijoux, *The Pierrot of the Minute*, with its delicate typographic ornaments and rules. I especially treasure the three typographic books he did for the Grolier Club –

Fra Luca de Pacioli, with its majestic title page; *Of the Just Shaping of Letters*, the only book B.R. physically printed with his own hands; and *Champ Fleury* in a special binding. But perhaps the one that gave me most satisfaction in discovering was the scarce prospectus for *Fra Luca*, which was printed on the same Kelmscott handmade paper *of* the book. It shows B.R.'s first design for the book's famous title page, printed in red and black with a border, but here the lettering is half in majuscule and half in miniscule. The final title page design in the book is all majuscule, and in *Bruce Rogers: A Life in Letters* (Thomas Taylor, 1989) his biographer Joseph Blumenthal called this 'a page of true grandeur tempered with grace – a beautiful title page unique in the whole history of the printed book'.

It was from the excellent book arts dealer in the UK, Barry McKay, that I bought this – one unsuspecting day I opened my Recently Matched Want List on ABE and lo and behold there it was. I bought it in a flash. He had – I felt – underpriced it, but I wasn't going to complain! In the many years I had been collecting, I had never seen the prospectus listed, while at least three copies of the book show online at any given time.

Fra Luca is usually a $2,000 book, and just once I saw it listed at $750 (from Blue Sky Rare Books) and I hesitated – stupidly – and it was gone. I had to pay a great deal more the next time a copy came around that I could afford. John Dreyfus, the scholar-printer, says 'this volume fulfils BR's expressed hankering for a book that "ought almost to be identified in the dark, merely by the feel or sound of it." Turn off the light, touch it – and listen.'

Rogers tended to dismiss his work, pointing to only 30 books as his personal favourites from the hundreds he designed. Born in 1870, in Lafayette, Indiana, his early years were spent as an illustrator. He turned to typography and design after his first glimpse of a Kelmscott Press book which he recalled as being a 'revelation'. This William Morris book made him see that a page could be made beautiful with type, ornament, and paper.

He immersed himself in the craft of the printed book, heading a special department at Riverside Press devoted just to the making of fine limited editions. From 1900 to 1912, B.R. produced many fine books, several of which were hand-set and printed on dampened handmade paper. These would constitute some of his best work, and his favourite work, leading to his reputation as a striking designer and typographer. Later, when his books were printed dry, he bemoaned it.

Blumenthal notes that B.R. shook off his William Morris influence quickly enough, and turned to the 'sophistication of the sixteenth century French printers'. B.R. felt restless at Riverside, and when in 1916 Emery Walker, William Morris's friend and advisor, invited him to come work with him in England, he jumped at the chance.

He wrote to Walker, 'I still have dreams of doing something finer in a fully developed style of my own that has yet been accomplished. I do not, for an instant, think that I can ever surpass Morris or Sanderson or Hornby on their own grounds – but my own ideal book is still far from being a realization and I must keep working towards it, however slowly and painfully.'

A book he printed in England after his arrival was *Of the Just Shaping of Letters*, for the Grolier Club, a bibliophile society in New York. Because of the war, Walker was left with no pressmen, leaving Rogers to print the book in the cold without proper heating. He fed each sheet of the dampened Kelmscott handmade paper to a press that had seen better days. He had never printed before yet, says Blumenthal, Rogers attained beautiful presswork – so finely attuned was he to the physical book.

Though Rogers loved England and felt more at home there, the business side of the partnership did not flourish, and he decided to return to America, although Walker and he continued to be close friends till the end, with Rogers returning later to England again to print three of his masterpieces, *The Odyssey*, *Fra Luca*, and *The Oxford Lectern Bible*. Of *The Odyssey*, Blumenthal writes that it is 'indisputably one of the most beautiful books printed'.

Fra Luca de Pacioli of Borgos Sepolcro, 1933, is one more book on the history of Roman lettering that the Grolier Club commissioned, a companion volume to *Of the Just Shaping of Letters* (1917) by Albrecht Dürer and Geoffrey Tory's *Champ Fleury* (1927). Fra Luca was a Franciscan friar who was a mathematician fascinated by letters. *De Divina Proportione,* Venice, 1509, is his seminal work. Stanley Morison wrote a scholarly essay for the book on Fra Luca and the importance of his diagrammatic drawings of letters. Blumenthal describes it as 'a noble tall quarto of 118 pages, printed on a magnificent paper handmade by Batchelor of England, in an edition of 390 copies, with seven copies on large paper and 23 majestic Pacioli letters printed in an intense black ink of great depth.'

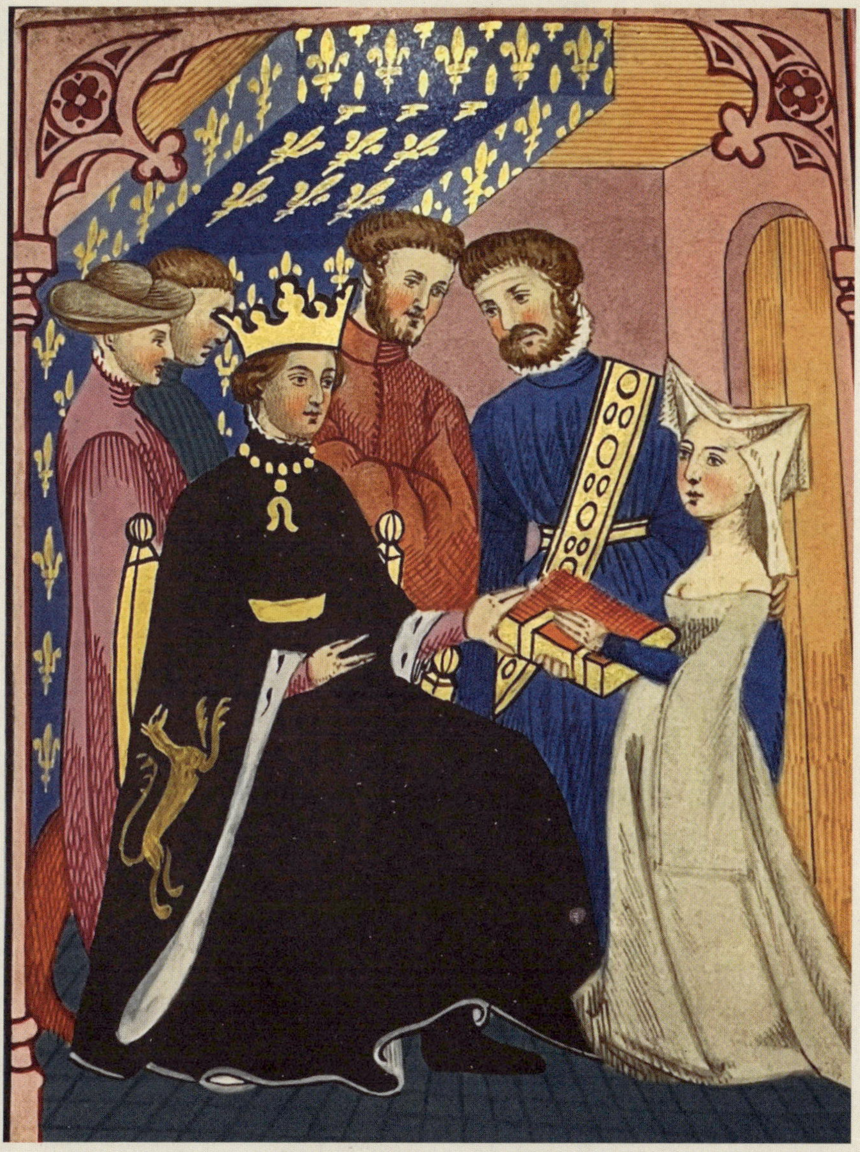

A miniature in gold and colours on paper by Louisa Costello, *Specimens of the Early Poetry of France*, William Pickering, 1835

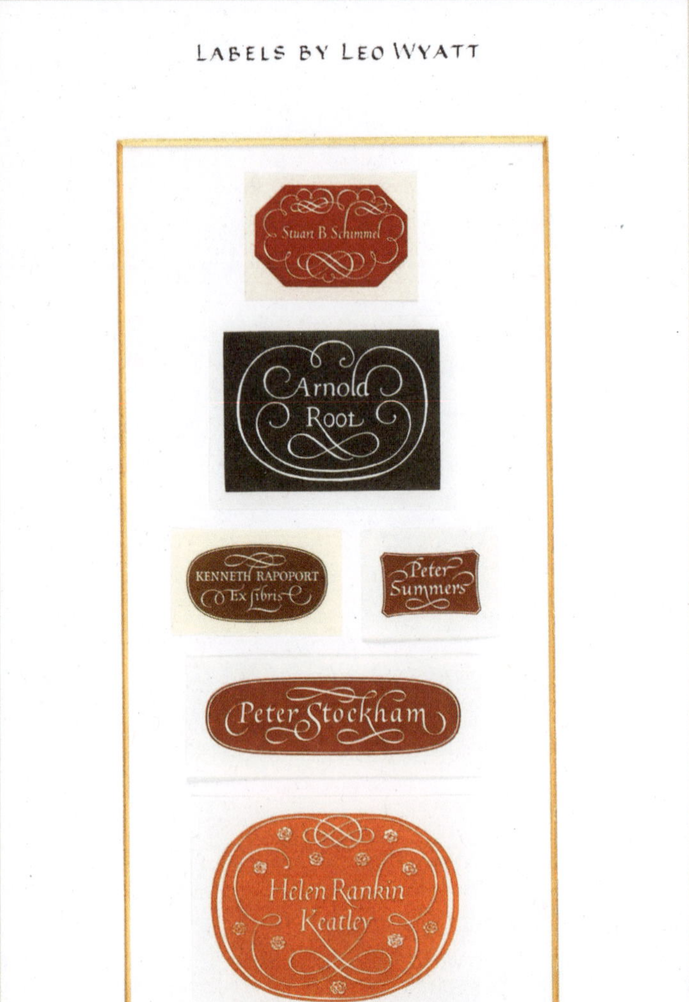

Calligraphic bookplates engraved by Leo Wyatt

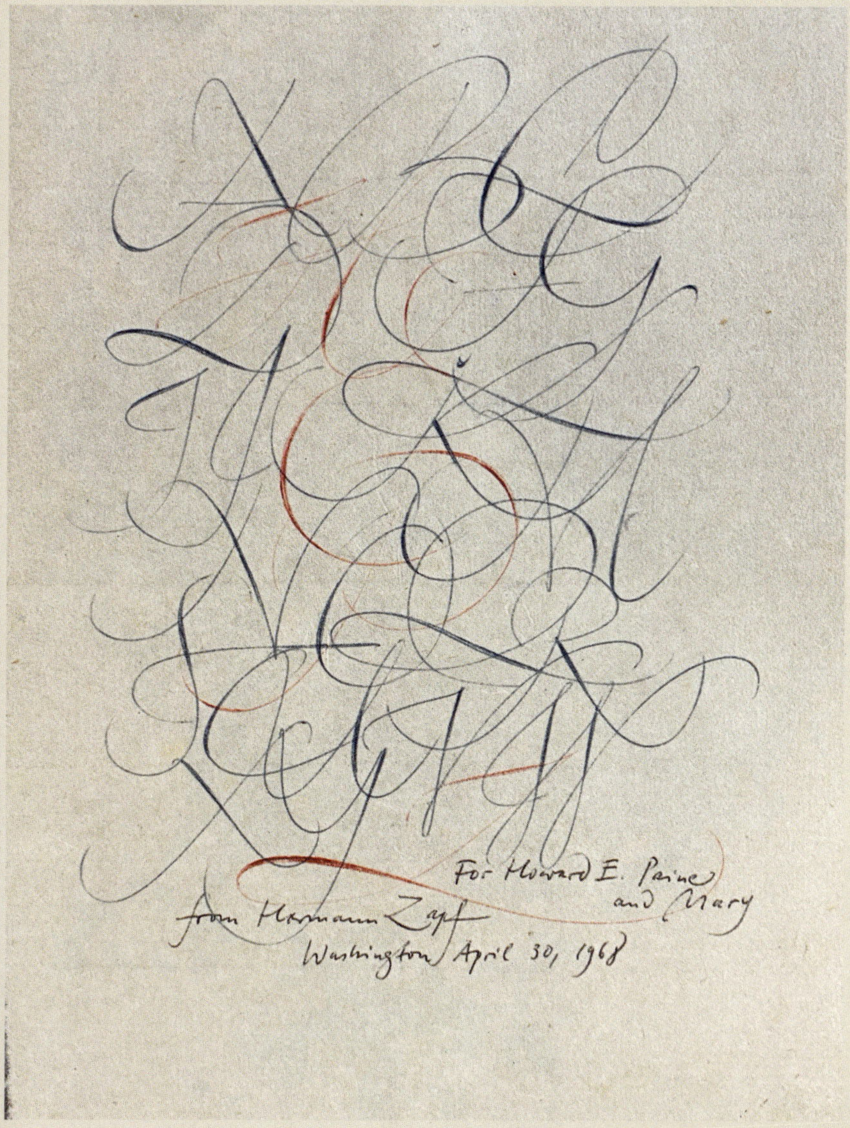

Original calligraphic Alphabet by Hermann Zapf in red, blue and black ink

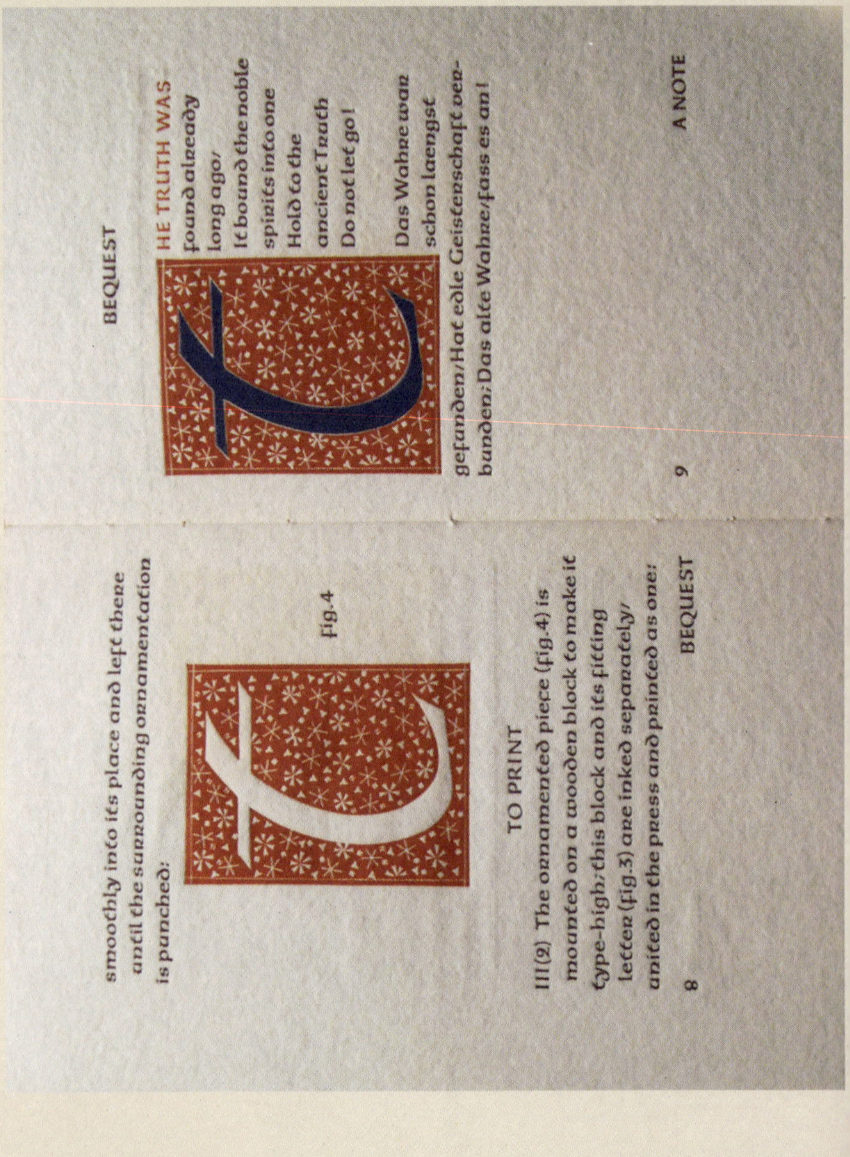

smoothly into its place and left there
until the surrounding ornamentation
is punched:

fig.4

TO PRINT

III(2) The ornamented piece (fig.4) is
mounted on a wooden block to make it
type-high; this block and its fitting
letter (fig.3) are inked separately,
united in the press and printed as one:

8 BEQUEST

BEQUEST

THE TRUTH WAS
found already
long ago,
It bound the noble
spirits into one
Hold to the
ancient Truth
Do not let go!

Das Wahre war
schon laengst
gefunden, Hat edle Geisterschaft ver-
bunden; Das alte Wahre, fass es an!

9 A NOTE

Carolyn Reading Hammer, *Notes on the Two-Color Initials of Victor Hammer*, cut in brass, uncial type, Stamperia del Santuccio, 1966

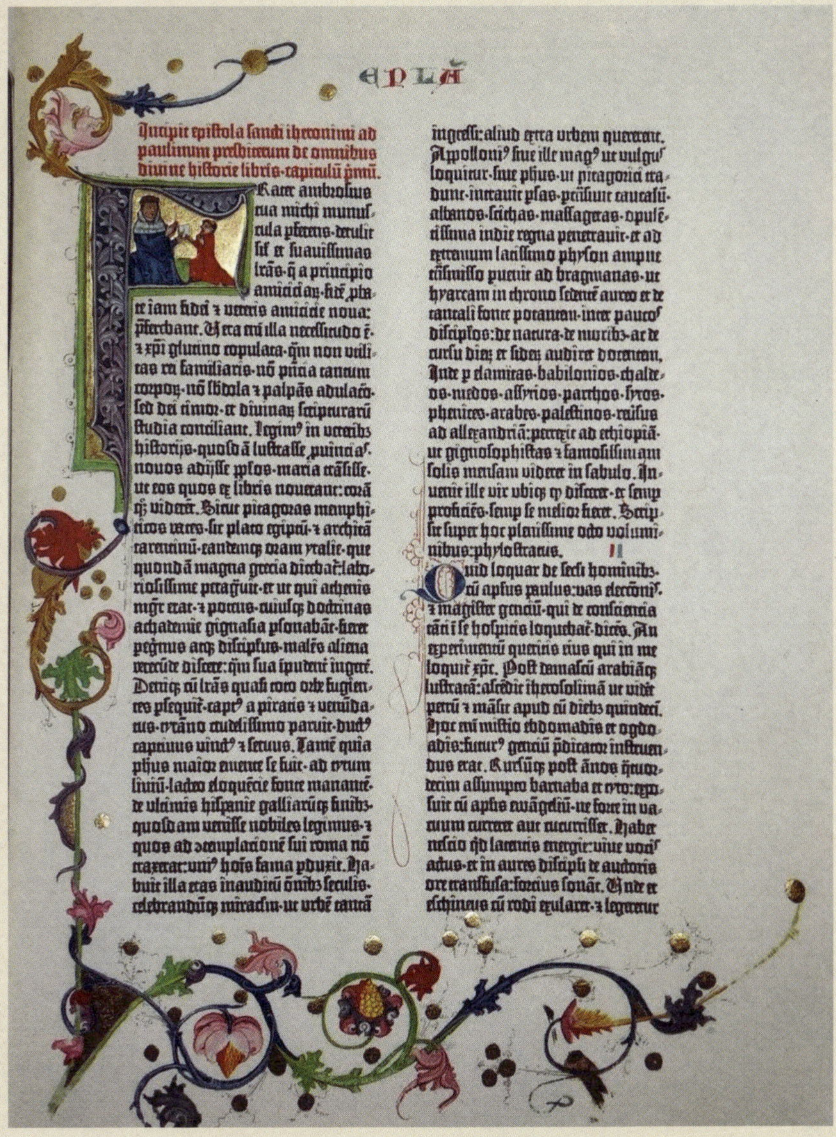

Idion Verlag Gutenberg Bible facsimile page, in gold foil and colours, 1977–78

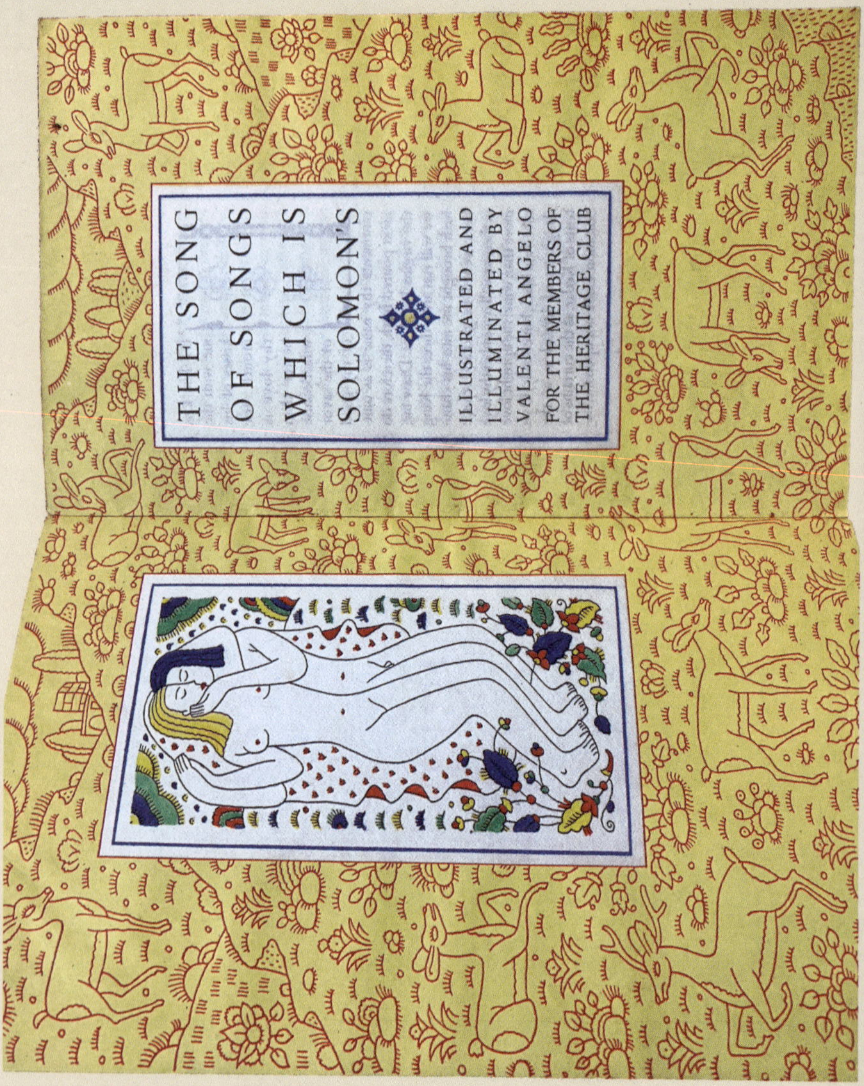

Valenti Angelo hand-coloured frontispiece in an extra-illustrated copy of the *Song of Songs*, 1935

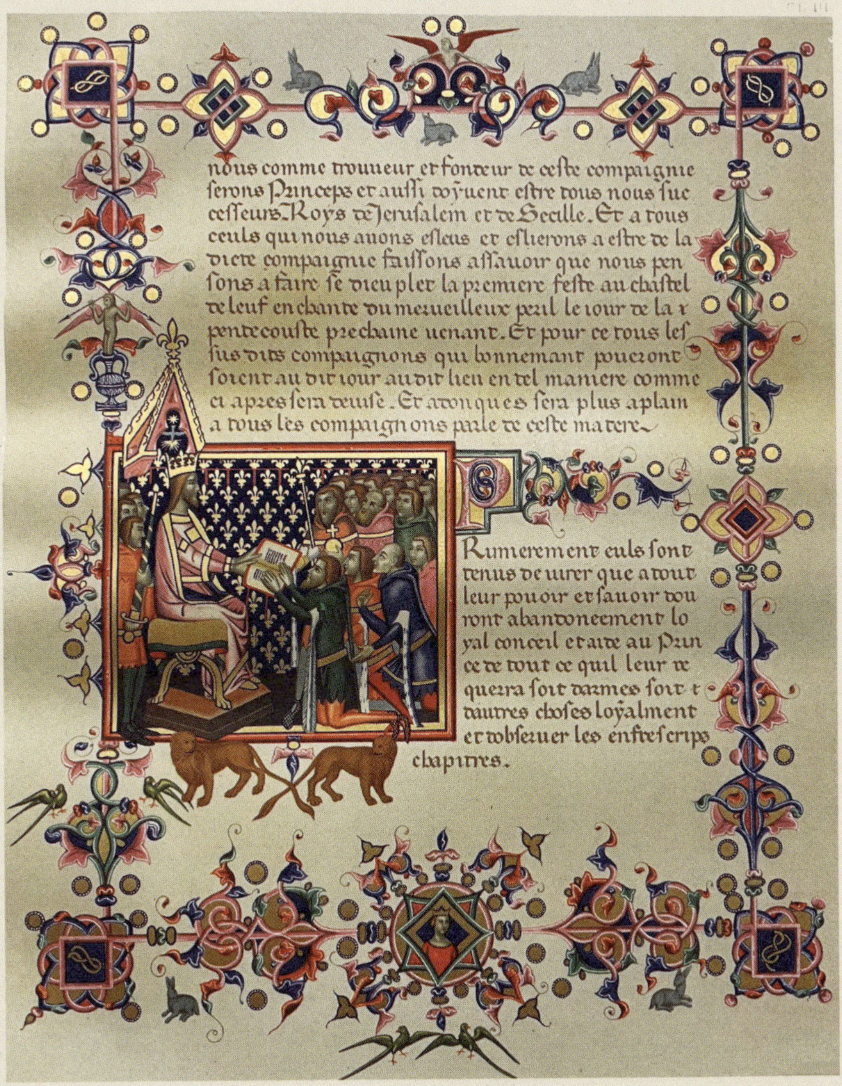
nous comme trouueur et fondeur de ceste compaignie
serons Princeps et aussi doyuent estre tous nous suc
cesseurs Roys de Jerusalem et de Secille. Et a tous
ceuls qui nous auons esleus et eslierons a estre de la
dicte compaignie faissons assauoir que nous pen
sons a faire se dieu plet la premiere feste au chastel
de leuf enchante du merueilleux peril le iour de la x
pentecouste prechaine uenant. Et pour ce tous les
sus dits compaignons qui bonnemant poueront
soient au dit iour au dit lieu en tel maniere comme
ci apres sera deuise. Et adonques sera plus a plain
a tous les compaignons parle de ceste matere.

PRimerement euls sont
tenus de iurer que a tout
leur pouoir et sauoir dou
ront abandoneement lo
yal conceil et aide au Prin
ce de tout ce quil leur de
querra soit darmes soit d
dautres choses loyalment
et dobseruer les enfrescrips
chapitres.

Statuts de L'Ordre de Saint-Esprit, 19th century facsimile of a 14th century manuscript, Gruel and Engelmann, 1853

HISTORICAL AND DESCRIPTIVE SKETCH

AND NOTICES OF

The Conventual Church & the Parochial Church

of Tynemouth.

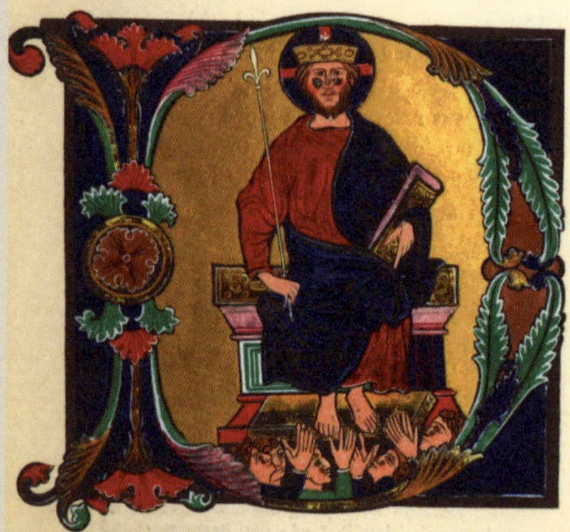

URING[1] THE REIGN OF EDWIN, KING OF NORTHUMBRIA, AND PROBABLY BY THE ROYAL CONVERT HIMSELF, AN EDIFICE WAS ERECTED AT TYNEMOUTH, AND DEDICATED IN THE CHRISTIAN FAITH TO THE WORSHIP OF GOD, WHO, PROCLAIMED BY THE BLESSED PAULINUS, WAS THEN RECENTLY ACKNOWLEDGED IN EDWIN'S COURT AND REALM, TO BE THE GREAT KING ABOVE ALL GODS. THIS RELIGIOUS STRUCTURE WAS BUILT OF WOOD, AND WAS REBUILT WITH STONE BY EDWIN'S ROYAL SUCcessor, S. Oswald.[2] It is not improbable, that the monastery so rebuilt was destroyed by the Danes in their ravages during the reign of Ecgfrid, and was restored by his pious

[1] This magnificent illumination is derived from a diurnal of the 13th century in the British Museum. Harl. MS. 2895.

[2] "Edwinus, rex Northumbrorum, sacellum erexit Tinemutæ ex ligno, in quo Rosella ejus filia postea velum sacrum accepit. "S. Oswaldus monasteriolum de Tinemuthe ex ligneo lapideum fecit." Lel. Collectanea, tom. iii. p. 43, citing 'Chronicon auctore Monacho Albanensi, sed incerto nomine.' The MS. from which Leland quoted, appears to be codex 134 in the Library of Corp. Chr. Coll. Oxon.

Large historiated initial, hand-coloured and gilded by Henry Shaw from *The Monastery Founded at Tynemouth*, 1846

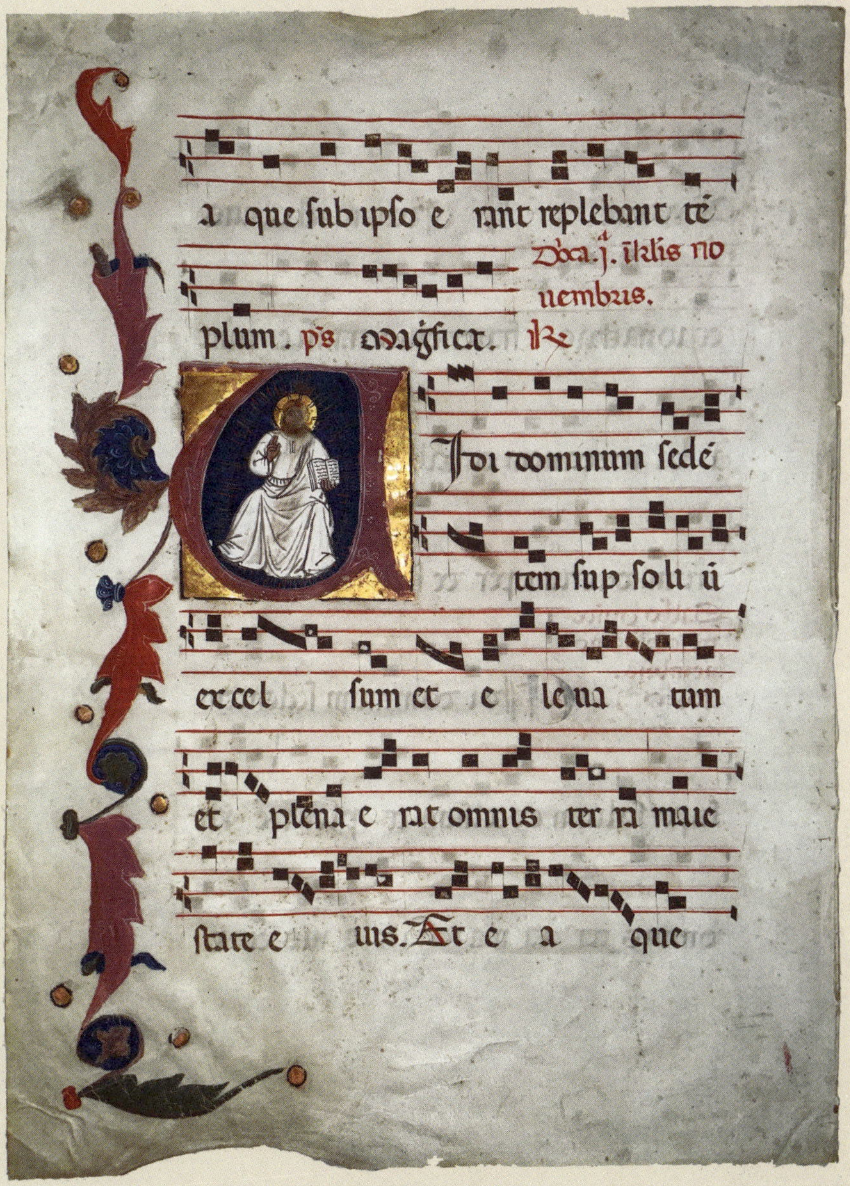

Illuminated historiated initial, from a 15th century Italian antiphonal leaf on vellum

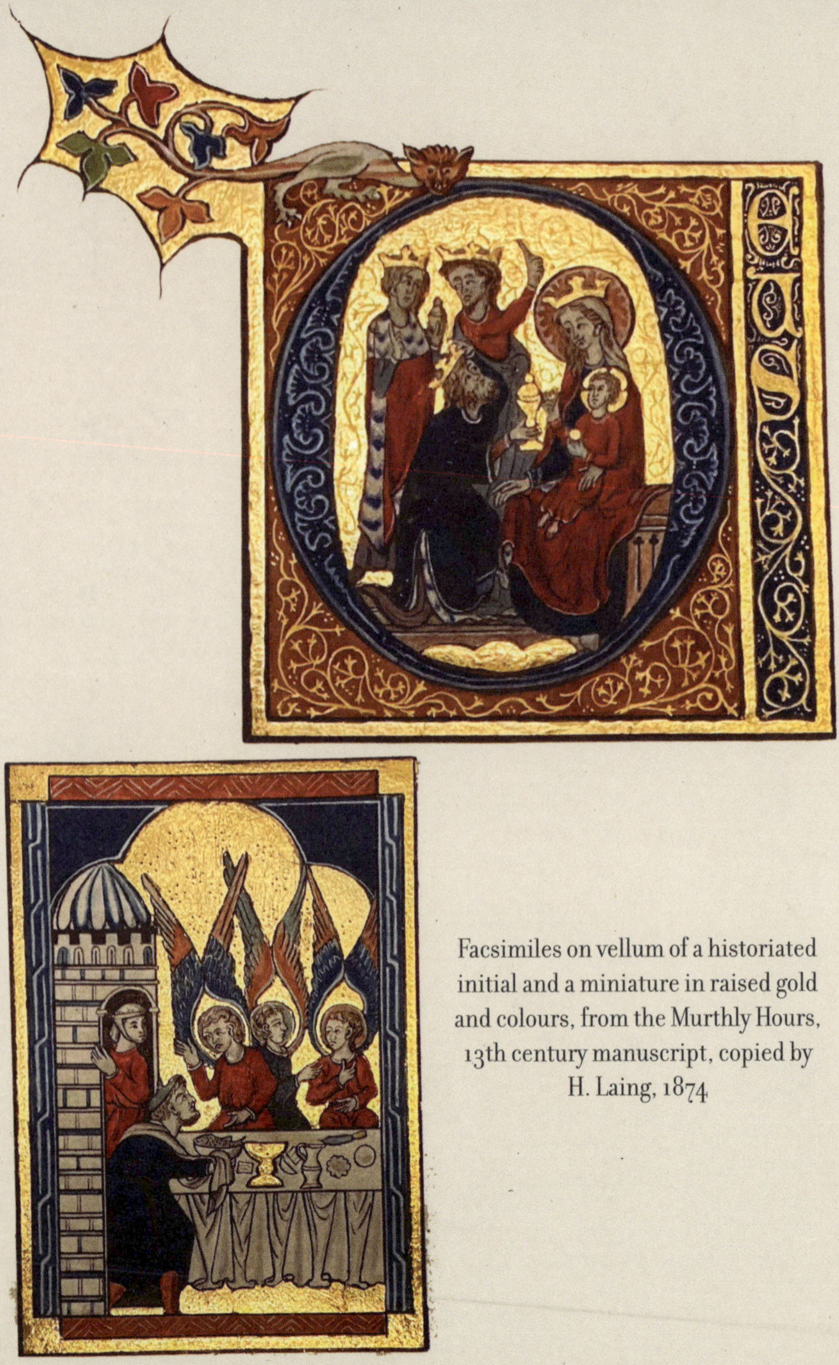

Facsimiles on vellum of a historiated initial and a miniature in raised gold and colours, from the Murthly Hours, 13th century manuscript, copied by H. Laing, 1874

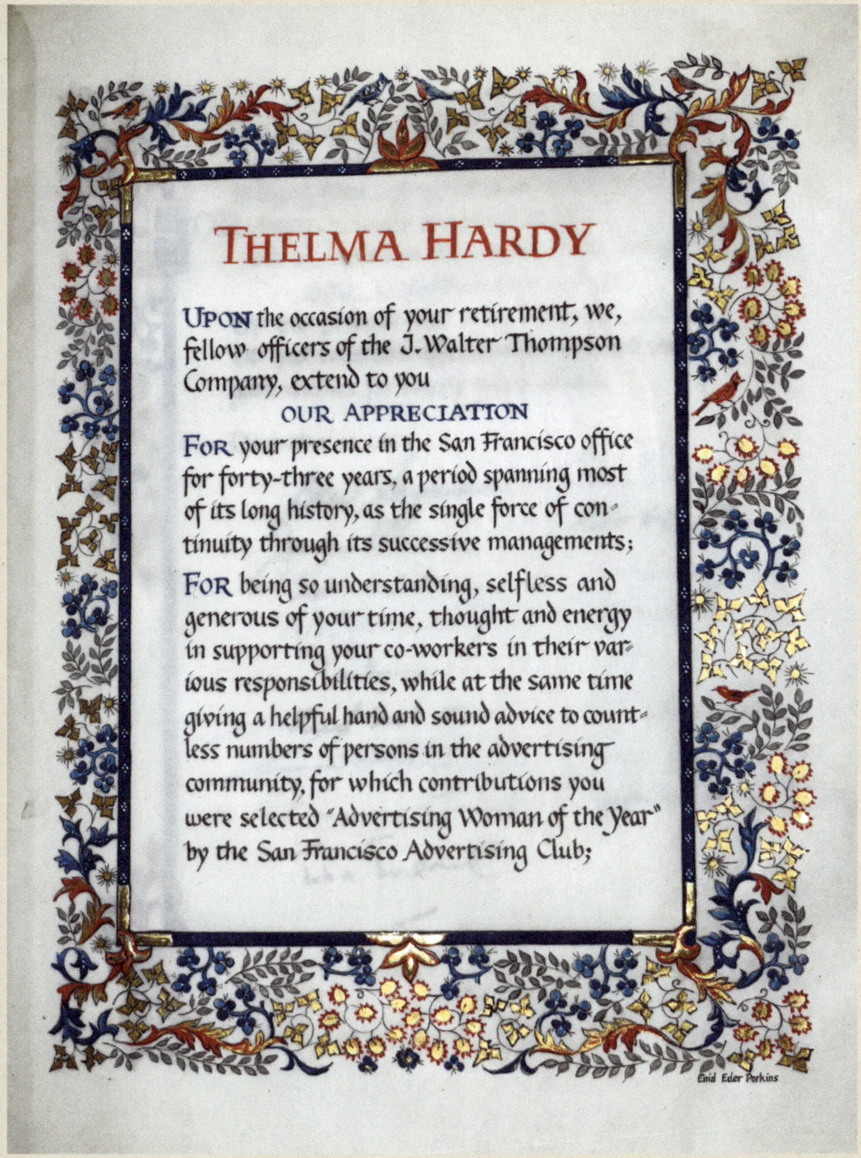

THELMA HARDY

UPON the occasion of your retirement, we, fellow officers of the J. Walter Thompson Company, extend to you

OUR APPRECIATION

FOR your presence in the San Francisco office for forty-three years, a period spanning most of its long history, as the single force of continuity through its successive managements;

FOR being so understanding, selfless and generous of your time, thought and energy in supporting your co-workers in their various responsibilities, while at the same time giving a helpful hand and sound advice to countless numbers of persons in the advertising community, for which contributions you were selected "Advertising Woman of the Year" by the San Francisco Advertising Club;

Enid Eder Perkins

Illuminated testimonial on vellum, calligraphically written out and illuminated in liquid gold and colours by Enid Eder Perkins

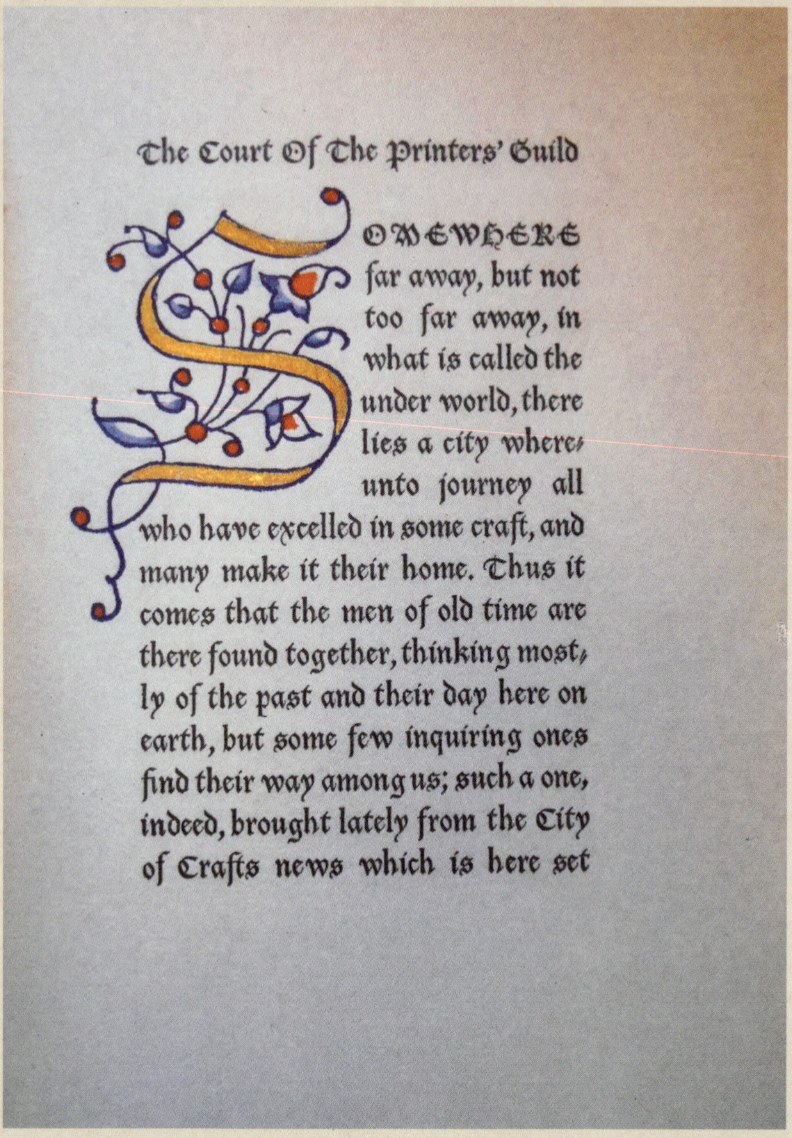

The Court Of The Printers' Guild

SOMEWHERE far away, but not too far away, in what is called the under world, there lies a city whereunto journey all who have excelled in some craft, and many make it their home. Thus it comes that the men of old time are there found together, thinking mostly of the past and their day here on earth, but some few inquiring ones find their way among us; such a one, indeed, brought lately from the City of Crafts news which is here set

Hand-drawn initial decorated and illuminated by Valenti Angelo, *The Court of the Printers' Guild*, 1975, an edition of 50 copies done on his small handpress

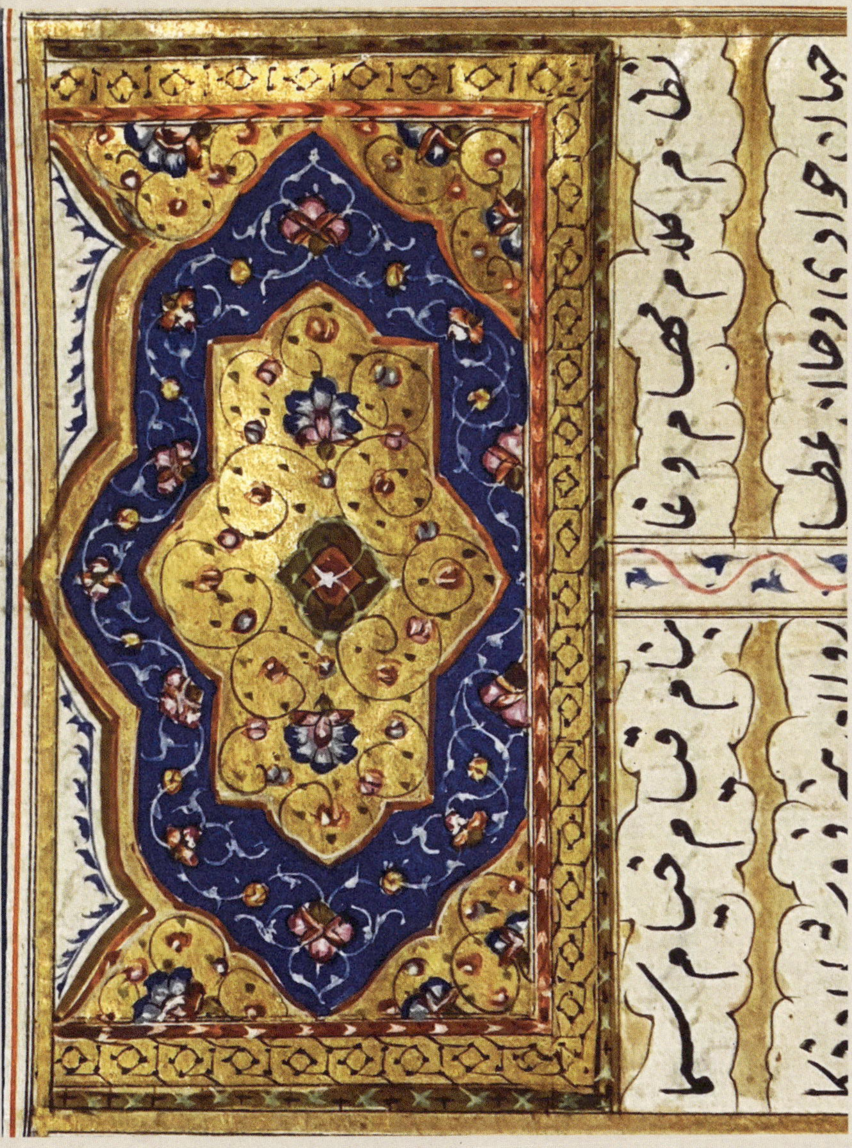

Polychrome gold panel, from a fine, lavish 19th century Mughal manuscript

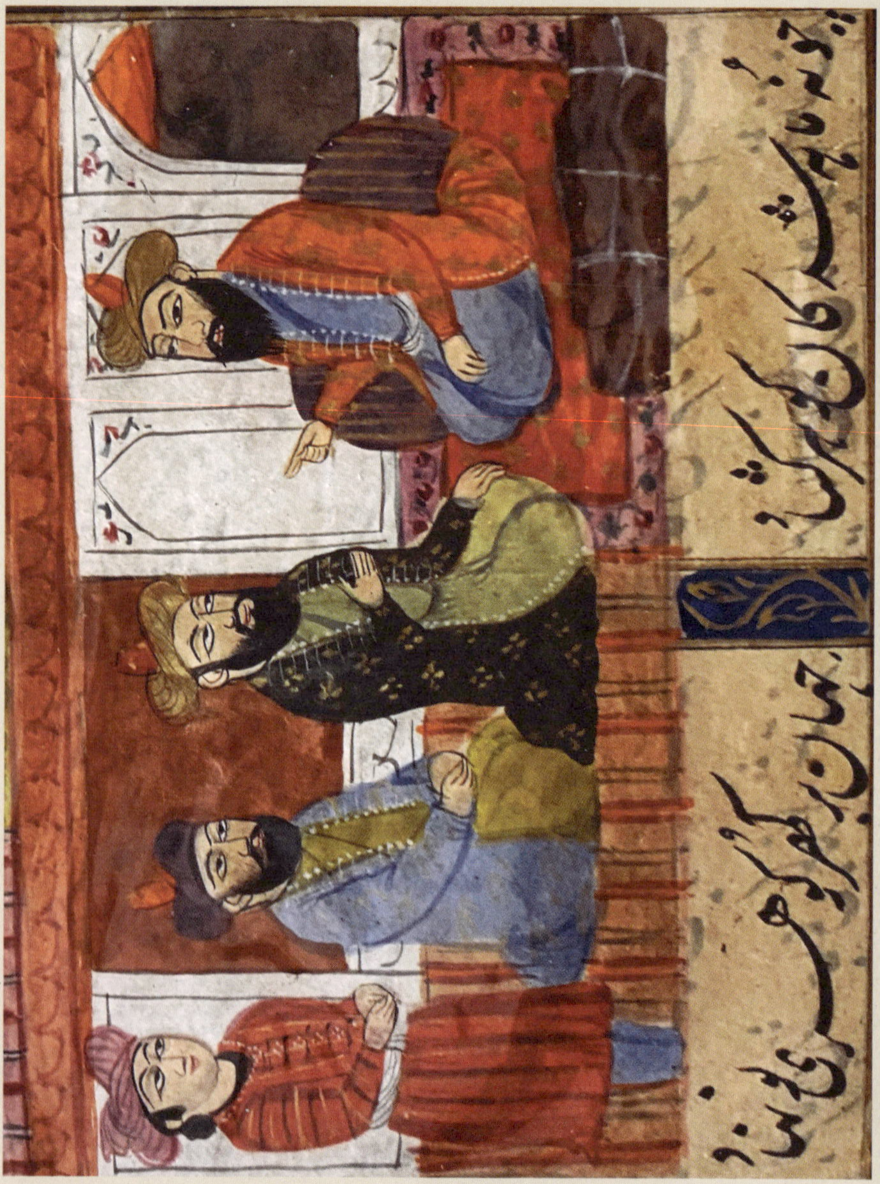

Persian miniature from *Iskandernama*, manuscript on paper, 1812

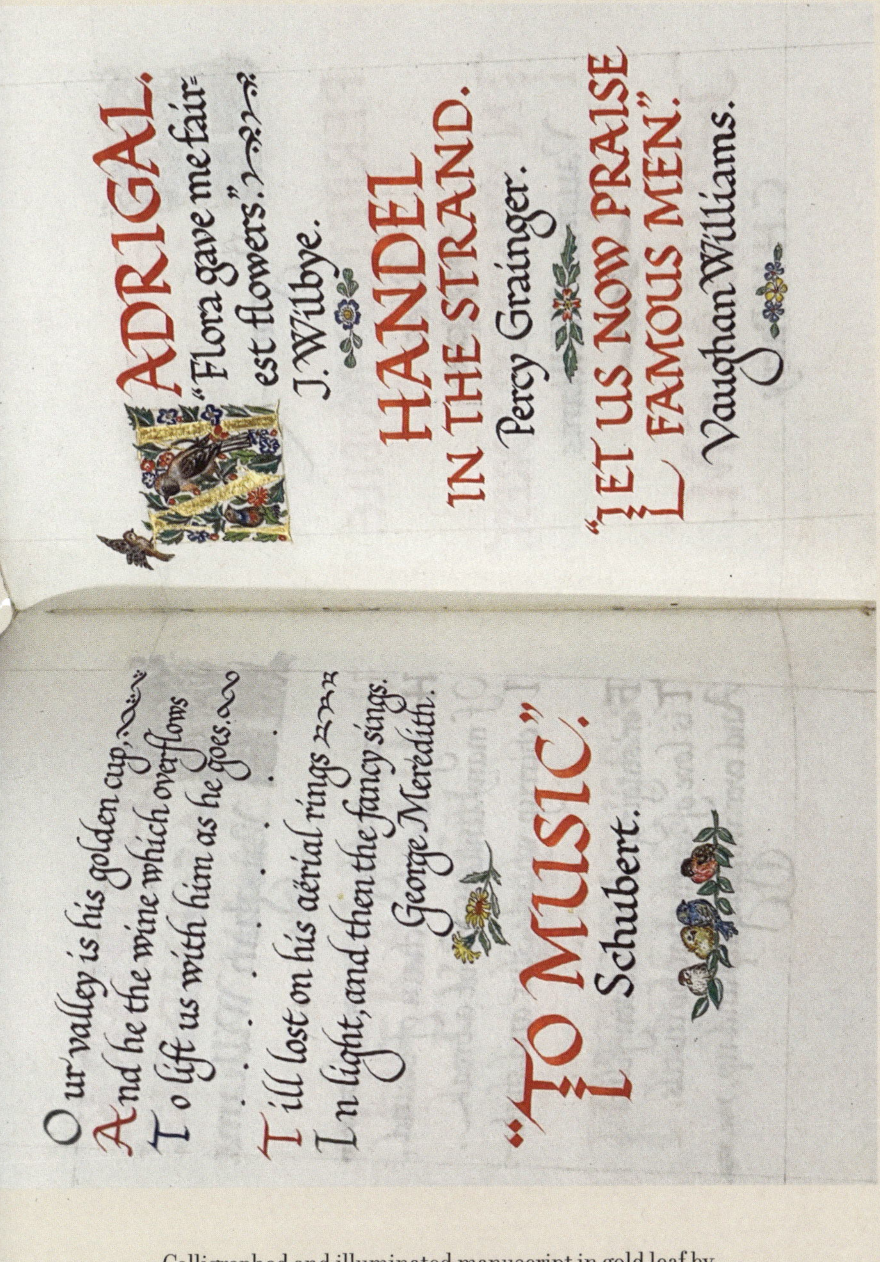
Our valley is his golden cup,
And he the wine which overflows
To lift us with him as he goes.
. . . . .
Till lost on his aërial rings
In light, and then the fancy sings.
George Meredith.

"To Music."
Schubert.

Madrigal.
"Flora gave me fairest flowers."
J. Wilbye.

Handel in the Strand.
Percy Grainger.

"Let us now praise famous men."
Vaughan Williams.

Calligraphed and illuminated manuscript in gold leaf by Margaret Alexander, 1934

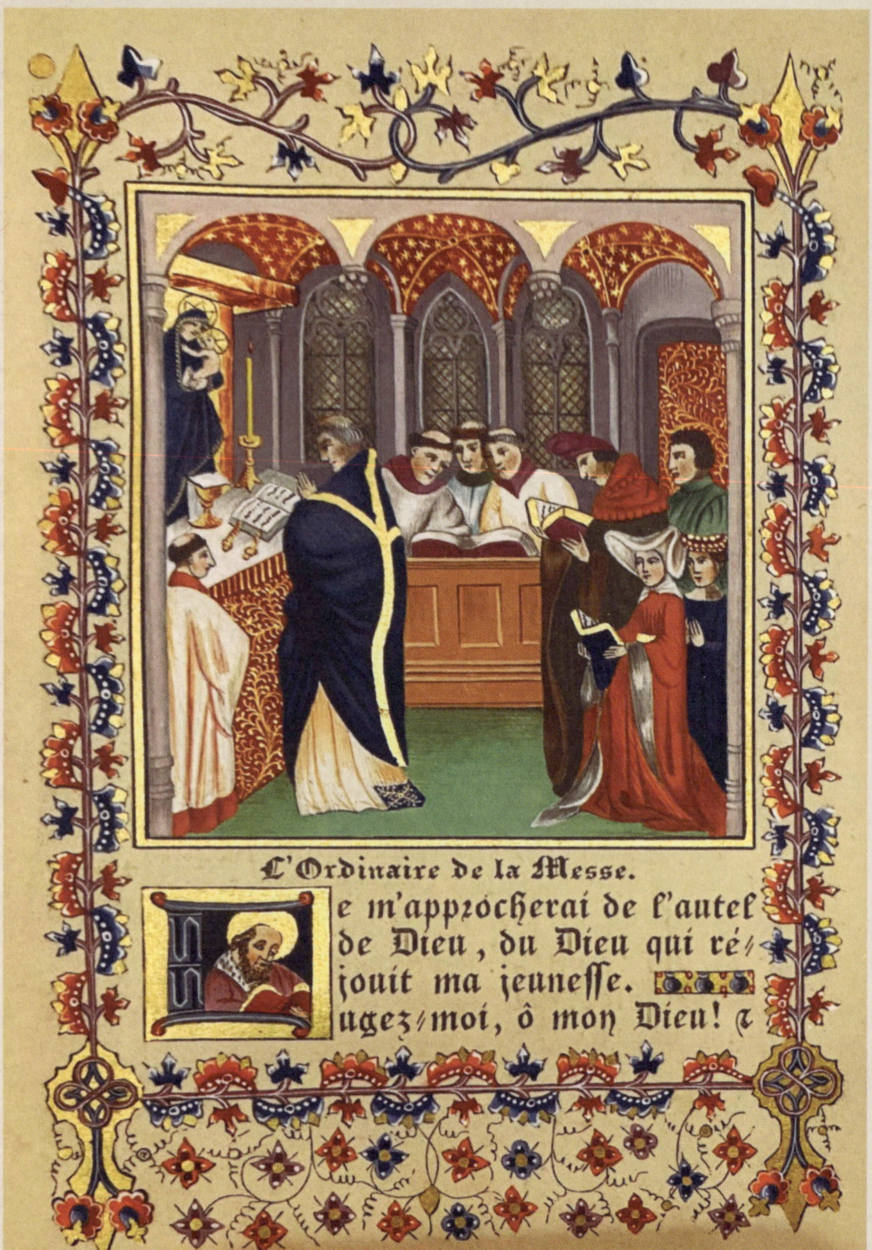

A Book of Hours, hand-coloured and illuminated in gold by
Aline Guilbert, 1843

On the *Oxford Lectern Bible*, which many consider his greatest achievement, Rogers reflecting on the making of the book many years later said something beautiful, something to the tune of giving a reader handling these volumes the feeling that he, Rogers, was given to knocking off such majestic folios on a regular basis! That is, the volume shouldn't come across as heavy and deliberate and highly fiddled with, but as having been accomplished with a sureness of touch and grace.

He continued to freelance for the next few years, and in the 1920s joined the printing house of William Edwin Rudge where he at last got a chance to make the kind of fine books *he* wanted to make. The wonderful thing that happened at the Rudge shop was that he became a mentor to many young printers training there such as John Fass who would go on to become a legend himself, his work playfully reflecting B.R.'s influence in the way Fass handled type and ornament.

Rogers had a tragic family life. His daughter died young, and his wife who would fall sick often, died in her sixties while Rogers lived till 87. He died in 1957, still working on a few books. In the eyes of his biographer, 'he was the first great artist-typographer.'

Talking of the artificer of the book, Rogers in many instances physically worked on making a page look better typographically, 'crafting' it with his hands, painstakingly and expertly: the gold leaf procured to be applied in the roundel devices for *The Odyssey* turned out to be too little and too thin. Rogers had to begin from scratch and have the gold leaf specially beaten to fill the circular background of the devices against the figures in black. In *Geoffrey Tory* as well as *On the Just Shaping of Letters*, he retouched the weaker or lighter letters in such minute detail, and yet with such delicacy in each copy that he would develop severe headaches that would not go away.

Coming back to the nicer B.R. things I have, to be honest I have hankered more after a book *about* him than any done by him. Being part of the B.R. cult, naturally when one comes to know there is a highly desirable and fairly scarce tribute book to him from his own contemporaries, some of the most revered and beloved printers, typographers, designers, and illustrators of the day, you want the book desperately. The book is *Barnacles from Many Bottoms*, the second title from the Typophiles, a happy, informal gang of graphic artists and bookmen who pooled their considerable talents and resources to print typographically playful books and keepsakes, and at the same time celebrate their illustrious members.

Barnacles is one of six scarce and highly sought after books the Typophiles did and it had always been out of my reach for the way it is priced. (The other five sought after titles are: *Spinach From Many Gardens*, *Diggings from Many Ampersand Hogs*, *Left to Their Own Devices* and the two portfolios – not just scarce but rare, unbound tributes to Beatrice Warde and Fritz Kredel.) I had given up hope of owning one. Then, fortunately, a bookdealer I often swapped books with, emailed me to say he had just won some very nice books in an auction, and *Barnacles* was one of them. I immediately asked him to set it aside for me, and offered up as many high-end press books from my collection as I could let go – including some I didn't think I ever could – in order to secure it.

The second item is a bargain coup (at least for the likes of this impecunious collector) that I happened to stumble on: a two-page ALS from B.R. stuck in the back of a book. This was a copy listed on ABE from a bookstore in California of a Riverside Press edition he designed, *Georgics of Virgil*, with ornaments and on handmade paper. The description for this listing said: *'Limited Edition (1904); this copy is No. 287/330; 100pp; 'B.R.' edition, his initials are on title page and letter is tipped in between back endpapers.'*

My finger was on the page down to keep scrolling further when I backtracked and considered that line 'B.R.' edition, his initials are on title page *and letter is tipped in between back endpapers...'* The B.R. edition is common enough, since it became a source of pride for the Riverside Press to advertise a book had been designed by the famous B.R. but what was that bit about a letter tipped in at the back? A facsimile letter or a real holograph letter? And letter from whom? Surely not from Bruce Rogers? Such a letter would at least be $300 (even if it was just two lines from B.R. to say he wouldn't be home for dinner or attending a party), and this one was priced $40, so I didn't have much hope that it could be a tipped in ALS.

I called the bookshop hastily, and asked the young woman who answered the phone to pull the book. 'Your description mentions a letter at the back, I'm guessing that's printed, and part of this edition, and not an actual letter?'

'Hmmm, let me see.' Silence on the phone as she riffled to the back. 'It's a two-page letter and looks to me hand written, not printed.'

'Who is the letter from? Does it say?'

'Let's see – uh, I can't quite make out but I think the last name of the signature could be Roger or Rogers?' I kept my voice as even as I could: 'I think I'd like to take the book. Can you please send me a PayPal invoice?'

The letter turned out to be quite a find, from very early in B.R.'s career, replying to another typographer – Frederic Goudy!

And the third and most singular of all B.R. ephemera I have is a trial or proof page with not only annotations in pencil from B.R.'s hand indicating measurements and spacing, but also hand-drawn borders, initials and ornaments!

A ZAPF RARITY

There are two rarities in my possession from the hand of Hermann Zapf, the widely admired German calligrapher and type designer, that I treasure. The first is *Feder und Stichel* (*Pen and Graver*), a lovely calligraphic manual drawn by Zapf that was cut in metal by hand into 25 plates and printed letterpress, and the other – a serendipitous find – is an original hand-drawn calligraphic alphabet broadside from the hand of Zapf himself. I could never have dreamt such a thing would be available in the market. And yet, there it was at an auction, an original hand-drawn example of calligraphy by the master at a price that was just possibly within my reach.

But would mine be the winning bid? Could I win such a high-stakes auction? After all, we are not talking about a printed broadside from Zapf, but a calligraphic display of letters from A to Z drawn with three different inks by Zapf in his own hand for a friend.

For those not familiar with Zapf, he was the greatest type designer the modern world has ever known, and an equally elegant calligrapher and book designer. His calling he once said was 'to create beautiful letters'. Jerry Kelly,

Zapf's biographer, famously said, 'What Michelangelo was to sculpture and Beethoven was to music, that's what Hermann Zapf is to type design and calligraphy.' His celebrated 2019 biography – *Hermann Zapf and the World He Designed* – explores Zapf's prodigious work intimately, while warmly evoking his life.

Zapf's story properly begins in 1935, when he was 16 and chanced on a calligraphic exhibition in Nuremberg of the German master, Rudolf Koch. Then and there, Zapf decided to become a calligrapher. He came from a family that was struggling financially, and with the meagre pocket money he had, Zapf would buy lettering manuals and teach himself calligraphy. Soon, he was writing out calligraphic manuscripts; one of the most striking was written in gold and silver ink on a Japanese paper dyed purple. His stellar career in type design began when he was just in his twenties, for the Stempel type foundry in Frankfurt.

Before I get to more details about my hunt for Zapf rarities, a word about his other celebrated book – *Manuale Typographicum*. He loved arranging specimens of type in inventive ways, and in 1954 came this gorgeous display of the complete alphabet in various typographic arrangements. Published as an oblong 12 x 9 inches folio, it was an entirely new kind of type specimen book, points out Kelly. Zapf set some rules for himself – each page had to show a complete alphabet (A to Z) and it would be only in two colours, red and black, and the text used would be evocative quotations related to the felicity and beauty of letters. It was printed on a paper that had 'a sensuous, textured surface'. Kelly hails *Manuale Typographicum* as 'a masterpiece of the printer's art. It will forever rank among the greatest works of typography and printing'.

Now back to *Feder und Stichel,* which apart from being a thrilling display of Zapf's calligraphic hand, is also the first ever showing of his Palatino type in a book. A gifted punch-cutter named August Rosenberger at the printing house of Stempel, where Zapf worked, expressed his desire to engrave Zapf's various calligraphic letters in metal! That is, he would attempt to cut calligraphically drawn alphabets (with their elegant strokes and flourishes) in lead with his own hands, so they could be printed on to paper from these hand-cut engraved plates. Zapf had the highest admiration for Rosenberger and his craft, and gave him permission to go ahead. But even Zapf was shaken by the perfection and beauty of the 25 hand-cut calligraphic plates in relief that Rosenberger produced.

This calligraphic book was printed letterpress from these plates, and published in four limited editions, the first in 1949 in a deluxe edition of eighty copies on a delicate Japanese paper, and bound in full leather by Zapf's wife, Gudrun Zapf von Hesse (who was a considerable type designer, binder, and calligrapher in her own right – her Diotima italics and Ariadne initials are perhaps my most favourite type designs). I've never seen a copy of the Japanese paper edition in the market in all these years, either at an auction or a bookseller's catalogue, and if one surfaces, it will be forbiddingly expensive, to say the least. But I still hope to find a copy one day, even though there is a question about being able to afford such a thing.

In 1950, 500 numbered copies of *Feder und Stichel* on old Fabriano paper were printed, and one could say this was the first edition. It was bound in quarter leather and boards, also by Hesse. This beautifully printed edition is fairly scarce, too. The later, more common editions of *Feder und Stichel* that followed in 1952 are *not* printed directly from the hand-cut metal engravings, but from electrotype plates. This little bibliographical detail is unfortunately not known to auction houses and booksellers who continue to list these copies – the Trajanus Presse edition and the English version, *Pen and Graver*, from Museum Books – as being editions printed directly from Rosenberger's hand-cut plates.

It didn't take me long to find a copy of the 1952 English edition of *Pen and Graver.* A few months after I'd bought the book, I happened to mention to Jerry Kelly that I now possessed a copy of *Pen and Graver*, and he casually dropped that 'bibliographic secret' about *Feder und Stichel.* This meant, of course, that I just had to go after the two scarce editions done from the hand-cut plates.

Perhaps one reason why that very limited edition on Japanese paper is so rare today is because most of those copies on publication were sent out as compliments to famous typographers and calligraphers: Stanley Morison, Jan Tschichold, Giovanni Mardersteig, Jan van Krimpen, Brooke Crutchley, and Bruce Rogers, to mention just a few, had been the lucky ones to receive a copy.

However, I can offer a tip as to where you could acquire two original specimen leaves of the hand-cut plates either on Japanese or old Fabriano paper – thanks once again to Jerry who first told me where these leaves are safely and securely tucked away in a privately printed book by Hermann Zapf that was done as a tribute to his punch-cutter in 1996. *August Rosenberger 1893–1980: A Tribute to One of the Great Masters of Punchcutting, an Art Now All But Extinct* was designed by Zapf and printed letterpress on Rives paper by David Pankow and Jerry Kelly in an edition of 120 copies. Inserted into a back pocket in this book are four original specimen leaves from Zapf's work, two of them being those hand-engraved original leaves from *Feder und Stichel.*

August Rosenberger 1893–1980 is a scarce book; on these fine papers, the calligraphic letters feel exquisite. On 12 May 2021, the revered type specimen collection of Jan Tholenaar, a collector, came up for auction at Swann Galleries; included in the lot was a copy of the scarce 1950 *Feder und Stichel* on old Fabriano. Predictably, I missed the auction, and kicked myself for months after. Then, entirely by chance, not long after, I spotted a copy on eBay that looked like the Zapf manual but was titled differently: *Stift und Stichel.* On closer examination, it turned out to be a copy on old Fabriano in fine condition that the seller had mistitled.

But the listing already had 12 bidders vying for it. I placed a soft bid and hoped a last-minute max bid would secure it – in the ten-second countdown I changed my max bid to the highest I was wanting to go, but held it back until there was only four seconds to go. Such bids are a risk, even a little fumble and you miss registering the bid, but it's the only way to prevent a counter snipe bid. For a few seconds after the auction closes, there is no indication if you won or not, and then you either see the cold, matter-of-fact message, 'Sold for -------', which means you didn't get it, or the thing you want to see: 'You won. Pay now.' And I dutifully paid up.

I was delighted with it. Rosenberger's metal plates had been perfectly impressed into those textured Fabriano papers, wonderfully showing off various calligraphic hands drawn by Hermann Zapf – uncial, italic, black-letter, and chancery. The text itself was set in 10-pt Palatino roman. Jerry Kelly in his biography tells of a letter Bruce Rogers wrote to Zapf upon receiving *Feder und Stichel*: 'The book of schrifts is very handsome, and the beauty and variety of your hand-work is remarkable. As you can tell by this letter, I am not a calligrapher, but I can appreciate the beauty of your writing. The engraving, too, is remarkable.'

Now, finally, to that sweet, sweet find, a Zapf coup of sorts: stumbling on an auction for the scarcest and handsomest thing a typophile can dream of having from the hand of Hermann Zapf – an original calligraphic alphabet broadside hand-drawn by the master.

Finding is one thing, owning or acquiring it is entirely another, but this I managed by a combination of luck and timing that seemed entirely serendipitous to me. Zapf usually did these impromptu calligraphic broadsides for friends or colleagues as a token of his appreciation or friendship. Grabbing whatever pen and paper was at hand, Zapf would draw out a calligraphic alphabet in a flash.

It was exactly such a Zapf original that caught my attention when it came up for auction. This was really quite incredible because no one who owns a Zapf calligraphic manuscript ever parts with it. But apparently someone *had* done just that – to my great good luck. But could I hope to win the auction and be the owner of it?

The opening bid was already high, and I put in a slightly higher bid and waited. Zapf had drawn this calligraphic alphabet in three colours, blue, black and red, using light and heavy strokes, with some letters leaping out at you and others hidden in a flowering of calligraphic flourishes. Further, it was inscribed and signed in his hand, mounted and framed. With a few minutes left for the auction to end, I was sure a last-minute bidder would turn up with a fantastically high snipe bid and snatch it away from me, so I got ready with a high bid of my own that would more than triple the current bid, hoping this would secure it. As the seconds ticked by for the auction's ending, my fingers hovered over my laptop, poised to click the tab that would significantly raise my max bid, in the hope that this would secure the prize for me. Stunningly enough, *no one else* bid, and I won the auction without a contest.

The only answer was that no one had seen the listing – no one that is to whom something like this would have mattered.

And just like that an original Zapf alphabet, the loveliest and most prized thing from the hand of our greatest calligrapher and typographer, was now suddenly and sweetly in my hand.

A CALLIGRAPHIC TUESDAY

The most sumptuous and loveliest 'calligraphic' find I have saved for the last. The way everything unfolded on the day I made this fabulous find reinforces what collectors have often experienced or seen: one lucky find leads to another unexpected find. A confluence of finds happened all in a day, and I christened this – after the day was done – 'my calligraphic Tuesday'. Each item I bought on that Tuesday was not just related to calligraphy, but was an actual original, hand-lettered specimen of fine calligraphic writing.

There are days in a collector's online book hunting life that pass by without a single satisfactory find, and there are days when you make a huge, fulfilling find – both are exciting, though common, aspects of the book hunt. But it's only once in a while that a day is filled with a flurry of jaw-dropping finds, and it is my contention that such things happen more (or even only) to a collector hunting books online. By the end of this account, I hope to have illustrated this.

On a mild Tuesday evening in October 2019, as I was indifferently browsing the antiquarian market online, a virtual storm of finds – books, letters, and manuscripts of a calligraphic nature – engulfed me. And some, if not all, were even thrilling bargains. It was vastly pleasing because it was all about an area of collecting that had always fascinated me – an area, in fact, that was really lacking in my book arts collection – original works of calligraphy and lettering.

I had become increasingly fascinated with original examples of calligraphy – hand-done, not printed – after I acquired, in a virtual auction coup on eBay, a hand-calligraphed alphabet by Hermann Zapf, inscribed and signed. After this, I would on occasion see other examples of original calligraphy in the market by other masters, but they were – as expected – very expensive. I had lucked out with the Zapf alphabet. You have to remember that any piece of original calligraphy – whether a book or a broadside or a card or a pamphlet – is a manuscript, making it the only copy in existence. That's one of the reasons why hand-done calligraphed works (versus printed calligraphed works) are pricey. Once you possess a calligraphic manuscript, you own the only existing copy.

On that Tuesday, I had been thinking all day about a beautiful calligraphic work on paper that had come up at an auction in London a year ago titled *The Owl at Alfriston*; this calligraphic manuscript was from the hand of Margaret Alexander, a renowned English calligraphic scribe, who had been a student of Edward Johnston and Graily Hewitt, two master scribes. The manuscript opens with a lovely gilded watercolour of an owl done in the fashion of a historiated initial, followed by six pages of calligraphic text in gold, green and black, ending again with another little watercolour that has burnished gold in it.

Alexander 'wrote it out' possibly in 1957, and the famous collector who had commissioned this work, J.R. Abbey, had it bound in marbled boards. The opening initial of the letter O has within it an owl painted in gold and watercolour, and the illumination at the end is again of this owl in a cage, painted also in watercolours and gold. I put in my maximum bid, but because of the high interest in it, guessed this would not come to me – Forum Auctions had estimated it would go for between £1,500 and £2,000, and it fetched a hammer price of £2,400.

That morning more than ever this beautiful calligraphed manuscript was on my mind and I thought why not look for something from the hand of this English scribe that might still be in the market? Such things are not just scarce but rare – perhaps once in five years or so you may see a manuscript in the market authored by English scribes in the calibre of a Graily Hewitt or an Edward Johnston or a Margaret Alexander. Imagine my surprise then when one search result actually came up on *via*Libri from a dealer in the UK titled 'Rutland Musical Festival, transcribed and illuminated by Margaret Alexander'. Predictably it was priced fairly high, though not exorbitantly. Still, it was a Margaret Alexander manuscript that was not only calligraphically written out but illuminated as well! I wrote quickly to the dealer asking for details and photos of the manuscript.

Feeling encouraged I continued searching on *via*Libri

with keyword searches like 'calligraphic letters' and 'calligraphic broadside', and got two promising results. The first was a packet of letters from Randall House Rare Books that apparently contained some nice examples of calligraphic writing, with one of the letters being from Thomas Maitland Cleland, a famous designer and calligrapher. The asking price of $45 seemed a bargain. I have admired Cleland's elegant calligraphic hand, and knew that in the market the price of just one handwritten letter from his hand can command $150–200.

The other 'calligraphic hands' in the packet went unnamed in the description, but that was fine with me; whatever else came with the Cleland letter would be a bonus. I placed the order, and followed up with an email asking for photos and more details. I looked for other calligraphic letters from Cleland, with one exciting result – an original calligraphic birthday greeting for Cleland from the Typophiles in the hand of one of America's most admired calligraphers, Fridolf Johnson. The calligraphically written out greeting, executed in black and gold ink, read:

> *To Tom Cleland, Admired by all for Your Magnificent Contributions to the World of Design – Your Friends The Typophiles send their Felicitations & Best Wishes for a very Happy Eightieth Birthday.*

Interestingly, this calligraphic sheet was Johnson's *worksheet* for the final finished broadside greeting; the final specimen is now housed at the Victoria and Albert

Museum in London. Again, I wrote asking for images from the dealer, George Minkoff. This item also came with a trove of correspondence between the calligrapher and the museum, and one typed letter signed by Cleland to Johnson, saying what a masterful piece of calligraphy the greeting was.

When the images came for the Fridolf–Cleland item, I beheld a nicely flourished hand, writing out a joyously worded greeting, done in a subtle gold ink (if you held it up in a certain light you could see the gold shine) and fascinatingly, in the margins were Johnson's practice letters, like a flourished C or T and practice strokes to be used for openings and endings of letters. And, thankfully, it was not done on a smooth card stock paper but a laid, watermarked, deckled paper.

Before going through with the purchase (there was no fear that someone else would grab it – it was being held for me, and I had asked for a day to think about it) I sent the only image of the worksheet I had to Jerry Kelly, the typographic scholar and calligrapher, to ask his opinion. At the time of emailing him, I didn't have all the information on the worksheet with me, such as whose hand it was – that came later in an email from the dealer. I wanted Jerry's impression of the calligraphic hand I was seeing.

There was mail from Jerry the next day:

Wed 23/10/2019 11.59 a.m.

Wow! This is really nice (even if it only a rough).

I'd guess that it might be by:

Hollis Holland
Alice (Koeth – but she always goes by just Alice)
perhaps Fridolf Johnson
Where did you find this?

I'll call Alice to see if possibly she remembers doing it.

best
Jerry

He was, as you can see, bang-on. I said so in my next mail to him, and asked him what he thought of the piece?

And he replied:

'It is a nice piece of lettering, one of the nicest I have seen by Johnson.'

The more I thought about it, the more attractive the worksheet grew – it made for a fascinating study, to see how the calligrapher had worked out the lettering. If you looked at the scans carefully, you could see the faint outline of pencil strokes still left in. What thrilled me the most in it was something more personal – just seeing the word 'Typophiles' calligraphically written out in such lovely strokes was reason enough to buy it.

Meanwhile, the images for the small lot of calligraphic letters from Randall House Rare Books had arrived in the mail, and even just glancing at them (the bookshop had spread out the letters with their original envelopes in about four images to show as many of them as possible to me) told me I had stumbled on a treasure trove. What a calligraphic stash, and the bookshop seemed unaware of what they had here or did not care: handwritten letters from Paul Standard, Leo Wyatt, Douglas Jackson, and Arnold Bank. They were some of the most revered calligraphers and lettering artists of the twentieth century.

And the contents! All talking about their work, about calligraphy, lettering, even mentioning the work of other calligraphers – exactly the kind of desirable content collectors and dealers look for in a letter to make it appealing and of greater value. It was quite something, to take in at one go, so many beautiful and flourished hands in these letters. Wyatt's letters and Standard's was on their letterheads, the Cleland letter was nice, even if a bit crumpled, but all the others were in fine condition.

The envelopes were a further bonus – each mailing cover had the name and address in the calligrapher's hand. I asked the bookshop to please send my order along, but via express shipping – I would pay the added charges. Now, this was a fine bargain. When the packet eventually arrived (ten days or so later), I read and re-read the letters, and then just spent some time looking closely at all the calligraphic strokes and flourishes among these famed hands. Looking through these calligraphed letters has given me several hours of pleasure. The experience of looking at hand-done lettering offers a different pleasure than that of printed letters.

The Wyatt letter must have been early in his career, when he was just beginning to make a name for himself as a calligraphic wood engraver and bookplate maker. Wyatt says to the client he is addressing that he could send along samples of his calligraphic bookplates, based on which a collector could commission bookplates from him.

Several hours had passed and there was still no response or images from the UK seller with the Margaret Alexander manuscript. Impatient, I called the landline number listed for the seller, and got the machine and left a message.

I had become very interested in collecting typographic and calligraphic bookplates and had begun collecting them in a small way. And while I was waiting anxiously to hear back in some fashion from the UK dealer, I hit the jackpot with a luscious bookplate find. This time rather than me hunting for a find, the 'find' found me! I received an email from a rare book dealer I bought from regularly, asking if I would be interested in a beautiful set of Leo Wyatt calligraphic bookplates, all handsomely mounted and framed. The two masters of the calligraphic bookplate are Reynolds Stone and Leo Wyatt. As engravers, both had an affinity for letterforms that drew them to making calligraphic bookplates on commission for collectors.

This framed and mounted display of Wyatt bookplates had first come up for sale at Heritage Auctions.

> Bookplates by Leo Wyatt. [London, mid-twentieth century]
>
> *Attractively matted, glazed, and framed in three separate frames. The largest frame features four bookplates including Wyatt's own that show the tools of his trade and commemorates his years of work as an engraver in South Africa. The other two frames contain fourteen bequest and individual book labels. Printed in color these labels are fine examples of Wyatt's use of space and letters on wood blocks. From the James M. Goode Collection of Bookplates.*

I managed to secure one of the three framed bookplates – the most attractive one, I'd like to think, showing seven original calligraphic bookplates done for collectors in different colours, beautifully displayed in a matted frame, 19 x 10 inches. I acquired it through Frederic Shearer, a bookdealer, who had won all three framed Wyatt bookplates at Heritage. All three sold quickly, one of them of course to me. The one I bought has labels for collectors and other bookmen and bookwomen of the arts of the book such as Stuart Schimmel, Arnold Root, and Susan Otis Thompson to name the three I recognized instantly, and they were absolutely beautiful.

Unlike the bookplate done with a pen and ink where you can reduce a large drawing to the size of a bookplate, the engravers of calligraphic plates in wood have to work to original scale – which means working within that small space. And there is no room for re-doing a calligraphic bookplate in wood, no second chances. These lettering artists work in miniature spaces, and still produce elegant letterforms with flourished calligraphic strokes.

I acquired this at a more than fair price (to be translated as a price I am happy or able to pay!) and this remains one of the most cherished things in my bookplate collection. And of course this was the only calligraphic item I bought that Tuesday which was not an original, hand-done specimen, but had been printed.

It was perhaps an hour or so later when I had all but forgotten about my query on the Alexander manuscript that a mail from the British dealer finally landed.

I could see there were images attached, and I opened

them. And gasped. Was I really seeing what I was seeing? It was written out in a fine hand, six pages, and featured four exquisite watercolour miniatures with gold in them. They were done as large initials beginning a page, with the letter gilded (in the finest gold leaf I have seen in a modern manuscript) and showed little birds done as a watercolour miniature. Four of them – *four* – when even *The Owl at Alfriston* had only two.

I wondered briefly if perhaps it was printed – a copy made from the original manuscript. But no, I had seen enough examples of original calligraphic writing to know what I was seeing in the scans was hand-done. You can get the text and the watercolours to look almost the same in a manuscript and a printed book, but not the gilding. The gold in Rutland Musical Festival, with the burnishing raised prominently in all the four initials gave it away as a hand-illuminated manuscript.

Before the bookseller could change his mind, I bought it. It arrived a couple of weeks later via tracked airmail. The covers were stiff vellum boards, another sign of how precious it was. The colophon read: 'Transcribed and Illuminated by Margaret Alexander.'

I still can't believe I own a Margaret Alexander calligraphic manuscript; this is the kind of thing collectors fantasize about, making an enormous find at a price you can (just about) afford.

ILLUMINATED IN GOLD AND COLOURS

It's always the one that got away that haunts a collector. Acquisitions hotly pursued and won don't take up the same head space as books that you failed to acquire. All collectors will have their own stories, and I have a few I could tell. The one that I regret the most for not being able to secure is a nineteenth-century hand-illuminated manuscript, done as a Book of Hours, on vellum, with eight full page miniatures in gold and several illuminated initials, and all 40 parchment pages written out in a black gothic script, the margins with lushly decorated borders in blue, green, pink, and red.

It came up for sale at Ader, one of the oldest auction houses in Paris, on 3 July 2021, with a hammer price estimate of between €1,000 and €1,200. I called the auction house and left an absentee bid of €1,750 with them (which does not factor in the 25 per cent buyer's premium on top of the hammer price), and felt somewhat confident that I might have a shot at winning it. I really should have known better, especially since I had spent the last couple of years looking for modern manuscripts, researching them, going through catalogues, auction records and even acquiring a few. In the process I found out how highly valued and desired they were in the market, with a ready collectorship eagerly pursuing them, paying top prices. The one from Ader I was looking at was one of the finest examples of a modern illuminated manuscript I had seen.

The next day I tuned into the auction on Ader's website, a small window opens to stream the auction in real time. The manuscript I was after, *Recueil de Prières*, was Lot 53, with the opening bid of €500. When it came up, I straightened up to follow it closely, but in no time the bids had raced to €1,300, past the estimate. There were bids from the floor, from the internet, and absentee bids like mine which Ader would call on my behalf. When it ticked up to €1,600, my counterbid was quickly offered against it. A pause in the auction room. I held my breath. And was summarily dismissed from a bid on the floor. It fell at the hammer for €2,432. Now looking back, I think even that was low. It really was more a €5,000 to €7,000 book. But if I'd stood a chance at all of acquiring such a fine illuminated manuscript it would have been here – at this reasonable hammer price. If anything of this quality were to come up again, it would be at a price I could not possibly meet. I should have put in a bid of €3,500, and even though such a price would have been more than anything I had paid so far, the manuscript would have been secured.

I must confess to why I am still obsessing over it, even willing to stretch myself financially to acquire it – because, you see, I have become infected by Victorian bibliomania, the taste for illumination and colour that ran rampant in the nineteenth century. I hasten to add that I don't mean those overwrought, gaudy chromolithographed books in metallic gilt that were – and alas still are – popular. These are also known as 'Victorian Illuminated Gift books', and I find them dull. They are, in fact, to blame for keeping those who love illumination and colour in books from going after the most beautiful and brilliant examples of nineteenth-century illumination in the market. That is, original hand-executed manuscripts on vellum, facsimiles of manuscripts that were partly printed, partly hand-finished on paper, and a few even finely accomplished illuminated books that were entirely printed.

Part I: Collecting Facsimiles of Illuminated Manuscripts.

The best work in this field comes not after chromolithography was fully established (which would be around 1850) but what came *before* when woodblocks and copper plate engravings made into lithographs would then be coloured and gilded by hand. A costly, laborious and skilful process that gave these plates an authenticity and richness that chromolithographed plates never achieved.

A.N.L. Munby was one of the first scholars to trace the revival of a gothic taste for illumination among eighteenth century bibliophiles that had begun around 1750, and then peaked in 1850 in his *Connoisseurs and Medieval Miniatures* (Clarendon Press, 1972). The most groundbreaking, expansive study of this is to be found in *Manuscript Illumination in the Modern Age: Recovery and Reconstruction* (Sandra Hindman, et al., Mary and Leigh Block Museum of Art, 2001).

I think the most astonishing and joyous discovery I made in my collecting pursuits is learning about the existence of such modern illuminated manuscripts. Victorian England had skilful copyists who learnt how to calligraph and illuminate documents, testimonials, addresses, and entire manuscripts. They spent several hours studying original medieval and Renaissance manuscripts in the British Museum to be able to hand letter gothic and humanist scripts and draw faithful facsimile versions of illuminated and historiated initials, decorated borders and miniatures; and perhaps best of all they figured out a way to replicate the colour paints and raised gold leaf found in those ancient manuscripts.

Simultaneously, this was happening in France as well, where bibliophily had always been very advanced, with a longer tradition of engagement with illumination and colour in books. And America, with its arts and crafts books that peaked around the turn of the century, drew a new generation of scribes who used hand-done illumination to decorate printed books, not manuscripts.

To list just a few of these gifted scribes and illuminators from the period from the second half of the eighteenth century to the first half of the twentieth century – Joseph Strutt, Henry Shaw, J.O. Westwood, Caleb Wing, C.L. Ricketts, Florence Kingsford, Graily Hewitt, Alfred Fairbanks, Edward Johnston, Margaret Alexander, Alberto Sangorski, Henry Laing, Margaret Adams, Philip Mortimer, Nestore Leoni, Albert Cousins, Louisa Stuart Costello, Enid Eder Perkins, Mary Hoke, John H. Tearle, Mary Cheney, Robert Wilson Hyde, William Cushing

Bamberg, Esther Faithfull Fleet, Phoebe Anna Traquair, Augustus Pugin, Henry Noel Humphreys, Owen Jones, Aline Guilbert, and of course the Spanish Forger, whose copying skills were so developed that for a time his facsimiles were passed off as sixteenth and seventeenth century Renaissance manuscripts. These scribes worked as professionals and commercial artists, taking commissions from wealthy patrons, collectors, and institutions to execute by hand either exact facsimiles of an existing medieval manuscript, or creating an original manuscript. (An exception was William Morris of the Kelmscott Press who was also a highly accomplished, self-taught scribe, and illuminator who wrote out and decorated manuscripts for the pleasure and beauty of it, either to go into his personal collection or created as a smashing gift for a friend.)

From this tradition of writing out and decorating modern manuscripts by hand, these same copyist-scribes ventured into publishing printed books that were partly lithographed and partly hand-finished in polychrome colours and gold leaf illumination by the foremost publishers and printers of the day – William Pickering, Day & Son, Longmans, William Smith, Henry Bohn, and Joseph Cundall.

I had become completely besotted with these facsimile reproductions in England and France. The idea behind these lavish creations was to give a modern bibliophile a sense of the grandeur and beauty of original medieval illuminated manuscripts. To this end, various colouring and illumination techniques were tried to convey the dazzling beauty of the decorated and gilded manuscripts of the Middle Ages.

And I can tell you right off, having steeped myself in those reproductions of illuminated manuscripts, that the best of these is not, as widely heralded by dealers and collectors, the chromolithographed books of Henry Noel Humphreys, Owen Jones, or Henri Léon Curmer but the hand-finished work of Henry Shaw. One marvels at Shaw, a devoted antiquary and a skilled architectural draughtsman who was so besotted by illuminated manuscripts that he set out to painstakingly copy them by hand (as a medieval scribe would have), reproducing an initial or a miniature or a portrait with remarkable accuracy, engraving them on a copper plate, and then hand-colouring and illuminating the printed plates in gold leaf.

From these manuscript originals Shaw produced two acclaimed and influential printed facsimile books, *Illuminated Ornaments Selected from Manuscript and Early Printed Books from the Sixth to the Seventeenth Centuries* (1833) and *Dresses and Decorations of the Middle Ages* (1843), both published by William Pickering. In the large paper copies of his two celebrated books, the plates are exquisitely and expertly hand-coloured and heightened with gold leaf. There is one other masterpiece from the hand of Shaw that is not as well-known and is often overlooked – which I'll get to shortly.

The regular or small paper issue of *Illuminated Ornaments* and *Dresses and Decorations* measure approximately 11 x 8 inches, while the large paper edition is about 15 x 11 inches. These large paper copies, done in a small edition, are scarce and command (deservedly) high prices. Gold leaf was used in the large paper copy alone, and in the small paper copies, the gold is replaced with a yellow-orange watercolour. The print run of these editions is unknown, but contemporary bookseller and auction catalogues note that very few copies (between 25 and 50) were done of the large paper issue. While one or two large paper copies of *Illuminated Ornaments* can be spotted in the market, the large paper of *Dresses and Decorations* is extremely rare.

Illuminated Ornaments displays a series of decorations and initials from various existing manuscripts that Shaw meticulously copied with commentary by Frederic Madden, assistant keeper of manuscripts for the British Museum. The opening plates in the large paper copy of *Illuminated Ornaments* shows four leaves from a remarkably beautiful seventh century Greek manuscript where the whole leaf has been painted and decorated on – what is known in manuscript jargon as – 'gold grounds'. That is, the entire background of the leaf is in gold, and the script and ornamenting is accomplished on the gold. Shaw used a finely beaten gold leaf for this, and the result is as close to an original medieval illuminated leaf as you can get in a facsimile. The plates in the large paper copy are all hand-finished.

I had earlier mentioned Shaw's neglected masterpiece, the third book from his hand that also resembles an illuminated medieval manuscript. It was Ruari McLean who first drew my attention to it in his widely referenced *Victorian Book Design and Colour Printing* (1963). In his chapter on Shaw, just before he ends his essay on this antiquary-genius, he writes:

> Shaw's skill in copying medieval illuminated letters was also used in a magnificent work that deserves mention for its own sake... *The History of the Monastery Founded at Tynemouth*... published in two large quarto volumes in 1846. Initial letters were drawn by Shaw after models in specific manuscripts, and were fully coloured and gilded by hand. In addition, each volume contains lavishly hand-coloured full page plates by Shaw...

Even though McLean singles out *Tynemouth* and heaps praise on it, the book seems to have been overlooked by collectors and dealers, perhaps because it is only mentioned in passing. It is only after I saw these volumes for myself did it dawn on me that this, too, was one of Shaw's illuminated masterpieces. The two full-page engraved plates done as miniatures in volume 2 are not only brilliantly hand-coloured, they are also beautifully gilded, most likely by Shaw himself in all the copies. These plates are very like coming across two large, full-page miniatures from a great medieval illuminated manuscript. The polychrome initials, several of which are five to ten lines long, are sumptuously hand-coloured, with a few even gilded. The initials are all faithful facsimiles of actual initials from famous manuscripts, redrawn by Shaw.

However, beware of the second edition of *Tynemouth* from 1847 standing in as the original in the inventory of several booksellers. As of this writing, out of four copies on AbeBooks, only one is the 1846 edition with the hand-embellished plates. The 1847 edition is a reissue with most of the plates in monochrome and the two full page miniatures simply printed as lithographs. Booksellers seem to be genuinely unaware that this is the case since bibliographical details for this production is scant. If you are considering a copy, always ask the bookdealer if all the initials are in colour and if the three (there is one full page miniature in volume 1 as well) illuminated miniatures look hand-coloured and gilded and not mere lithographs. That first issue is scarce, but it does occasionally surface.

Another little jewel of a book from Pickering is worth noting here as an early and fetching example of illuminated miniatures in an early nineteenth century production. This is not the work of Shaw but of another copyist and illuminator, Louisa Costello, and the book is *Specimens of the Early Poetry of France* done as early as 1835. It contains four illuminated miniatures by Costello copied from medieval manuscripts in the British Museum and the Bibliothèque Royale. (Her job at the British Museum was to copy facsimiles.) Her miniatures here are beautifully accomplished with careful and delicate hand colouring, with the gold finely laid in. I acquired my copy of this bijoux of nineteenth century illumination in a rather procrastinated fashion. There were four copies in the market of *Specimens of the Early Poetry of France*, and at one time or another I explored all these copies, asking booksellers for photos and details of their respective copies.

Pricewise they ranged from $150 to $350. (There were two copies priced lower but in these the miniatures had not been hand-coloured or gilded but left black and white.) And though I ended up passing on all of them, I was unable to get those beautifully done miniatures out of my mind. I would often open the folder in my laptop that held the photos of these miniatures from the four copies, and study them intently, each time coming away with a newer appreciation for Costello's work. However, by the time I came around to realizing I actually wanted to acquire a copy, only the most expensive of the four was available. I dithered again for a while, then asked the bookseller to send me an invoice, and then asked to cancel it after I found myself dithering some more, cursing myself for not getting one of the earlier copies. Finally, I gave in realizing how close I was coming to possibly missing out on this one as well. Happily, all this turned out better than I could have expected – the miniatures in this copy were superior to the others I had seen, plus each of the miniatures had a black and white proof precede them (unique to this copy) and the book itself was in a signed Rivière binding.

Like Shaw who disdained chromolithography as being unsatisfactory, his close contemporary in Paris, Comte August Bastard refused to limit his facsimile to lithographs. For his project of publishing a series of facsimiles of famous illuminated manuscripts that he titled *Peintures et Ornements des Manuscrits* (*Paintings and Ornaments of Manuscripts*, 1836), he gathered a team of men and women who had been trained in drawing and illumination and created a workshop from which these facsimiles were hand-coloured and gilded. The plate would be first printed in just two colours, and all the other colours and gold would be hand-applied at the workshop. The result, as fantastical as it was, ended up being more expensive than an original medieval manuscript! Particularly, the complete portfolio set in its deluxe version where all the plates were fully coloured and gilded. I would give a lot to get hold of at least a few plates – but the rub is that *Peintures et Ornements des Manuscrits* is so excessively rare and so costly that no copy of it has been seen in the market for years.

Another beautiful facsimile work that is also scarce but does surface in the market every five years or so is J.B. Silvestre's *Paléographie Universelle* (1841). The plates here, nearly 300 in all, are quite beautiful, too, with bright colours and burnished gold to most of the illustrations. There's a better chance of locating a copy of the 1850 Henry Bohn reprint – *Universal Paleography*. This was issued as two folio volumes of plates, and two octavo volumes of text. I managed to find some disbound plates, eight plates from volume 1 and eighteen plates from volume 2, and fortunately they too, as in the original, are hand-coloured and gilded.

If you've had some interest in these nineteenth century chromolithographed books, you must have noticed I haven't yet mentioned the most iconic book from this period: Owen Jones and Henry Noel Humphreys's, *The Illuminated Books of the Middle Ages* (Longmans, 1849). I've had only a marginal interest in this work because it was mechanically reproduced, with no hand-embellishment. It was issued in various sizes, of which the elephant folio (22 x 16.5 inches) is the most lavish. This entirely chromolithographed book is not uncommon in the market, if not the elephant folio edition, then at least the royal folio edition turns up often enough. The gilt in the 39 plates cannot match the gold heightened copper plate etchings in the work of Strutt, Shaw, and Silvestre, but the breath, depth, and richness of colour in *The Illuminated Books of the Middle Ages* is very pleasing. Humphreys and Jones used the most sophisticated advances in chromolithography that nineteenth century Britain had to offer to faithfully reproduce manuscript illumination from the seventh century to the seventeenth century. Each plate required multiple runs in the press to achieve colour registration and saturation, while some plates used as many as seventeen colours to accurately evoke the range of colours found in those hand-painted manuscript illustrations. This book is often regarded as *the* great masterpiece of nineteenth century colour printing.

To take a little detour here to describe a juicy bargain that came my way unexpectedly, netting me the elephant folio copy of this work, could be instructive in showing how much our emotions or attachments to what we collect – how hot or cool we are towards them – become responsible at times for what prices we end up paying for them. As I said earlier, I wasn't all that keen on acquiring a copy of *The Illuminated Books of the Middle Ages*; I was rather cold towards it for not possessing those hand-embellished qualities one encounters in the work of Shaw, Strutt, and Silvestre. If at all it should be acquired, then the most desirable copy to buy would be that grandiose folio issue (22 x 16.5 inches) because here the illuminations are shown in their true and original size, and these plates were worked on most carefully and lavishly over six years. But whenever one of these came up for sale, they were invariably priced between $3,000 and $5,500. The Royal folio issue of 16 x 12 inches was priced usually at $2,500. I explored buying these copies over the years but in the end always opted out of acquiring them, even though I managed to negotiate a slightly reduced price with the dealers. I could never be sure how much I would like the Humphreys-Jones plates, especially in comparison with Shaw, and it felt like too much to pay for something I was only mildly interested in.

This lack of interest translated into a kind of stealthy approach for the right copy to come along; and this indeed paid off eventually. One fine day a copy of the elephant folio pops up for sale on AbeBooks for $299.99. It was in three quarter leather and marbled boards with the back board detached but present – that was all! Internally the plates – all 39 of them – were fine. The seller probably didn't research this copy enough and fixed an arbitrary price for it. There was no hesitance this time on my part to put the order through, feeling thankful that my 'coolness' towards this work had kept me from yielding to all those dearly priced copies in the market.

The Illuminated Books of the Middle Ages: An account of the Development and Progress of the Art of Illumination, as a Distinct Branch of Pictorial Ornamentation, from the IVth to the XVIIth Centuries centuries (to give its full title) was the culprit, though, that opened the floodgates to those florid chromolithographed Victorian gift books. It was so successful that it spurned endless imitations of middling illuminated books. Inspired by what Humphreys and Owens had done with chromolithography, all facsimiles of illuminated manuscripts that came after this production in Victorian England and Europe abandoned copper plate engravings and hand-finished plates (as Shaw had done so alluringly) and entirely resorted to lithography to print the gold and colours.

A work of illumination and hand colouring from Humphreys that I do admire is the first illuminated book he designed and executed, the two volumed *Illuminated Illustrations of Froissart* in 1844 and 1845, published by William Smith. Both volumes contain hand-coloured facsimiles of miniatures from manuscripts, from the British Museum, and the Bibliothèque Royale. And both contain lovely, delicate gold illumination. The deep blues and reds in the illustrations he is able to achieve with hand-colouring stand out. (These illuminated plates were subsequently used in two other editions of the *Chronicles of Froissart*, the 1855 Henry Bohn edition and the 1868 Routledge edition – while the gilt is still bright in these plates, the colours are not as deeply saturated – though beware: not all copies in these editions include the colour plates.) The 1842 Froissart Bohn edition, along with Humphrey's widely influential book that came later, *Art of Illumination and Missal Painting* (1849), were two of William Morris' long standing favourite books, and it is entirely possible that Morris came by his love of the gothic from Humphrey's experiments in colour and illumination here.

Two of Owen Jones's books that I have admired in their elephant folio editions but do not own are *Plans,*

Elevations, Sections, and Details of the Alhambra (1842-45) and *The Grammar of Ornament* (1856). Both are recognized as masterpieces of chromolithography. In this vein of entirely lithographed facsimiles, I can mention three fairly lovely examples – all of them the work of one antiquary, J.O. Westwood – *Paleographia Sacra Pictoria* (1843), *Illuminated Illustrations from the Bible* (1846), and *Facsimiles of the Miniatures & Ornaments of Anglo Saxon & Irish Manuscripts* (1868). All of them feature vibrantly coloured plates with gilt in them.

I have preferred to collect printed facsimiles that have some hand-embellishment to them, with at least partly hand-finished plates. An overlooked nineteenth century masterpiece of illumination and hand-colouring is the 1842 Henry Bohn deluxe edition of 25 copies only, of Joseph Strutt's *The Regal and Ecclesiastical Antiquities of England*. Like Shaw, Strutt – a skilful copyist – engraved on copper sixty miniatures taken from various medieval illuminated manuscripts. Strutt's *Regal and Ecclesiastical Antiquities* was first published in 1793 with the engravings in black and white. The 1842 Bohn edition with the hand-coloured plates is fairly common in the market. The 25 deluxe copies that were *extra* hand-coloured *and* illuminated in gold is scarce, but it is a real beauty, worth every penny of its stiff price. In the same exquisite fashion, Strutt's *A Complete View of the Dress and Habits of the People of England* (Bohn, 1842) in two volumes also had a deluxe edition limited to 25 copies where the plates, in addition to being extra hand-finished in more opaque colours, was also superbly heightened in gold.

Apart from the hand-finished colour plates, there was one other reason why I was so charmed by the work of Shaw, Silvestre, Costello, and Strutt – a favourite theme or subject in many of the illuminated miniatures in these volumes is the inclusion of bibliophilic illustrations redrawn from manuscripts depicting a scribe or an illuminator presenting a manuscript to a king or an abbot. These make for beautiful, exciting illustrations where the book being presented – with pomp and ceremony – is lit brightly with gold illumination. (The 'golden book' Valenti Angelo first saw as a child and venerated all his life!)

I must make mention of two other fabulous – even fantastic – works in illumination and colour from the same period: both were first issued in parts, and then bound in book form. *Facsimiles of Choice Examples Selected from Illuminated Manuscripts* (1898) by Bernard Quaritch, and *Illuminated Manuscripts in the British Museum: Miniatures, Borders, and Initials, Reproduced in Gold and Colours* (1899–1903). Though both are separate, unrelated publications, the illumination and colour in both are the work of another Victorian genius – William Griggs – who, not being satisfied with how illumination and colour had been reproduced in facsimiles published previously, invented a technique of gold embossing to make the plates feel slightly raised from the page, as seen in original medieval and Renaissance manuscripts.

I stumbled on these exceptional illuminated facsimiles by chance. Restless after the success of *Tynemouth* to unearth more fine examples of hand-finished gold burnishing in modern facsimiles, I would repeat certain keyword searches over and over again, such as 'hand illuminated', 'illuminated by hand', or 'illuminated in gold and colours'. The Quaritch volume – *Facsimiles of Choice Examples* – is a display in facsimile of actual illuminated manuscripts and early printed books from the bookshop's stock. Likewise, the final magnificent set of illuminated plates from *Illuminated Manuscripts in the British Museum* was published by the Trustees of the British Museum in a folder of four sets, from 1899 to 1903, each folder containing fifteen beautiful plates. The four parts were also bound as a book in an edition of 500 copies.

The 60 plates shown there were all from manuscripts held in the British Museum, and were printed and sold to commemorate the Museum's holdings. The trustees felt that all previous efforts by chromolithography, while artfully suggesting the hand-painted colours of illuminated manuscripts mechanically, had never been as successful in conveying the illumination from gold leaf in medieval manuscripts. For their experimental volume, they hired William Griggs to find a way. To convey illumination in an even more tactile, convincing way, again actual gold leaf was used. In their preface, the museum's trustees note that Griggs invented an 'embossing technique to mimic the raised surface upon which gold leaf is laid down in illuminated manuscripts' – as mentioned in the introduction to each volume to indicate why their facsimiles were different from anything else done before.

All these plates were reissued a few years later by the British Museum as black and white collotype plates. If you were to look carefully at the title for these inexpensive black and white collotype reprints, the title would read: 'British Museum *Reproductions* from Illuminated Manuscripts Series.' What's noticeably absent from the rest of the title here is, of course, what made the original set so special – 'reproduced in gold and colours'.

One last nineteenth century illuminated chromo-lithographed work needs to be mentioned: Henri Léon Curmer's *Les Évangiles des Dimanches et Fêtes L'année* published in 1864 in three volumes. The first and second part contain the illuminated colour plates, the third contains a whole lot of text material related to the production. Curmer, a French publisher of lithographed books, visited several museums around Europe, photographing miniatures and historiated initials from medieval and Renaissance manuscripts depicting the gospels and the prayers for feast days – the prints were then quickly lithographed, hand-coloured and gilded. The plates number more than 400, and show manuscript painting from the tenth to the sixteenth century.

All the nineteenth century volumes I have described are of interest for another reason – their text. The commentary these illuminators added regarding the origin and style of the manuscripts they copied these plates from forms one of the earliest sources of scholarly information on the history of illuminated manuscripts. Before 1800, there were no published texts on manuscripts – even those listed in the catalogues of dealers and auction houses confined their description to something along the lines of 'beautifully illuminated, bound in morocco'. The first book to talk about manuscripts in a substantial way was T.F. Dibdin's *The Bibliographical Decameron* (Bulmer and Co, 1817) where Dibdin, the father of bibliomania, devotes hundreds of pages to the burgeoning love for illuminated manuscripts among his peers, accompanied by copper plate engravings showing miniatures and initials from manuscripts from the fourth to the sixteenth century. I cheered when I discovered Dibdin himself disliked miniatures from the fifteenth and sixteenth centuries, and thought the earliest manuscript illumination – particularly from the thirteenth century – was the most beautiful for their gothic charm.

(A memorable rare book bargain find was purchasing the scarce large paper issue [one of only 50 copies] of the three-volumed *The Bibliographical Decameron* at an auction sale for $170. It is usually a $3,000 to $5,000 copy in the market. The standard edition itself is $800, even at its lowest. How did this happen? The copy at this auction was disbound, with all of its text pages present, but lacking 4 of the 37 plates [38 if you count the 'Presentation in the Temple' added later] called for. Which is why no one wanted to even put in the minimum opening bid of £150 – everyone, that is, except me who didn't mind a disbound, slightly defective copy. What no one – including the auction house – seem to have realized is that it was wider and taller than most copies regularly seen in the market. Only after the volumes arrived did I myself slowly figure out that the pages looked sumptuous with very wide margins and the plates done on various special papers.)

Dibdin's scholarship though has been faulted for inaccuracies but the next significant entry in manuscript description – that of Frederic Madden's in *Illuminated Ornaments* – was hailed as the first knowledgeable and accurate write up on manuscripts. Those who followed were fairly accomplished scholars in the subject: John Ruskin, Champollion, Humphreys, Westwood, M.R. James, Sydney Cockerell, A.N.L Munby, and Christopher de Hamel.

The next significant phase of modern illumination begins around the second half of the twentieth century, when German and Swiss publishers began creating very fine, lavish facsimile editions of celebrated illuminated manuscripts. They were entirely printed, and used collotype and sheet fed gravure processes to print vibrant colour plates with the illumination accomplished by gold foil stamping. (Some of the extra deluxe production used 23 carat gold.) The copies were restricted to 800 to 900 numbered copies, no more. (In England, the Folio Society did the same, but they were not nearly as exciting as the German and Swiss facsimiles.)

If you look them up on ABE, you'll find dozens of these European facsimiles listed, the price varying from $500 to $5,000, depending on how elaborate or lavish each production was. They were accompanied by a scholarly commentary volume, and the set would be slip-cased, with the illuminated facsimile volume itself in some fancy binding that was meant to mimic medieval bindings: blind stamped leather with brass fittings and clasps to jewel encrusted inlays and onlays. These mechanically reproduced mid-twentieth century facsimiles are not as beguiling as those copper plate engraved hand-finished nineteenth century facsimiles, but they are more pleasing and far superior to those chromolithographed Victorian 'illuminated' gift books. As you turn the pages of these Swiss and German facsimiles, and tilt them to an angle where the light can catch the gold-foil stamped illumination, they tend to light up beautifully.

Three that I want to single out are: the Idion Verlag edition of the *Gutenberg Faksimile Bibel* (three volumes, 1977–88, München), the *Faksimile Stundenbuch der Katharina von Kleve* (two volumes, Faksimile Verlag, 2009, Luzern) and *Lothringische Apokalypse* (two volumes, Edition Leipzig, 1988). The first ever facsimile in colour and gold of the 42 Line Bible attributed to the printing shop of Gutenberg in Mainz was the Insel Verlag in 1917, in a small edition of about 300 copies (the first five lettered copies we are told were done on vellum!). It was a faithful reproduction of two of the most decorated and illuminated copies of the Gutenberg, from the copy at the Königlichen Bibliothek in Berlin and the copy from the Ständischen Landesbibliothek in Fulda. We have to remember that only a handful of the extant copies of the 42 Line Bible are richly illuminated. Many remain in black and red with a touch of more colour to the initials and borders. (Perhaps even more beautiful than the Berlin and Fulda copies is the Gutenberg at the Huntington.)

It wasn't until 1961 that the next full colour facsimile was produced, the *Biblia Sacra* from Pageant Books, which was a facsimile of the 1917 Insel Verlag. This was in about 1,000 copies, and can be commonly found in the market in varying prices, from $4,500 to $5,500. However, in my opinion, the best of these is the third and last one – the Idion Verlag facsimile printed between 1977–78, which is again a facsimile of the Berlin and Fulda copies. This is priced about the same as the Pageant edition, and like the other two, the volumes are tall, impressive folios of about 18 x 12 inches. Unfortunately, though, bookdealers and collectors don't seem to have quite realized that this production is superior to the other two – they are all praise for the Insel Verlag and Pageant editions and seem to have entirely overlooked the Idion.

Having examined all three editions, I can tell you exactly why this is the most exciting Gutenberg facsimile to own – the 80 or so historiated initials with elaborate, decorated borders are truly illuminated. The other two facsimiles also have the same 80-odd decorated initials and borders in glorious colour, but the gold in them is flat and dull. The people behind the Idion Verlag seem to have wanted to change that to give the plates the effect of medieval illumination, and *raised* the gold foil in each miniature. So, if you run your fingertips over the illustrations and the borders, you can feel the raised gold ink. Even better, you can *see* the gold raised from the surface of the paper. To top this, the entire facsimile is printed on Van Gelder rag paper.

The original fifteenth century manuscript of *Hours of Catherine of Cleves (Stundenbuch der Katharina von Kleve)* is owned and held by the Morgan Library in New York. This is considered one of the most beautiful Book of Hours and the greatest Dutch illuminated manuscript with its 157 miniatures in gold and colours. (In 1966, the

Morgan Library itself produced a modest, handy colour facsimile of their manuscript and this can be had for bargain prices with numerous copies in the market.) In 2009 from Faksimile Verlag in Luzern came the gorgeous, illuminated facsimile in brilliant colours and illumination in 23 carat gold. Again, if held to the light, the miniatures shimmer and glint. Even if the whole thing reeks of the mechanically reproduced facsimile, it is still a delight.

The most beautiful of these mid-century European facsimiles, and the most extraordinary, too, is the Lorraine Apocalypse (*Lothringische Apokalypse*, Edition Leipzig, 1988) the early fourteenth century manuscript that I had just mentioned. I don't think I've seen anything quite like it in facsimile making: the colours in it look hand-painted, and the gold glistens like liquid gold. I don't think it is either – if it was it would have been forbiddingly expensive – and yet it is so thrillingly like a real manuscript than a printed facsimile.

There are 74 miniatures in colours and gold, with numerous illuminated initials. The pictures/illustrations depicted in these miniatures are mystical – a vision of the apocalypse as recorded by the creator of this medieval manuscript. It is also scarce; my bid of €500 at an auction didn't win, it fell at the hammer price of €1,300. That indicated to me that this facsimile must be worth acquiring and I eventually located a copy with a German dealer, and it has given me such pleasure to this day, to take it down from the shelf ever so often and lose myself in these other worldly illuminated miniatures.

An extravagant instance of modern illumination is the

notorious 'Bibliomaniac Edition'. In 1902, an American publisher called Frederic J. Quinby picked the novels of an obscure nineteenth century French writer named Paul Charles de Kock and turned them into the most lavish production of deluxe books imaginable. They were printed on vellum, with initials, head, and tailpieces painted in watercolours and gold, and bound in crushed red or green morocco with decorated doublures and floral onlays and inlays. Ten sets were printed, each containing 48 volumes! Quinby had planned 100 sets, but all of it got too much – the cost, the labour, the material – and the whole enterprise was abandoned. Each volume is about 300 odd pages – 48 books of such length into ten sets, all of it printed on vellum, with etchings, pen and ink drawings, and watercolour sketches hand-painted in gold. Each volume then bound in full levant with fine art-nouveau work on the cover, flyleaf, and spine, hand tooled in gilt. I count myself lucky to have found one of these volumes (some collectors own all 48 volumes, each decorated differently).

My modern manuscript collection has had some exciting additions recently, all of them acquired between 2021 and 2022. One day, not too long ago, I happened to be reading a survey of facsimiles of illuminated manuscripts in the *Private Library*, a journal for collectors. The survey was by the artist J.G. Lubbock, and he opens the article by remarking on how facsimiles have managed to reproduce the deep, vibrant colours in medieval manuscripts but the use of gold illumination in them has remained unconvincing. He then adds: 'Only one facsimile to my mind has succeeded brilliantly – *Les Heures de Marguerite de Beaujeu* – done in 1925 in Paris in a small edition of 300 numbered copies and signed by Madame Theophile Belin who published it. The gold leaf looks very like something from a medieval illuminated manuscript.' (The original manuscript is now at the Morgan Library and Museum.) I flung the journal down and ran to my laptop to look for a copy on *via*Libri, though I had little hope that I would find one, given the fabulous reputation of this facsimile and its limitation of copies to just 300. Incredulously enough, I located a copy (the only copy, by the way) in a provincial antiquarian bookshop in France. At least it was listed, but was it still available or had it sold out long ago? The price, fortunately, was not as high as it could – or should – have been. Writing an email and waiting for a response would take too long, so I called and got the owner who informed me that the book was there. Usually, I would negotiate a bit on the price or the shipping, but this time I bought it without demurring in the slightest. I was ecstatic to have found it, and amazed at the antiquarian market – one minute I was reading about a fairly rare and beautiful book, the next minute I had found it, and become its new owner. How's that for how instant rare book collecting can be done online? A few weeks later when it arrived, I could see at once what Lubbock had meant – the gold leaf had not dimmed one bit, and looked as fresh as the day it was made, and the whole effect was beautiful and satisfying.

More recently, I stumbled on another beauty – a facsimile example to rival *Les Heures de Marguerite de Beaujeu.* I spotted it at a PBA Galleries auction in September 2022, and the only reason I participated in the auction was for its temptingly low opening bid, but by the time the auction was over the hammer price had tripled. I'm still not sure why I chased it the way I did and won, but after the book arrived, I felt quite chuffed with myself. It is perhaps the most beautiful chromolithographed facsimile of an illuminated manuscript I have seen. *Statuts de L'Ordre de Saint-Esprit au Droit Désir* (Statutes of the Order of the Holy Spirit to Right Desire) is an 1853 facsimile of a fourteenth century illuminated manuscript with 17 plates reproduced in colours and gold. The gold shines brightly even today, and the deep colours, particularly the ultra-marine blue, is breathtaking. The facsimile was from the French duo of Engelmann and Gruel, the first a renowned lithographer, the second a much-heralded binder. There is in the market a glut of their chromolithographed books for sale, but only this and *this* alone has the shimmering beauty of an illuminated manuscript. The gold replication I can somehow fathom, but how did they achieve that medieval blue which has been near impossible to replicate in facsimiles?

Part II: Collecting Original Calligraphed and Illuminated Manuscripts.

Even such a trove of splendid printed illuminated facsimiles had still not prepared me for what I uncovered next – original, hand-executed manuscripts, hand-calligraphed, and hand-illuminated that seems to have flourished alongside printed book illumination. Some were facsimiles of manuscripts, while others were just original works of calligraphy and illumination. I had my first inkling of such handwritten and illuminated specimens when I chanced on a bookseller listing for an 'illuminated testimonial'. As strange-sounding as that was, such things were common right from the middle of the nineteenth century and continued into the twentieth. In particular, around the turn of the twentieth century, it became a tradition to present memorializing testimonials, tributes, and certificates in manuscript form – two to four pages of text would be written out calligraphically on vellum (or some form of parchment) and then decorated in hand-painted watercolours and gold leaf. Typically, these were undertaken by 'engrossing studios' that employed or commissioned professional lettering artists, calligraphers, and illuminators to make the manuscript. Often, they were accomplished with great skill and beauty. These engrossing studios were like modern-day versions of the scriptorium in medieval monasteries where monkish scribes and illuminators produced illuminated manuscripts on parchment. Some of these modern-day calligraphers and illuminators went on to become famous, creating their own version of an illuminated manuscript, taking for a text an excerpt from a famous work of literature. One of the most charming that I was lucky enough to find is a manuscript done by Enid Eder Perkins, a very gifted calligrapher, whose work in the testimonial looks hardly less beautiful than those original illuminated medieval manuscripts she had modelled it on.

I began obsessively looking for other examples of original – not printed -examples or specimens of modern-day illumination. You may recall that marvellous find I describe in the chapter on calligraphy of a Margaret Alexander manuscript – that along with the original hand-drawn calligraphic alphabet by Hermann Zapf was only the start. In quick succession I acquired several other entirely hand-done modern specimens, from whole manuscripts to single leaves. I'll limit myself to talking about a few that have given me particular pleasure.

The first is a facsimile on vellum of a thirteenth-century Scottish illuminated manuscript. The prize when you are a collector of fragments from medieval illuminated manuscripts like me is either a leaf with a miniature painted in colours and gold or a leaf with an illuminated, historiated initial.

A historiated initial is when the alphabet or letter that begins a page or a chapter or a paragraph (the opening initial, that is) has within it a hand-drawn human figure or figures, usually a famous historical or religious character. It is skilfully accomplished inside an elaborately drawn and decorated alphabet. They are usually hand-painted in rich colours, with gold in the background.

But I usually have little or no luck in acquiring one of these things as far as auctions go – for instance, sometime in 2018, I saw a leaf with an excellent historiated initial burnished with gold at an auction with a very high opening bid. I placed a slightly higher bid, hoping no one else would bid against me since the opening bid was already high. I lost it just as the auction closed – someone had been waiting patiently to put in a snipe bid that left me the underbidder with seconds to go. Nearly a year after losing that auction, I found *The Murthly Hours*, a vellum facsimile of a celebrated Scottish Book of Hours, on eBay. It was just a fragment, severely incomplete, disbound, consisting of five large historiated initials, one single miniature and a title leaf, all done in gold leaf and colours. The asking price was very high, almost as much as what fragments from an original manuscript might cost. It did not sell right away. Then the price was slightly lowered, and I was tempted. Though so slight, they were beautifully done, with deep saturated colours and thick gold leaf finely burnished.

And to be fair, it did not advertise itself as a whole facsimile of *The Murthly Hours* (the original is in the National Library of Scotland); instead, the title page of this hand-done facsimile on vellum called itself *Specimens of the Illuminations in a Missal*. The owner of the original Murthly manuscript, J.T. Gibson Craig, commissioned a skilled copyist and illuminator called Henry Laing, to execute examples of miniatures and historiated initials for him. This might seem odd to us – why, after all, should one get a facsimile made when you have the original? But this was fairly common for collectors in the nineteenth century who owned illuminated manuscripts: the facsimile enabled them to spend time with the manuscript without having to handle the original frequently; they used the facsimile to study the manuscript, lend it, and so on. For this reason, the facsimile had to be nearly on par with the original, and they spared no expense getting the best copyist and illuminator, and the best materials to make it. This is why these 'original' facsimiles on vellum with gold leaf and painted colours are so respected and desired by today's collectors.

I would check the listing every day, half hoping it had been bought (so that I didn't have to agonize over a decision) and half hoping it would still be there. But it would always be there. Then, perhaps after a couple of months had passed, and I had willed myself to forget about it, a best offer for *The Murthly Hours* found its way to my mailbox from eBay. This was one of those email prompts you receive from eBay when you've been checking a listing often. It was considerably reduced, but still too pricey for me. I could for that price buy two *original* historiated initials. But I couldn't get it out of my mind and a couple of weeks later I made a counter-offer and it was accepted. It was still a steep price but I knew all too well something like this would never come my way again. I am so glad I have it, particularly so for the unusually large size of the historiated initials in this facsimile – about five inches each; most specimens I have seen are one to two inches. The historiated characters and scenes depicted in the initials were from the Bible, as is typical of a Book of Hours. The original manuscript is the work of English and French scribes, and the miniatures and initials are charming for being early examples of miniature making.

For a time, connoisseurs of manuscripts had viewed the work of the scribes and illuminators of the fourteenth, fifteenth, and sixteenth centuries to have attained the highest achievement of manuscript art because the human figures in the books of this period look as accomplished and rounded and artistic as the work of Renaissance painters. Manuscripts from the fifteenth and sixteenth centuries, particularly from Italy, were highly sought after and collected. Today, however, there has been a complete reversal. Later manuscripts are seen as being too close to paintings, too much like 'easel painting', where the illustrations are there for their own sake. The more gothic miniatures from the twelfth and thirteenth centuries are now heralded as the glory of manuscript making – here they feel like true adornments to the text, and show more vitality, freshness, and originality in their cruder but more enchanting gothic figures.

I may have even been lucky, finally, with finding an original illuminated miniature – and a beautiful specimen of it – when I stumbled on a most unusual listing at Riverrun Books and Manuscripts for a very modestly priced cutting of an illuminated miniature. Medieval miniatures are the most expensive in this whole field of medieval manuscript hunting. You can secure a historiated initial between $950 and $1,200, but the miniature begins at $2,500 and goes up to $25,000. This dazzling specimen was priced at a fraction of what these things usually sell for; it was mounted and framed, and showed a great amount of blue and gold in it, and shone brightly. Titled 'The Annunciation', the miniature depicted an angel visiting Mary. It must be a facsimile I concluded, and even if it was, it was a fine example, going by the highly burnished gold grounds in it, and was surely worth the asking price. But when I went on to read Riverrun's description, I was pleasantly shocked and delighted – apparently a genuine miniature taken from a thirteenth century German manuscript that had been priced low because the miniature at some point had been retouched or overpainted by a later hand, embellishing the miniature further.

This was too good to pass up. I had to find out more, and perhaps talk with someone at the bookshop that could further back all this up. I got the owner himself, Tom Lecky, who said the auction house that had looked at it felt fairly sure it was not a facsimile but an original, but one that, alas, had been worked further on by some hand – when this may have been interfered with the appraisers had not been able to say. In order to absolutely verify it, the surface it had been painted and gilded on – vellum most likely – had to be closely examined, but since it was mounted and glazed that wasn't possible anymore. And therefore it was being offered cautiously, as is – w.a.f. in the jargon of auctioneers, 'with all faults'.

I said I wanted to think about it and asked that it be put on hold for me. After I had rung off, I looked up Mr Lecky and was pleasantly surprised. He had formerly been head of Books and Manuscripts at Christie's auction house in New York. It was now an obvious guess that the people Mr Lecky had shown the miniature to must have been his former colleagues at Christie's – though of course I couldn't say for sure. I called him and said I was keen but would he consider revising the price? He agreed, and we came to a mutually satisfactory sale price.

Well, all I can say is as each day goes by, I am so happy that I bought it, doubts and all, because each time I look at it, I am convinced more and more that it is the real thing – recent manuscript scholarship has shown that cutting out a miniature from a manuscript was a known practice as far back as the fifteenth century – and became more common and even rampant in the following centuries. A connoisseur of illumination or a religious devotee would either commission an atelier to produce an illuminated miniature or cut it out from a manuscript to either have it glazed – as seems to have happened with my miniature – or paste it into another manuscript to adorn it further, or just even stick it into an album.

A pity about the later, additional handwork in my miniature, but that too has only made this radiant miniature more interesting. After all, manuscript experts at a big New York auction house couldn't be all that wrong, could they?

Perhaps the one I am personally most thrilled and proudest of, as well as the one I am most affected by each time I take it off the shelf and look through it, is an original nineteenth century Indian illuminated manuscript – a history of the Mughal kings, 219 leaves calligraphically written out in *nastaliq* in black and red ink, several other gilt-ruled leaves, five pretty miniatures and three richly illuminated polychrome panels. This was a true find. Only the most lavish Eastern manuscripts have miniatures in them, so this must have been commissioned by a royal. There is page after page of colour and gold in it, with calligraphic writing from various hands, all of it of the highest order.

A more modest but fetching little example of a little

book with just calligraphy, no illumination, done in two inks in a fine hand is 'The Green Door', a short story by A.A. Milne. This was not of course a Winnie the Pooh story, but something the author had written early in his life, a kind of modern fairy tale. I found this, as ever, by chance on ABE, buried as it was under a pile of listings. In 1925, a lettering artist named Harry B. Dorr was commissioned to write out this story as a gift for a couple. He wrote it out on a watermarked Barcham Green handmade paper and bound it in green crushed morocco. It was one of the loveliest examples of calligraphy I had seen, and I pounced on it the very second I came upon the listing.

In the end, though, nothing can quite compare to the glory and beauty of medieval manuscripts. If I could, that's all I would be collecting but they were – and always will be – out of my price range. This hasn't stopped me from going after medieval and Renaissance fragments. I'm guilty as the next collector of chasing after those single medieval illuminated leaves that are auctioned not just on eBay, but at every premier auction house doing business today. I don't feel as guilty as I should perhaps feel, since many of them come from imperfect or disbound manuscripts, though that may not always be the case. It's well known that a trade in breaking up manuscripts has flourished since the 1920s, and will probably continue to flourish since it brings such quick gains and large profits.

Anyway, I digress. A transaction I want to conclude with – which is related to medieval leaves – happens to also be the strangest collector–dealer transaction I've had so far, as well as being, unexpectedly, the most generous.

And it had to do with a spectacular incunabular leaf. Browsing in a desultory fashion on eBay one day, I came across a stunning early printed leaf featuring five large highly illuminated initials in blue, green, magenta, orange, and burnished gold. It was a leaf from a luxurious Breviary printed by Nicolas Jenson in 1478, and the five initials sparkled as though they had been painted and gilded just that morning, so fresh did they look.

The crisp handmade paper measured 13 x 9 inches, and had a few flaws: the paint and gold had bled through the paper a little, and a tiny tear at the bottom of the leaf had been expertly repaired. The seller had slightly reduced the price to take this into account, but in addition, he had a 'best offer' option on the item. This lovely leaf with five sparkling initials was priced $650, and I made an offer of $500. He countered with $550, and we settled at $525.

With the flaws, was it still worth what I had paid? It absolutely was, because at that very same time leaves from the same Jenson Breviary from a very well-known dealer of manuscripts was priced $1,200 each. And those leaves had only a single illuminated initial, not five!

When the parcel arrived, I had a good mind to scold the seller for how casually he had packed this, as if it was a $20 broadside or pamphlet. Just a large cover which contained two sheets of blank paper between which he had placed the leaf. As I removed the leaf between the paper to examine it, I hoped hard that it was still intact. Luckily it was, but I still felt like writing to the seller to point out how easily it could have been damaged – but all that evaporated as I found a handwritten note from him saying, 'Dear eBayer, by way of compensation for the slightly flawed leaf you bought, I am enclosing another leaf (of the same book) with no flaws in it and with one initial illuminated in the same gorgeous fashion. Enjoy.'

It was indeed a perfect leaf with it's one initial illuminated in the exact same way as in the leaf I had bought. I was thrilled and perplexed. He could have sold this leaf for about the same price quite easily and quickly on eBay, but he had let me have it for nothing. Incunabula leaves with such elaborate illumination are scarce and pricey – not to forget that this was the work of Jenson – so instead of cursing I blessed him, and wondered all day at my luck.

PART TWO

THE PLEASURES OF BIBLIOPHILY

Rare Book Dealers, Collectors, and Other Bibliophiles

'A FULL TIME OCCUPATION'

A.N.L. MUNBY

'I am an incurable book collector', wrote A.N.L. 'Tim' Munby, 'and have haunted the antiquarian bookshops for forty -five years; I still have on my shelves the first old book I ever bought: the tenth edition of a volume of sermons printed in 1744 which cost two pence and which, without wishing to boast, I claim is worth at least double today.' My favourite English bibliophile has always been Tim Munby, not John Carter. Carter is the more famous British bibliophile, but Munby's wit, style, and collecting connoisseurship outclasses not just Carter, but the rest of the Biblio-Boys (Michael Sadlier, Simon Nowell-Smith, Graham Pollard, and Percy Muir).

I first encountered the bibliophile writings of Munby in *Essays and Papers* (1977), and thought it a treasure. Though published posthumously by Nicolas Barker, then editor of *The Book Collector*, it has become a modern classic of bibliophily. Munby's best-known essays here are 'Floreat Bibliomania' and 'Book Collecting in the 1930s'. Such was his modesty that in looking at 'Floreat Bibliomania' later, he commented, 'I'm afraid that the bloom, if ever present, has rather disappeared from this lightweight piece...'. Not true at all; rather, it is redolent.

Even as a lad, Tim Munby frequented antiquarian bookshops, though as he notes, not all of them were friendly to a child-collector. Some were downright curmudgeons, and one of these wits once chided him, 'Don't pull the old stuff about, you won't find a Shakespeare quarto.' Munby came to King's College as an undergraduate in 1932, and fit nicely into the tradition of bibliophily there. At Cambridge, he discovered the company of collectors was plentiful, and revelled in it. King's College, Munby notes, had a strong book-collecting tradition with the likes of John Maynard Keynes, Arthur Cole, and Stephen Gaselee; a few years junior to him were John Carter, John Hayward, and Desmond Flower.

And like so many Cambridge book collectors before and after him, Munby would visit the bookshop of Gustave David, who ran two places, one a rare bookshop in town, the other a stall at the marketplace.

'Cambridge in the early 1930s,' writes Munby, 'was dominated by Gustave David, who spent four days a week in the London salerooms, and on Friday offered his new purchases at the most modest of profits to his besotted customers.' David, a Parisian *bouqueniste*, left his city to set up shop in Cambridge, and lucked out. He was a chain-smoker, always sitting in a little chair outside his cramped shop sucking a dead cigar. He was also, 'somewhat of a tyrant, and *awarded* his books rather than sold them... he preferred the undergraduates to have the bargains and was known to snatch a book from an older collector to give it to a younger man in the bookshop'.

David was a much-loved Cambridge character, and at the end of his career, as he closed his bookshop, he was offered a choice between an honorary MA and a luncheon in his honour at Trinity Hall. He chose the latter, says Munby, and 'endearingly dozed throughout the speeches in his honour and broke down with emotion when he rose to reply'. David died in 1936, and a slender tribute with the title *David of Cambridge* was printed in his honour, with several collectors recalling their time in his bookshop; the proceeds from the book went to Mrs David.

After college, Munby joined the antiquarian firm of Bernard Quaritch and learnt the basics of the rare book trade here. He did not stay very long at Quaritch and moved in 1936 to Sotheby's and came under the tutelage of G.D. Hobson and Charles Des Graz, two of the most influential auctioneers of their time. While there, a most unusual assignment was presented to him that would change the course of his career. The Robinson Brothers, another well-known London rare bookshop, had negotiated the rare book buying coup of the century – they had bought, paying through their noses, the entire remaining manuscript collection of the vellomane, Thomas Phillipps.

Before they catalogued it or put it up for auction or did anything with the Phillipps collection, the Robinsons felt it might be good to have someone study the collection as well as the collector. It was Des Graz who recommended

Munby to Lionel Robinson to be the chronicler of what came to be known as the *Phillipps Studies*, which quickly gained a reputation as 'a magisterial study of bibliophily'. It resulted in a five-volume study of the Phillipps manuscript collection by Munby, as well as a portrait of Thomas Phillipps. In researching this monumental collection, Munby became an authority on the history of rare bookselling, and his personal acquisition of thousands of bookseller catalogues down the ages revealed the collecting and dealing practices of the book collecting world.

After this, he was a bookman to be reckoned with, and his old alma mater, King's College, came calling, asking him to become librarian to its vast special collection. This gave him some spare time to write and collect, but not travel. (John Carter's profession as Scribners' London dealer gave him many opportunities to travel and roam, something Munby missed.)

Munby wrote in 'Floreat Bibliomania', 'For antiquarian booksellers I have the liveliest affection and admiration. There is only one trait for the bookseller, not fortunately a very common one, which I find hard to forgive, and that is showing a customer a book and then announcing that it is not for sale. There is a book in the West Country... but no, I have hopes of it yet.' Later, that same West Country bookseller offered it to him, a large paper copy of a folio Prayer book of 1661.

> Even more agonizing are the memories of books which one might have bought but declined... And for every book which one regrets having bought, in

> my experience there are ten which one regrets having failed to buy.

Munby can hardly bear to think of the books he let go. He was miffed at fellow undergraduate philistines who asked him foolishly if he read the rare books on his shelf in his Cambridge digs. 'For the most part. However, I just look at them or take them down and stroke them from time to time. Book collecting, I would have you know, is a full-time occupation, and one wouldn't get far if one took time off for frivolities like reading.'

Elsewhere he wrote,

> The education of collector's wives must be started early; a visit to at least one bookshop a day throughout the honeymoon is to be recommended. I have twice observed the fearful object lesson of the *secret* book collector. Two men of my acquaintance owned hundreds of books which they dared not bring home and which remained for years in parcels at their booksellers. Such a compromise between retaining one's books or one's wife seems to me a dubious solution, but I have the problem continually in mind.

Nicolas Barker, former editor of *The Book Collector* described Munby in his recollections: 'The ruddy face, white hair balding to a monkish tonsure secularized by his military moustache, the sturdy figure, brisk walk, the baggy tweeds, poacher's pockets ready for a rabbit or a folio – all this lightened the hearts of everyone he came to meet. But most of all he was the consummate book collector.'

(I always wince at such hunting references, unable to comprehend why such a gentle and kind man should think shooting geese and rabbits was a relaxing, fun pass time.) Once at a book fair in 1973, Barker spotted the first book printed in 1781 on the construction of library steps, with a colour foldout plate illustrating the inventor's patent construction – just the kind of book about books Munby would cherish. It was priced £42.

And Barker said to Paul Grinke, at whose stall he had found it, 'Oh, I do wish I could give that to Tim.' Such was the respect for Munby that Grinke said, 'I'll knock off 20 per cent if you do'. Thirty-five pounds – 'most of my purchases were in single digits then, but how could I refuse? I took it to Tim. "*Where* did you find that?" He asked almost angrily. "I have been looking for it for 35 years." Suddenly £35 seemed ridiculously cheap.'

Delighting in Munby, I searched bookseller catalogues for anything signed or inscribed by him, and found a nice, inscribed copy of one of his *Phillipps Studies*. I was quite content with that find, with no plans to get anything else associated with Munby in his manuscript hand. But a fat temptation was waiting for me just around the corner; perhaps a few weeks after I had bought the inscribed *Phillipps Studies* volume, I saw a little thing I had hoped in vain to find.

The celebrated modern private press, Rampant Lions Press of Will and Sebastian Carter, had printed two of Munby's essays, each in a small, limited signed edition, 'Floreat Bibliomania' in 1953, and 'Book Collecting in the

1930s' in 1973. I wrote to Sebastian Carter expressing my deep desire to acquire both or at least one of these things. Alas, he replied, he didn't have any, and he imagined they'd now be quite scarce.

Sometime in late 2019, when I had all but forgotten about these two Munby pamphlets, I saw on eBay, quite casually listed, a fine copy of 'Book Collecting in the 1930s', with a photo of the colophon showing the limitation and Munby's signature. I bought it happily. I have, though, never so far been able to locate a copy of 'Floreat Bibliomania'.

In June 1993, a Sotheby's sale of the fine books and manuscripts from the library of the celebrated English dealer, Alan G. Thomas, featured a copy (in three volumes) of Phillipp's monumental catalogue of his collection. A complete set had become rare, and this copy up for sale was the most desired – this was the famous 'interleaved' copy of the catalogue featuring annotations in the vellomaniac's hand as well as in the hand of Munby, who had made extensive margin notes while writing the *Phillipps Studies*. Munby had acquired this from the Robinsons in 1947, and Thomas had bought it in March 1976 at the Munby sale, also at Sotheby's. It was estimated to go for between £5,000 and £7,000. And sold to H.P. Kraus for £29,900.

A STUDENT OF THE CHASE

NORMAN H. STROUSE

Norman Strouse, a book collector I've admired and feel a strong affinity with, had a favourite game going: pitting the modest collector against the wealthy collector, and showing how the small-time collector can still come out ahead of the moneyed collector. He held forth entertainingly on this in his book, *How to Build a Poor Man's Morgan Library.* (This was beautifully printed by Leonard Bahr at his Adagio Press on dampened Venezia handmade paper; the presswork is lovely.) 'Morgan' here as in J.P. Morgan, whose vast and fabulous collection of books and art is housed at the Morgan Library and Museum.

I may not have, writes Strouse, the limitless funds Morgan had, but I can still show in my collection one or two things that Morgan missed getting. Beautiful, singular, rare things that should have gone into Morgan's collection, but now won't because he beat Morgan to it. And, so what, he goes on to ask, if I can't afford a whole illuminated medieval manuscript, I can still content myself with buying a choice medieval leaf that has a gorgeous illuminated miniature. Morgan, he says, began collecting after he came into a lot of money, while he began collecting before he had much money. The modest collector can still experience all the pleasures of collecting that a wealthy collector can, and a few pleasures not even known to the affluent collector.

> Much as I admire these men (Huntington, Morgan) for their accomplishments and the generosity with which they gave their collections to the public I do not envy them, because they missed the greatest pleasure of the collecting game – item by item building of their collections, a sense of personal relationship to each volume owned and a quickened memory of the circumstances surrounding their most interesting acquisitions. They have in a word missed the emotional experience of collecting, the element which traps most of us modest collectors and gives us the greatest joy of reminiscence.

(Strouse wasn't to know then, but we know better today from recent biographies of these wealthy collectors that they not only knew their rare books well, they also knew the prices they'd paid for each copy – especially Huntington who, even when negotiating million-dollar purchases, would look for thrifty bargains! I'm charmed, amused and even reassured that hunting for bargains seems to be in the very blood of all collectors, middle class or rich. Lessing J. Rosenwald, another wealthy and formidable collector, who could have bought rarities at any asking price, was himself unable to resist looking for a bargain within the pages of a just arrived catalogue. In his 1976 memoir *Recollections of a Collector*, he confessed, 'There is no more delightful pleasure for a bibliomaniac than to satisfy his avocation on his day of rest by perusing his accumulation of sales catalogues...one always has the hope [seldom realized] that somewhere buried in such a miscellany is an item may be overlooked by the more astute dealers and the more catholic collectors.')

I am often tempted to view my own collecting efforts as 'a poor man's Norman Strouse Library'. So what if I can't afford a leaf with a miniature, I can content myself with a medieval leaf that has a beautifully historiated initial! And I just may have a thing or two that Strouse missed getting himself!

Of the hundreds of accounts on collecting books out there, perhaps only a dozen – if that – are on collecting fine press books. And no one has written as well or as much on collecting press books and the book arts as Strouse. I've thoroughly enjoyed his reminiscences of how and what he collected, the bargains he found, and the ways he pursued them. Strouse is my idol; he writes well, without sentiment, but always with deep feeling. He didn't write to brag about his conquests but to share his pleasure in the chase. He was a diligent student of the chase. He began collecting with modest, limited funds, but made a great deal of money later in his hugely successful career, even owning a penthouse apartment in Manhattan, the entire floor filled with his collecting treasures. He decided quite early in his collecting path that he would focus on rare and beautiful things from the field of the Art and History of the Book. Though he owned everything from the Kelmscott Press, his love for Doves Press and his admiration for its printer, T.J. Cobden-Sanderson, was so intense, that he traded his best William Morris material with fellow collector John L. Crawford for his extensive archive of Doves Press material.

His first idol was Thomas Bird Mosher and his pleasingly designed books, and having foolishly passed over some scarce Mosher material for a lack of funds, Strouse was ready the next time for anything interesting in the Mosher line of collecting that might turn up. And so it did: an auction of Mosher's own personal library, with several copies of his best editions, some printed on pure vellum, as well as Mosher's copies of the great press books, including the Doves Bible. Later, he regretted he hadn't gone beyond the tight budget he had set apart for the auction. In 1953, the famous bookdealer, Warren Howell, offered him two prize items: an original Gutenberg leaf and the *Nuremberg Chronicle*, each priced at $500, but if he would take both, it would be $700. Strouse knew a collector friend who had been looking for a Gutenberg leaf, and they teamed up to buy both, splitting the cost. Of course, Strouse kicked himself later for not getting the Gutenberg leaf, but lucky for him, not long after he was able to secure an original leaf for $450. (Pity Strouse is not around anymore to find out what a bargain he got: today that same leaf would easily sell for $175,000.)

His collecting deepened in new directions after his earnings shot up; press books were frequently and commonly acquired, but now he set his sights on incunabula, illuminated manuscripts, and original calligraphic works. He acquired in quick succession two important books printed by that justly famous Venetian printer Nicolas Jenson, one of which he describes as being 'magnificently illuminated'. Another substantial collecting coup came unexpectedly when a dealer Strouse would buy regularly from casually mentioned to him one day that a fantastic horde of rare and beautiful books was being offered by the family of a collector who had just died, but he didn't have the capital to buy the lot. Strouse asked if he could see what the collection contained, and the dealer provided him an inventory taken down after an appraisal had been done. Strouse's heart began pounding: the collection included several illuminated manuscripts, including a stunning Book of Hours featuring many miniature paintings. Strouse quickly arranged with his bank to provide the dealer with a loan, with the agreement that he would get first crack at the material. He even lent him his station wagon to fetch the books back. Strouse made sure that he bagged the Book of Hours, along with some other choice illuminated manuscripts – and this set him off on a hunt for calligraphed and decorated manuscripts. This Book of Hours had previously been owned by Robert Hoe, Henry Poor, and Courtland Bishop – 'one could not ask for a more resplendent provenance,' adds Strouse with satisfaction.

Of the many pamphlets that reprinted talks by Strouse on what and how he collected, the following are my favourites: *A Collector's Decabiblon* describes ten of his most exciting book-collecting experiences, in *The Pleasures of Packing A Library* he reminiscences about how he collected the treasures he is now packing in boxes because he is moving home, *A Certain Gaiety of Treatment* is on the Ashendene Press, and *The Lengthened Shadow* is his views on the great private press printers. Of these, only one is a fine press book: the aforementioned *How to Build a Poor Man's Morgan Library*. (There is a more ordinary, inexpensive edition of this talk, which he gave again to a university.)

One time, in 1954, Strouse sneaked out of a convention in Philadelphia when he realized the antiquarian firm of Charles Sessler was only four blocks away. He was quickly ushered into the inner sanctum of the bookshop which held their best material, presided over by Mabel Zahn, who had headed this section for many years. She asked Strouse what his interests were, and he rattled off: Doves, Ashendene, Nash, Kelmscott – at the mention of the last, she stopped him and quietly said, 'I may have something of interest to you there', and disappeared into another room that customers could not enter. She then emerged, Strouse says, with the richest and most beautiful copy of a book by William Morris he had ever seen. It was a book authored by Morris before he began the Kelmscott Press; it was printed on vellum and bound by T.J. Cobden-Sanderson. The glory of it was the embroidered work on the cover – which had been done by none other than May Morris, William Morris's daughter. He began to worry now if he could afford a treasure like this, and expressed his concern in this respect. Ms Zahn replied: 'Of course you can afford it. I've had it for several years and have been waiting for the right person to walk in to buy it. I shall show you the receipt for the original price I paid for it all those years ago, and you shall pay me ten percent more on that price.'

Strouse couldn't believe his ears. This was not just a low, low price, but a collecting coup of the first water. He left happily with the book.

After moving to New York in 1955, Strouse would drop in frequently to see what new things the famous dealer Philip Duschnes had acquired. He would also visit the Chiswick Bookshop of Herman and Aveve Cohen. He acquired fine books from Chiswick, and magnificent manuscripts from Duschnes. One Saturday morning in 1959, Duschnes showed him several manuscript choir book leaves with large miniature paintings on them. The Morgan Library had first choice at the lot, and picked two, and Strouse could only afford to buy one, but he was torn between two lavishly illuminated miniatures. One was of Mary and the Christ child, the other of the Ascension.

He reluctantly left the bookshop with one purchase – Mary and the Christ child – and in the days that followed bitterly regretted not getting the other. Hurried enquiries to Duschnes only revealed that all the leaves had now been sold, three of them to an anonymous Ohio dealer. Three years later wandering into Duschnes' shop, he discovered the leaf had returned to the shop – that Ohio dealer had passed away, and Duschnes had bought it back. Strouse bought it on the spot – he had acquired more funds for his collecting in the passing years, and though the leaf must have cost a good deal more than what it had been priced then, he didn't hesitate to add it to his collection. He goes on to remark that he does not expect to see two choir leaves with more beautiful miniatures in his lifetime.

The last of the significant and exciting rare book transaction from Strouse is my favourite. In the basement of Bill Fletcher's bookshop in Cecil Court, London, Strouse had once seen a Persian manuscript of exquisite beauty. He coveted it instantly, but it was priced at $12,000. Though he felt it was possibly worth more, it meant he would have to refrain from buying anything for a long time if he spent as much as $12,000 on just this one thing. Years passed but this manuscript never left Strouse's mind; it had lodged there, beckoning him. So, in June 1969, with some trepidation, he wrote to Bill Fletcher to ask if he perhaps still had the Persian with him, and if he did, what was the rock-bottom price he would accept for it if paid in cash? He braced for disappointment, expecting to hear that the Persian had long sold – which would not have surprised him.

The reply came back in a cable: the Persian manuscript was available, and Fletcher could offer it for $11,000. The collector cabled back that he had never purchased a book beyond the price of four figures, and as much as he wanted the manuscript, he could not break this precedent. Bill replied, this time via airmail:

> Your cable received a few days ago contains the most specious excuse you should think of for not buying a lovely manuscript, if you'll pardon my frankness.

> Precedents are made only to be broken, but since you treasure yours so carefully, I'll overcome this difficulty by saying that you can have my Persian manuscript for four figures, i.e., Nine Thousand Nine Hundred and Ninety-Nine Dollars.

Fletcher went on to add that he was being a bit tough on this sale because he thought the Persian item a real beauty:

> It's the only one I've ever had in anything like this class...and it is the last one I shall ever have... I am pretty sure that the longer I keep it the less I want to part with it and the more I shall get for it when it finally has to go.

This last sentiment from bookdealers has sent a chill into the hearts of many a collector, and Strouse immediately cabled: 'Please send manuscript nine nine nine nine.'

Within 24 hours a cable was received; 'Four nine manuscript is on its way. Congratulations.' This was soon followed by an airmail letter from Fletcher: 'Noble Sir, I am your fervent admirer and devoted servant. Your cable for the four nines manuscript was brilliant in its brevity and magnificent in your acceptance of the inevitable.' Strouse notes that since the day he's had the Persian in his hand, it has remained a permanent source of pleasure.

'A MAGICAL BIBLIOPHILE PAST'

THE CHISWICK BOOKSHOP OF HERMAN AND AVEVE COHEN

If I could time travel to just one antiquarian bookshop from the past, it would be the Chiswick Bookshop of Herman and Aveve 'Viv' Cohen located once upon a time in New York City. It opened its doors in 1935, and closed in 2001, and had specialized in fine press and illustrated books. A customer reminiscing about Chiswick remarked that being there and talking about private press books with Herman and Viv was like revisiting 'a magical bibliophile past'. One of their regulars, the collector Ken Auchincloss, recalls that Herman and Viv

> introduced me to the Five-Year Rule. 'If only you had been here five years ago,' they said. 'The things we could have shown you! The prices we could have offered!' And, of course, I think the five-year rule is still in effect. I think it'll continue to pass into the future – we'll always be five years beyond the golden age of book collecting. But the golden age of Herman and

Viv and Chiswick is one that I will treasure forever, because it changed my life.

My enchantment with Chiswick began in 2015 when I bought a monograph called *Reminiscences and Remembrances of Herman and Aveve Cohen and the Chiswick Bookshop* (2002). Naturally drawn to stories of rare bookshops, I began reading this slim booklet of 32 pages, and found I had fallen under its spell even before I had got halfway into it. Under the spell of the bookshop *and* the spell of this finely designed monograph. Jenni Matz, the granddaughter of the Cohens, compiled and edited this remembrance tribute, and noted typographer Jerry Kelly designed it. In her preface, Ms Matz writes: 'This Monograph is offered as a bookman's tribute to my two role models. It is comprised largely of letters written to and from my grandparents and correspondence sent to me by their friends. Of course, the most vivid telling of this tale comes from Viv herself, in transcribed interviews.'

In the second part, Ms Matz brings together recollections by various friends and customers of Chiswick – of time spent there with Herman and Viv, the beautiful books they found there, and the way this bookseller-couple were able to turn the premises of the bookshop into a meeting place for collectors and typophiles. Herman and Viv emerge as booksellers who were absolutely devoted to their job, and enjoyed selling books to collectors. A little after they were married, much to their family's dismay, the young couple announced that they were going to open their own bookshop. They were told right off it would fail but both felt – having dropped out of college to clerk in bookshops – their life was books, no matter what. The first location was 3 West 51st Street, NY. A lot of hard work, passion, and few lucky breaks saw them through the first years.

Viv recalls three lucky breaks soon after they opened: one day the then doyen of antiquarian booksellers, A.S.W. Rosenbach, happened to be passing by Chiswick, and stepped in to chat with the Cohens. He generously offered his mailing list and gave them a marvellous piece of advice (something I simply delight in): *'You're going about it the wrong way. I see new books in your window. That's nonsense. That's for the birds, those new books. Every time a new book is published you buy an old one and then you'll amount to something in the book business.'*

The second break was Herman's daring move to buy the entire stock of an antiquarian bookshop (Dunster House Bookshop) that had just closed down for $2,700 when all they had was $500 in the bank. This move brought the renowned scholar-collector Philip Hofer to their door, making it their third lucky break. Hofer had just heard Chiswick had bought the Dunster stock, and was sure he wanted many things from it. The Cohens, however, had no idea who Hofer was and were stunned when he spent almost the entire weekend picking their stock. It was Hofer's own collecting interest in fine press books that tilted the focus of Chiswick from a general antiquarian bookstore to a deeper focus on the book arts. Hofer urged them to be not just one more bookshop for bibliophiles, but to be a bookshop for collectors.

After Herman passed away in 1997, Aveve continued to run the bookshop. One of her fondest memories in the book is of their first meeting with two of the most admired and beloved artists of the fine press world: the wood engraver John DePol and fine press printer John S. Fass of the Hammer Creek Press. On any given day you might run into one or both of them in the bookshop – people who made beautiful and fine books who also happened to be their regular customers. (Indeed, the Chiswick seemed to be a kind of rendezvous point for The Typophiles.) One lucky customer (among many lucky ones) who trusted the Cohens implicitly about what he should acquire as a collector was Richard Schimmelpfeng. In the early 1970s, he recalls getting a call from Viv Cohen urging that he buy the work of printer John S. Fass at his Hammer Creek Press. Though Richard had never heard of Fass before, he bought everything Chiswick had in stock from Hammer Creek. Imagine this collector's fortune to have everything by this skilled fine printer at those prices, when Fass was just beginning to be known!

This affecting, beautiful monograph furthers ones interest, curiosity, and affection for Chiswick, the Cohens, and that whole 'magical bibliophile' period when everyone seemed a typophile, everyone a young collector.

Henry Morris the fine press printer who used to be a customer wrote a little limerick tribute for them in his *The Private Press Man's Tale*. It went like this:

> Once dwelled in Gotham, bookish giants, With numerous well-heeled clients. The noble Herman, fine Chiswickian, Of many great books, he took his pickian. Books on Paper, Type and such, Did Chiswick sell to

> readers much. Many fine scholars he supplied, And with Master Duchness often vied. This Duchness was a shop-man clever, Who took his losses almost never. And both these gents gave fine advise: 'Buy the best and hang the price.' What seemed so dear in former years Now looks so cheap it bringeth tears.

I felt so intimate with the Cohens and their bookshop that I wanted something touched by their hands, a catalogue they had hand-annotated or a signature or inscription from one or both of them, so I trawled through the antiquarian market. But nothing of that nature would ever turn up. Several years later, I chanced on a rather sparkling association copy, a book presented to the Cohens by my bibliophile hero, Norman Strouse, who had inscribed inside: *'To Herman and Aveve: Such good friends of many years who have helped me build my Poor Man's Morgan Library.' Dec 21, 1966. Norman Strouse.*

The bookseller I bought this from told me this copy had come from the collection of the Cohen's grand-daughter, Jenni Matz, the very person behind this tribute monograph. I immediately shot off a letter to her, a rather long, rambling email, part of which read:

> Dear Ms Matz,
>
> I have long wanted to write you a note about how enchanted I have become with your grandparents, Herman and Aveve, and the magical Book Arts bookshop they created with Chiswick. Like so many bibliophiles my first introduction to them was through your 'Reminiscences & Remembrances'. If there

> was one bookshop I could go back in time to visit, it would be Chiswick. To step into the bookshop and be welcomed warmly by your grandparents, to linger a while and hear them talk with so much devotion about fine printing, to perchance meet there John Fass or Valenti Angelo, or some other fine press enthusiast, seems like a bibliophile's dream.
>
> Thank you for making 'Reminiscences & Remembrances' happen – it is a bibliophilic jewel. I can't tell you how many times I have re-read it – I keep buying copies of it to give away to friends and family, and every one of them have been touched by the book.

I was thrilled to hear back from Ms Matz:

> *Pradeep! Thank you so much for writing to me, and apologies it's taken a few days to respond!*
>
> *I was so touched by your words about my grandparents and Chiswick. I am thrilled you enjoyed the monograph that the Typophiles put out. Not many people have seen it!*
>
> *I have shared your lovely note with my mother and sister.*
>
> *Jenni Matz*

I would like the spirited, moving closing lines of Aveve Cohen's words spoken to her granddaughter to be Chiswick's epitaph: 'The reality remains that I lost a wonderful husband, a business partner and my best friend... I live very simply. I was extremely happy in my marriage to my husband. I've been in this business for God knows how many years. I love this. I love their world. That's all there is to it.'

THE WARDEN'S MEETING

JOHN SPARROW AND THE OXFORD BIBLIOPHILES

The first association copy I bought still remains my favourite in the modest collection of books I have in this line of collecting. I had been keen on having a book signed by John Carter, that elegant, stylish English bookman, and found a lovely copy of his *Books and Book Collectors* with Forest Books, UK. It was also, to boot, a presentation copy, from Carter to J.R. Abbey, a distinguished collector of private press books and illuminated manuscripts. In Carter's elegant handwriting, it had a fine inscription: 'A small tit for a large tat.'

To possess something from the hand of the patron saint of bibliomania, T.F. Dibdin is something all collectors desire – a signed copy of the first ever treatise on *Bibliomania*, or an inscribed copy of his finest book, *The Bibliographical Decameron*, or even better, an entire letter in his hand. Every signed copy I came across was priced well above what I could pay; inscribed copies were pricier.

What hope did I have to find a letter from him in my price range?

But one letter in the market from R.K. Manuscripts, a UK dealer, got my attention in 2015. Though it was steeply priced, Dibdin makes a reference in the letter to a fellow collector that made it very desirable indeed. In this two-page letter to the antiquary, Thomas Aymot, sent on the noon of 24 July 1823, the patron saint of bibliomania talks of making a visit to Blickling Hall in Norfolk to see its famed library, and adds: *'Heber, who has called on me today, says, he will go with us to Blickling. He is at present desperately occupied with my "Companion" up to the chin.'*

A letter from Dibdin referencing Richard Heber, the great English bibliomaniac, was too good to pass by. I could just picture it: as Dibdin composes this letter, his friend Heber who has called on him earlier in the day, is now reading Dibdin's manuscript of *The Library Companion!* Also, just as attractively, the letter included its original postmarked envelope with the address written out by Dibdin, and the stamp of his famous red wax seal. The letter itself, according to the seller, is an octavo on bifolium. In good condition, lightly aged and worn. Addressed on reverse of second leaf to 'Thos. Amyot Esq | 13. James St. | Pimlico', with two postmarks and a good impression of Dibdin's red wax monogram seal.

The dealer was willing to reduce the price slightly, and I asked him if he could include shipping, to which he readily agreed. Something as light and small as this would not incur high shipping charges even with insured tracking. I waited expectantly for it. Usually parcels from the UK would reach me within ten to fourteen business days. Two weeks had gone by and nothing had arrived. I wrote to ask for a tracking number, and he replied: 'You didn't ask for special post. So, no tracking. Haven't lost more than two in 30 years.'

I stared at his email in disbelief. Most antiquarian booksellers in the UK I've ordered from over the years automatically send anything that's even slightly expensive by tracked and signed Royal Mail. There was nothing to do but hope for its safe arrival. A few days later when I collected my mail, I found a small envelope, like a letter to me, with my address handwritten. I didn't for a moment imagine this would be it, and I was about to tear open the envelope casually, assuming it to be from a friend, when I saw the sender's address.

For a second time I found myself staring in some disbelief. He had not even used one of those cardboard mailers, simply having slipped the Dibdin ALS inside a regular paper envelope, licked the gum, stuck it, and sent it on its way. When I shared this with some of my dealer friends in England, they were aghast at the risk this seller had taken; again, very routinely anything ephemeral like this would have been packed in layers of paper and cardboard before it was airmailed by a dealer. Somehow, this little envelope had not only not got lost or misplaced, but on finally getting it open, the letter inside had miraculously remained intact.

Curiously, everything I've bought connected to English bibliomanes from this period seem to always come close to being a mishap, or a disaster averted in time.

From bookseller Christopher Edwards, I bought a one-page ALS from Richard Heber that got shunted from post office to post office because the pin code was off by a digit before it finally found me. After negotiating the purchase of a letter in the hand of the vellomane Thomas Phillipps from another British seller, I got a frantic phone call from him saying this was the painter Thos. Phillipps, not the collector! He had made a mistake – however, he did have a letter from the Phillipps I was looking for, and that's the one I should be considering for purchase. Except it was priced, naturally, three times higher.

The scholar-collector who devoted himself to looking minutely at association copies was John Sparrow, once the warden of All Souls College, Oxford, and the guru to a host of notable English bibliophiles. For over a quarter century, at the end of every term, the Oxford University Society of Bibliophiles (OUSB) persisted with a tradition of meeting at the warden's house for book talk, usually on a Thursday evening in the last week. How I wish I could have been there, at the warden's meeting, where young collectors would gather at John Sparrow's lodgings to talk about the rare book finds they had made. You were required to bring to the meeting a fine, recent bargain you had managed to make over a rare book purchase, show it off to this circle of bibliophiles, and talk about it. An enticing, stimulating display of 'bibliographical show-and-tell'. John Sparrow, Esq, OBE, MA, warden of All Souls would preside over these meetings, and would himself in the end bring out *his* most recent rare book find, and tell you the story of the lengths he had gone to obtain it.

Additionally, every term this bibliophile society would organize talks by notable collectors, followed by excursions to private libraries and book collections. Just the roll call of these speakers and hosts strikes a thrill through you: A.N.L. Munby, Stanley Morison, C. H. Wilkinson, John Carter, William A. Jackson, Graham Pollard, Simon Nowell-Smith, Harry Carter, William Rees-Mogg, Ruari McLean. Anyone who was anyone in English bibliophily had participated.

Lucky indeed were the undergraduates that joined the OUSB. The society began in the Hilary Term of 1951, and continues to the present.

In all this, it is the warden, this beloved scholar-collector who fascinates me. He has been a kind of bibliographic guru over the years to young English bibliophiles desiring to follow in his footsteps and become a scholar-collector like him. One of the OUSB members, George Story, reminiscing about their guru in *The Warden's Meeting* (1977), a tribute book to Sparrow, writes, 'the Warden, through precept and rich example, tutored us all in the taste and technique of collecting. To misquote Houseman, he helped us as no one else did to enter into the pleasure of collecting which "differs from other pleasures in this, that it is shadowed by no fear of satiety. Other desires perish in their gratification, but the desire of books never".'

Sparrow, an astute collector right from his undergraduate days, was noted for his love of books bound in limp vellum, which occupied apparently one whole large wall of his library (imagine nothing but white or cream spines filling every shelf on a wall). A founding member of the Oxford Bibliophiles, Bent Juel Jensen, recalls: 'No one can forget the loving care with which the Warden treasures and handles a 17th century English book in limp vellum, and for his perceptive study of association copies'. An association copy is usually a book or a pamphlet signed and inscribed by the author to someone famous or someone significantly associated with the author.

In *The Warden's Meeting,* several OUSB members reminisce about the book they brought to these meetings, and narrate how they made their rare book finds. Nicolas Barker says he spotted his find displayed prominently in the window of a bookshop. And tantalizingly, the shop was closed for the weekend and he had to uneasily wait for Monday to come to examine it. 'What was it that had caught my eye? It might have well been its contemporary vellum binding, a taste formed (I rather think) in the Warden's Lodgings.' Looking around leisurely in one of London's famous antiquarian bookshops, Christopher de Hamel finds what looks like a defective copy of an early printed book, circa 1509. Though in poor condition, it is attractive for its illumination in raised gold, green, and red, and since the copy had been marked down in price, he decides to buy it.

Because the warden had always stressed that they should look carefully for signs in the book of ownership and provenance, de Hamel later uncovered, on the final paste down of this tatty copy, a rather grimy inscription: 'Mei Jo: grolier Lugdunen & Amicorum'. Good God, it was a hitherto unrecorded Grolier binding! The prince of bibliophiles, Jean Grolier, whose books were some of the earliest in book collecting history to have been clothed in beautiful bindings.

Another bibliophile, Helen Peters, joined Oxford in 1972, and at her uncle's suggestion joined the society, and quickly came under the influence of John Sparrow. She was taken to the warden's sanctum, where three walls of shelving contained fine bindings, and the fourth wall – that famous wall – held bindings in limp vellum. Not long after, Helen spotted a beautiful seventeenth-century book in limp vellum in a bookshop, and it looked just like those she had seen with the warden; the price, too, was temptingly low. But foolishly she didn't buy it because she told herself she did not need it for her study. A year or so later, she was again in this bookshop looking for a seventeenth-century book, and remembered the vellum-bound copy. She looked for where it had been shelved then, but it was no longer to be found there. Sold, obviously; nevertheless, she asked, and was told all the books on that shelf had now been moved to a locked bookcase. Her heart sank: locked cases were something beyond her purse. Still, she looked to see if her book was still there...and it was. To her further delight, it still had the old price, and she quickly bought it, and proudly showed it off to the warden.

Another publication celebrating Sparrow and the Oxford bibliophiles is *Bibliophiles at Oxford* (2006), which is a brief history of this society, and its activities. It is 1950 in Oxford, and a young man takes out a notice in a magazine called *The Isis* in its 25 October issue, asking: 'It seems odd to Mr. John S. Granger that no society or club caters for bibliophiles in Oxford. So, he is now trying to form a bibliophile club...anybody interested is invited to contact Mr. Granger at Jesus.' A few students came forward and the society was founded. Giles S. Barber recalls one of the warden's meetings, with all the members seated around in a semicircle and a fire before them – Giles had brought with him a Flaubert story printed at the Eragny Press by Lucien and Esther Pissarro. When it was the warden's turn, he suddenly disappeared for a minute or two, only to return with a first edition of *Madame Bovary*. *Bibliophiles at Oxford* also lists all the programmes and the Term Cards. These little cards given to the members at the end of term lists the speakers who had given talks, the title of their talk, as well as the printer of the card, the type used, and the paper it is printed on. I somehow managed to find a copy of *Bibliophiles at Oxford* with an actual Term Card laid in! Mine was the Michaelmas Term of 1978. The main talk was: 'J. Maggs: Why I enjoy Bookselling.' Printer; RT Risk, type, Bembo, in a pale blue grey card.

The card had a moving passage from a George Gissing essay, that is set between head and tail piece ornaments by the printer.

> Gissing: 'Many a time I have stood before a stall, or a bookseller's window, torn by conflict of intellectual desire and bodily need. At the very hour of dinner, when my stomach clamoured for food, I have been stopped by sight of a volume so long coveted, and marked at so advantageous a price, that I *could* not let it go; yet to buy it meant pangs of famine. My

> Heyne's *Tibullus* was grasped at such a moment. It lay on the stall of the old book-shop in Goodge Street – a stall where now and then one found an excellent thing among quantities of rubbish. Sixpence was the price – sixpence! At that time I used to eat my mid-day meal at a coffee-shop in Oxford Street, one of the real old coffee-shops, such as now, I suppose, can hardly be found. Sixpence was all I had – yes, all I had in the world; it would purchase a plate of meat and vegetables. But I did not dare to hope that the *Tibullus* would wait until the morrow, when a certain small sum fell due to me. I paced the pavement, fingering the coppers in my pocket, eyeing the stall, two appetites at combat within me. The book was bought and I went home with it, and as I made a dinner of bread and butter I gloated over the pages.'

The cards would always carry this information on them: 'Meeting at the Warden's Lodgings, All Souls College, by Kind Invitation of J.H.A. Sparrow, Esq.' Later on, after the warden had retired, they still met at his residence, Beechwood House, Iffley Turn. Sparrow was the president for many years. There were mouth-watering topics covered by the most illustrious bibliophiles: things like 'The Origins of Modern Bibliophily', 'Four Decades of Collecting', 'Collectors Progress', 'Bookselling; A view from the Inside', 'The Collector and the Bibliographer', 'Who Deals Better: Auctioneer or Dealer?' Sparrow himself spoke once on collecting, John Maynard Keynes on collecting Blake, Barker on the giant Bibliotheca

Lindesiana collection, Colin Franklin on private presses, Will Carter on fine printing, David Butcher on fine printing in the cloisters, the Stanbrook Abbey Press, Paul Nash on adventures in typography (on Carlow and his Corvinus Press), Simon Brett on wood engraving, Christopher Edwards on association copies, theory and practice. Printers who participated in making the Term Cards included Strawberry, Whittington, Rampant Lions, Libanus, Alembic, Old School Press, and Incline among many others. One excursion was to King's Library, where A.N.L. Munby showed them around. There were also visits to top bookdealers, to private presses, while some excursions were just old-fashioned picnics!

Once a whole archive of these Term Cards was listed by the London rare book sellers Collinge and Clark. As usual Oliver Clark's catalogue list appeared in my mail, and I did what I always do – quickly scanned it for things of deep or immediate collecting interest to me. One of the very first items was a clutch of Oxford University Bibliophile Society memorabilia, with many Term Cards included, from the collection of a prominent member. Idiotically, I came to the preposterous conclusion that this wasn't something collectors would be eager to acquire (that they would be far more preoccupied with the other fine press goodies on the list) and decided not to contact Clark by phone as I have done in the past for items that have caught my interest, and emailed him instead, asking for his best price (for orders from the list, he offers a discount). When I heard from him a little later, it was to say that the OUSB packet was the first thing that had sold – almost at once;

and that he had had more enquiries for this one item than anything else.

Not long after, the antiquarian market had another present waiting for me one morning: a scarce Sparrow pamphlet, *Some Reflections of a Bibliophile,* that I had not seen a single copy of in years. I lunged at it, and was delighted with this essay on book collecting from this wise and witty collector. Sparrow lists four rules here for a collector (which he freely admits he doesn't always follow):

> Never lend a book
> Never sell a book
> Never give anyone a book
> Never read a book

About the last rule, Sparrow writes:

> I am reminded of the experience of an old friend – long since dead – Richard Jennings, the most sensitive book collector I have ever known. He was entertaining in his library the doyen of booksellers, Percy Dobell. Dobell took down from the shelves a volume which he recognized as one that he himself had sold to Jennings some years before. He turned over a few pages of the book, and then putting it down on the table, fixed on poor Jennings an accusing eye: 'Mr. Jennings,' he said in shocked tones, 'Mr. Jennings, *you have been reading this book*!

A strange doctrine, not reading a bought book, says Sparrow, and then goes on to describe a number of other things you can do with a book: 'It can be first acquired, lovingly and leisurely examined and admired, it can be catalogued, it can be taken down and admired again, it can be dusted and protected, it can be re-catalogued and rearranged, it can be repaired, it can be put in a fine binding – it can be again rearranged or shown off to a fellow collector – so many things other than reading it!'

One summer at the Bodleian Library, Sparrow remarked to a staff member how quiet the place was, this seemed to be the Bodleian at its best, and the man replied with a sigh: 'Yes, Mr. Sparrow, you are quite right: we would get on very well in Bodley, if it wasn't for the readers.'

It is in this pamphlet that Sparrow famously summed up the essential emotion in all collectors: 'But the desire for a find is not the essential element in the collector's make up; the essential desire is a desire for possession. A collector may enjoy *finding* things but he may also want to *have* them. "I rather think you haven't got a copy of *this*," is a remark that one book collector will make to another when showing him around his library, and the note in his voice is not the note of compassion.'

He describes what draws a collector to a fine edition:

> As an association copy appeals to a sort of sacramental instinct in the collector, so a copy of the first or original edition of a book, particularly if it is in pristine state, appeals to his historical imagination...the collector with a fully awakened historical imagination will insist upon the original edition... The appeal is entirely physical, and plays upon the sense of touch as much as upon the sense of sight...in the relation of the

> typeface to the whole page...in the feel of the volume, the crispness of the paper, the sound the leaves make as you play upon them with your fingers – 'le papier chante', is I believe how the French describe it – in the rightness of their edges, if uncut...all that goes to make up a fine copy of a book.

In 1977, Jonathan Hill Booksellers published *Association Copies*, a finely printed pamphlet (printed by Henry Morris of Bird and Bull Press on Barcham Green handmade paper, with lovely green marble wrappers) containing Sparrow's notes on association copies down the years, with examples taken from his own collection. I couldn't resist purchasing this even though it was steeply priced, since each copy was signed by Sparrow.

'A WONDERFUL WAY OF LIFE'

THE VEATCHS

I first began taking notice of the Veatchs when nearly every scarce or beautiful fine press book I wanted to buy or learn more about – bibliographical details and price – via a search on the rare book market would invariably show up, repeatedly, in one of their catalogues. Since nothing in their stock was priced anything less than $100, I didn't have an opportunity to buy from Lynne and Bob Veatch in those early years of my impecunious collecting. But I never failed to periodically check their New Arrivals, as well as scrutinize their catalogues, about 99 of them, most of which are online to access. Their catalogues became an excellent and constant reference point in my hunt for fine press books.

Finally, in September 2015, I bought something from them. It was a special printing of the Hammer Uncials cast by the Dale Guild Type Foundry, one of only ten copies on Umbria handmade paper with the four large initials in gold. I had the previous year bought the regular edition on Fabriano mould-made paper with the four initials rubricated, but not gilded. I just had to have this being a fan of Victor Hammer and his uncial type, and so the moment I spotted this on their website, I put the order through quickly. And I followed it up with a letter.

> *Dear Lynne,*
>
> *Though I have, regrettably, bought little from you, I have immensely admired your bookshop, and its beautiful stock. Of all the book catalogues I receive in the post and read, yours give me the most pleasure. One of the delights of browsing on the Internet has been coming across your pdfs of older catalogues, which are instructive, fascinating, helpful and enjoyable. Your current stock, along with what you've carried in the past – glimpsed through your series of catalogues – reveals an unrivaled inventory where the arts of the book is concerned. The kind of high-end books and prints that have passed through your hands over the years, many private press books in their scarcer, deluxe imprint, is truly impressive and exciting. I've also noticed how many books arts events, projects, seminars and publications you have supported at one time or the other since Bob and you began your bookshop.*

Lynne Veatch emailed back a single line, saying that these were probably the nicest things anyone had ever said about them.

It was very kind and modest of her to say so, but I know that the Veatchs have been heaped with praise from famous collectors, special collections libraries, rare book institutions and fellow antiquarian dealers. I've had testimony from numerous fine press collectors who speak of how instrumental the Veatchs have been in forming their collection. Their inventory is always priced just right – neither overpriced nor underpriced. You can confidently buy what is of interest to you in their stock, and know you paid a fair price. They know their books, so you won't find any bargains or bookseller's mistakes here! I've had the opportunity more recently to offer books, broadsides and bookplates from my collection to the Veatchs in exchange for trade credit. A significant, thrilling moment for me was receiving catalogue number 92 from 'The Veatchs, Arts of the Book' in the post, and opening it to see three items in it that had come from my collection. This probably didn't mean much for these eminent booksellers who've catalogued and described countless rare, fine and elusive things in their stock that had originally come from the collection of other collectors, but for me, with my long-standing fascination for their catalogues, it meant I hadn't done so badly as a collector if I had some things in my collection that even the Veatchs wanted for stock!

Much before I had bought anything from them, I had been eager and curious to learn more about them as dealers, and after a few interactions with Lynne related either to purchases or queries regarding items in their inventory, I asked her to tell me how they got started. I'll let Lynne herself give an account of the Veatchs. I think you'll agree with me even before you've got to the end of her account that the life of an antiquarian bookseller, especially as lived out by the Veatchs, is indeed enviable.

The first private press book Bob and I ever bought, in 1969, was Dard Hunter's *Papermaking by Hand in*

America. We had just finished graduate school and married. We both had full time jobs, but outstanding student loans, and no cash reserves. Still, the book was irresistible. The way it looked, the way it felt, the way it smelled. And the fascinating subject matter. Hunter not only did a great deal of research for the text, he also designed and cast his own type for it, made the ink and the paper for it. He recreated all kinds of old papers for the facsimiles in the book. It is an amazing work. The book cost $2,000. Herman Cohen, of the Chiswick Bookshop, let us take it home with a year to pay.

When Bob and I could finally afford to buy more books, we collected private presses who were active in the 1970's and 80's – Bird & Bull, the Allen Press in California, Walter Hamady's Perishable Press, Leonard Baskin's Gehenna Press. Henry Morris's press was a favourite because almost all of his books concerned bookish subjects, mostly papermaking and marbling, but also early color printing, bookbinding, and bibliography. He has made a lasting contribution to the book arts. Lewis and Dorothy Allen spent an entire year, full time, on each book. Every element of an Allen Press book – type, ornaments, illustrations, binding design & materials – contributed to an organic whole, beautifully printed on dampened handmade paper on an old Washington handpress.

Bob had begun learning to print on his Albion, and Henry Morris and Lewis Allen were generous with their help. Bob sent Henry the first piece he printed; it came back entirely and humorously marked up with everything that was wrong.

Hamady's books were valued for their handmade papers, creativity, and humour. Baskin's *Flosculi Sententarium* and *Cancelleresca Bastarda Displayed* are masterpieces of pure typography.

We had standing orders with several presses. In those days, we were 'completists' – i.e., we tried to acquire everything a press produced. That meant relying on booksellers to search for us and to send quotes. Pre-internet, it meant scouring booksellers' catalogues (Maggs, Quaritch, Dawsons, Chiswick, Duschnes) the moment they arrived. And of course the AB: Antiquarian Bookman, which arrived weekly with lists of books for sale. It meant visiting the shops along New York's 4th Avenue and uptown, weekend drives to country barns, scouting the many local bookfairs, and braking at every 'antique' shop along the way.

We also collected all the Roycroft Shop books and ephemera designed by Dard Hunter. More importantly, we collected biographies of antiquarian booksellers, such as David Randall's *Dukedom Large Enough*, Edwin Wolf's *Rosenbach*, and Everitt's *The Adventures of a Treasure Hunter.* What a wonderful way of life antiquarian booksellers enjoyed! Summers spent in England and on the continent amassing trunkfuls of great books; the rest of the year spent poring over them. The reality, during the last third of the century, was rather different. And despite Everitt's (somewhat suspect) tales, we never found a *Tamerlane* in anyone's attic.

But those books were responsible for our becoming booksellers. And it is an enjoyable way of life for the people we've met and become friends with. It is a small, closely knit world of shared interests and camaraderie.

Building an antiquarian book business – acquiring both stock and customers – in those days (the late 1970s) was a slow and laborious process for us. We both had full time jobs, but managed to issue mimeographed lists of books for sale and exhibited at the Long Island and MARIAB book fairs. We joined the ABAA in the early 1990s, and had exhibited at numerous international book fairs in California, Washington, DC, Boston, and New York. In 1996, we felt established enough to quit our day jobs and become fulltime booksellers. These days we do fewer fairs and devote more time to research (one of the best parts of this job!) and catalogues – and our grandkids.

You've asked how we replenish our stock these days, and about collections we've purchased. Our books come mostly from collectors. We have been in business a long time and have a reputation for expertise and fair dealing. Our customers sell their collections to us when they downsize or, less frequently, change their focus. They recommend us to their book collecting friends or their heirs.

Of the many collections we've purchased, three were outstanding for their focus and depth. Harold Hugo's and John Peckham's (both of Meriden Gravure) were rich in books illustrated by the great British wood engravers. These formed the basis of a catalogue on wood engraving, to which we added original wood blocks by Bewick, Nast, and Harper's stock blocks.

Two very different Bruce Rogers collections were

offered to us in the same year. One was a working collection intended to form the basis of a definitive bibliography of B.R. (There is still no definitive bibliography.) The other was a collection of B.R.'s 'high end' books in fine condition. These also made up a handsome catalogue.

The largest and most exciting collection was formed by Jack Golden, a graphic designer in New York. The history of printing and printing technique, rare type specimens and periodicals, and beautiful examples of nineteenth century chromolithography. Eighteen months and seven trips with a van were required to shift them from Manhattan to Northampton. We still have many of these books.

You also asked what we think are the 10 greatest press books. What a question! There are so many splendid books. Martin Hunter and Jerry Kelly made a valiant effort to keep the list to 100 books in their *A Century for the Century*. Some of my favourites are the Ashendenes, the Elston Press, Eric Gill's *Four Gospels* and the *Canterbury Tales* for the Golden Cockerel Press, the Gregynog Press *Fables of Esope*, Bruce Rogers' *Odyssey* and *Fra Luca*, all of the Hammer Creek Press, the Officina Bodoni Aesop, and the Arion Press *Moby Dick* illustrated by Barry Moser.

If I could have only one book, it would be the *Hypnerotomachia Poliphili* printed by Aldus in 1499. If book choices were rationed to only one press, I would choose not a press at all, but the output of Bruce Rogers.

ON COLLECTING WILLIAM MORRIS

JACK WALSDORF

John Jack Walsdorf nearly went broke collecting William Morris, and was forced to sell his collection of Kelmscott Press books. When he had recovered and was financially stable again, he put together a second collection of Kelmscott and came to the brink again financially, and sold this one, too. His fascination for William Morris and his admiration for Kelmscott moved him again to put together a third collection, starting from scratch, which he subsequently had to also give up, only to begin a *fourth* collection – this one perhaps the trickiest since it involved Kelmscott ephemera, notoriously harder to find than the books.

Each time it got more difficult, the prices shot up year after year, and Kelmscott Press books became scarcer to locate in fine condition or with special attributes. But Walsdorf could never resist the pull of Morris and Kelmscott – and he is a collector I can feel some kinship with, because unlike almost every major collector of Morris (Marsden J. Perry, Sanford Berger, John L. Crawford, and Mark Samuels Lasner) he didn't have the ready funds to collect the books of the most expensive, the most sought after private press in the antiquarian market.

I'm grateful to Jack Walsdorf for another reason: in 2007, he and a private press printer – Kay Michael Kramer of The Printery – felt a memoir of how Walsdorf collected Morris would make an attractive fine press book. They titled it simply, *On Collecting William Morris: A Memoir*. Bound in quarter leather with decorated sides, the book contains an original leaf from a disbound copy of a Kelmscott Press book tipped into it. Each chapter begins with a stylized initial surrounded by vine leaves and boxed in a green border. Fine press books with the subject of book collecting are uncommon, so this was exciting. (My favourite in this small clutch of finely printed collector's and dealer's memoirs is Colin Franklin's *Bookselling, a Memoir* (1986) printed with austere typographic beauty by Bob Baris of The Press on Scroll Road from an iron handpress on a beautiful Twinrocker handmade paper.)

Like Norman Strouse, Jack Walsdorf was a collector who didn't shy away from writing about collecting, feeling a similar urge to combine his collecting stories with bibliographical histories. Once a collection is fully formed and you learn everything about it and you've spent enough time with it, what do you do next? For both Strouse and Walsdorf (and Colin Franklin, too) the answer was: write about the collection. And luckily for us they both chose to entertain us with notes on how they collected, in addition to making bibliographical explorations. What is most resounding in everything Walsdorf says and writes is the joy of the hunt, to quench his constant thirst for book hunting everywhere he goes, and to write and speak of it.

On Collecting William Morris: A Memoir is a slender book recording Jack's four forays into putting together a fine and interesting collection of all things related to Morris, his arts and crafts circle, his private press and his life. One of Jack's more interesting initiatives in these cycles of collecting Morris was to go beyond gathering a complete run of the Kelmscott Press and focus on Kelmscott Press books that were either signed or inscribed or had inscriptions of association, as well as to augment this with other limited editions and fine press books that had either printed Morris's work (he was the author of many novels and essays) or were about him and his private press.

At the end of this sparkling collection, Walsdorf published a trade edition titled *William Morris In Private Press & Limited Editions: A Descriptive Bibliography of books by & about William Morris* (1983). It bibliographically itemized each copy in this collection supplemented by photographs of the pages showing inscriptions and signatures along with a brief commentary on how he put this collection together. I'd recommend getting a secondhand copy (they sell at $20–45) for the useful resource it is to books and pamphlets from *other* private presses on Morris and Kelmscott, as well as giving you a visual display of an entire collection of association copies.

His second and third collection were documented in two finely designed and printed catalogues: in 1994, William Morris and the Kelmscott Press; and two years later, the third was documented in Kelmscott Press –

William Morris and His Circle. Except for short introductory notes, none of them tell the full story of his Kelmscott adventures in the way his elegantly printed memoir does.

In a nod to Strouse, he titles the first chapter 'How to Build a Poor Man's Morris Library.' One notable difference between him and Strouse he says was this: he didn't have the ample funds Strouse had to begin collecting. Strouse, you may recall, said the same thing of J.P. Morgan, that he was no millionaire, but still managed to acquire a few things that even Morgan lacked. I don't have even a small part of the funds Walsdorf once possessed, buying in Indian rupees, but that didn't stop me from buying what I desired – exactly how Strouse and Walsdorf went about spending their money.

He was a poor man as a collector, and had to make many sacrifices to assemble his collection of Kelmscott Press books, many of them signed or association copies. As mentioned earlier, Walsdorf would sell his scintillating collection after having painstakingly assembled them over forty years. The first time around he bought 30 Kelmscott Press books, 16 of which were signed or association copies, often referencing principal players around the press and Morris, from Emery Walker to Sydney Cockerell to Edward Burne-Jones.

Walsdorf got started when as a young man he spent a brief time as a librarian in Oxford in the 1960s. He was fortunate to have Blackwells Antiquarian bookshop in the vicinity, and he says he learnt all about private press books for the first time at their antiquarian department.

He was able to examine many private press treasures here without having to buy them. Around this time, he came across Will Ransom's *Private Presses and their Books*, one of the earliest seminal references to this world of fine bookmaking, and not being able to afford it, typed the 180 odd pages, leaving out the bibliography. This way he imbibed the book fully!

And it was here, in the process of slowly typing out the book, that he began noticing how influential Morris and his press had been, and the number of connections or throwbacks to him in the present. Several contemporary private presses had printed books or ephemera relating to Morris and his Kelmscott Press. Thus was formed the idea to collect copies of Kelmscott Press books that had association marked in them, as well as private press book about Morris and his press. This was more challenging and costly but obviously a fun line of collecting. It immediately meant scores of book hunts would have to follow. He began to equip and gear himself for this by reading up as much as he could about the history of the press, the life of Morris and all the people associated with the British private press movement. He took his wife to Blackwells to see Kelmscott books, the shop man showed them three examples, and simply walked away from these $2, 000 books, saying 'You can leave them on this table when you are finished.' Walsdorf writes that both were 'impressed by the fine cream coloured paper, the deep black ink, and the decorative borders.' In June 1967, his year at Oxford came to an end. He left England with a trunkful of books, of which two were Kelmscott and the rest were from these presses: Doves, Stanbrook Abbey, Golden Cockerel, Daniel Press, and Gregynog.

By 1983, he had fulfilled what he had set out to do, and had a fine collection of Morris related private press books, but was also in debt. Tired of being short of money, and tired of running out of shelf space, he sold some 800 books to a University Special Collections library. Some of the significant items that sold in the collection were Morris letters, the Basilisk facsimile of the Chaucer, the scarce Village Press printings of Morris titles from Goudy, and one vellum copy of *The Wood Beyond the World*, and the most scintillating: Edward Burne-Jones's copy of the Kelmscott *Keats* with Morris's presentation to his friend and collaborator. But now all that was gone, and friends and family wondered if he might get depressed, asking him to stay away from Morris for a while. One day, picking up his son from school and telling him the collection had gone in the mail, his son asked him 'Well, Dad, are you okay?'

A year would have been a proper time before a second round of collecting, but true to a collector's instinct, Walsdorf didn't wait very long. In the flyleaf of his copy of William Peterson's *Bibliography of the Kelmscott Press*, 1984, he has written: 'With this book – I start my second "Quest for Morris" – a quest for a copy of every Kelmscott book.' The idea was to keep it simpler: no signed or association copy that would be too dear to acquire.

And he bought them more slowly, just one or two every year. The passion for collecting is really about the joy of the hunt.

This collection went on sale *en bloc* at The Colophon Book Shop, who published a splendidly printed catalogue in 1995. One of the best guides, Jack adds, to modern prices of Kelmscott books. This time he made sure to put in a note that he was not done with Morris as he had avowed before – but was just clearing the deck. While the Colophon sale was a success, some books did come back unsold, and they numbered about 220 in 1998, giving him something to start his third round. 'I was happy to get my little flock back', he says, rather than being disappointed that they did not sell. But just as everything was looking good, in 1999, he lost his job to downsizing, and a mortgage remained to be paid on his house. He was now forced to consider selling his Morris books, but this time making his own catalogue, a list, that he would send out to librarians and collectors, with a personal note. By 2001, he had sent out three lists; the books were selling well and quickly. This made him solvent in those lean years, even leaving over money to buy more books.

In the last chapter in *On Collecting William Morris*, Jack Walsdorf lists ten books that are still special in his collection, that he has held on to because of the special meaning they have for him, among which are: a William Morris manuscript poem, Hermann Zapf's *William Morris Sein Leben* (1949), his copy is inscribed in blue ink by Zapf in a calligraphic hand: 'William Morris: the Letters should be designed by an artist, and not an engineer' followed by the inscription 'For Jack Walsdorf, fellow lover of WM and the KP, from the author, HZ.'

In an afterword, Walsdorf tells us how he came to

acquire loose leaves from disbound copies of Kelmscott Press books that went into the making of two press books with original tipped in Kelmscott leaves: *The Kelmscott Press Golden Legend: A Documentary History* (1990) from the Yellow Barn Press, and *On Collecting William Morris* from the Printery. At the Boston Antiquarian Book Fair in 1978, he found for sale a whole bunch of the Kelmscott *Golden Legend* leaves for sale. This led to the idea of a Leaf Book on the making of the *Golden Legend*, beautifully printed by Neil Shaver with an unforgettable portrait wood engraving by John DePol of Morris. Printed on dampened handmade Batchelor paper, it has a brief history of the production of *Golden*, plus Walsdorf's and Shaver's note – Shaver writes of the luck *he* had in finding a stash of the Batchelor handmade paper the Kelmscott Press had used. The main contents are letters from and to Morris on its production and printing.

In April 2005, a seller on eBay was offering what he had listed as 'antique William Morris KP book Typography', noting that they had been the remnants of a sale from Swann Galleries in 2002, and even then the book had been missing many leaves. Walsdorf was the successful bidder, and when it arrived, he was pleasantly surprised to see a stack of *Child Christopher* leaves looking new. This gave him the idea for the second Kelmscott Leaf Book, *On Collecting William Morris*. Morris apparently loved the small octavo books, and the leaf in my copy of this book is a lovely one: the facing leaf is in red and black with two beautiful paragraph leaf marks. On the other side, a two inch initial in black of the letter that S. Virginia Kramer of the Printery had picked out herself when I bought a copy of their book directly from the press. I had forgotten to mention to her to find a copy with a nice leaf, but she assured me, when I called her after she had mailed the book, that she had done exactly that.

Jack Walsdorf passed away in 2017. I think a majority of his books were bought up by Blackwells Rare Books, Oxford – the place where he had first encountered the books of William Morris. Blackwell's made a nice catalogue of the collection. I wrote and asked for a copy – digital and printed – and for sentimental reasons ordered a few things that carried his bookplate or ownership signature. The most charming was a miniature book, *Printers on Morris*, with a wood engraving by Barry Moser of William Morris on Japanese Hosho paper. When asked once in an interview why collect Morris again and again? he said: 'So here I am, at age 70, collecting Morris again. Why? Because I truly love the whole subject of William Morris, his Kelmscott press and the other varied activities which made up his very full and interesting life. The many aspects of William Morris can be collected, read about and studied forever it would seem.'

ACQUIRED FROM ALAN G. THOMAS

Though I am not able to say exactly why, I've had a particular fondness for the English antiquarian bookseller, Alan G. Thomas. I didn't know him personally, nor have I bought anything from him but every time I learn a little more about him, I wish I had known him, and had bought from him. Is it perhaps because when a 12-year-old boy wrote to him one day asking to buy some good examples of illuminated manuscript leaves for the princely sum of £5, he replied kindly and with encouragement rather than scoffing at the boy's desire? Or was it because as a 22-year-old he skipped meals and starved himself to save up to acquire a few choice rare books; or for that time when a customer deeply desired a beautiful rarity in Alan's stock he could not afford, and the bookseller generously offered to swap it for anything from the collector's library he didn't mind letting go of?

Is it any wonder that for his 70th birthday, his customers and colleagues in the trade published a festschrift in his honour, each one writing about one extraordinary book or manuscript they had bought from Alan, to acknowledge his rare book connoisseurship? The salutes to him read like a who's who of the antiquarian book world: Nicolas Barker, Lotte Hellinga, Mirjam Foote, Bernard Middleton, Lawrence Durrell, and Anthony Hobson to name just a few. After Alan's death in 1992, Sotheby's auctioned his stock. The festschrift was called *Fine Books and Book Collecting: Books and Manuscripts acquired from Alan G. Thomas and described by his customers on the occasion of his seventieth birthday* (1981) edited by two famous manuscript scholars, Christopher de Hamel and Richard Linenthal, both of whom had been his grateful customers.

Alan Gradon Thomas had been a tall, lean man with gentle eyes and an extravagant beard. For the best part of his life, he had sold rare books and manuscripts from his Chelsea home, issuing catalogues to anyone who was interested. Such was his scholarship, and the fine quality of his stock, that the most seasoned book collector would find something in his catalogue to be tempted or dazzled by. The writer Lawrence Durrell and his famous household (brother Gerald Durrell, their mother, et al.) knew Alan in Bournemouth when he was in his early twenties, and would often drag him to their house to fatten him up because he was the leanest person they had ever seen.

Lawrence, who at this time was about the same age as Alan, remembers once when he visited his bibliophile friend in his small, meagre room, seeing a suitcase under Alan's bed that held just four or five books, but of such bibliographical taste and importance, that he was sure Alan was skipping meals to buy them.

This starving, slim young book collector turned book

dealer would go on to become 'the doyen of the British antiquarian book trade', serve as the president of the Antiquarian Booksellers Association in 1958, and launch the first London antiquarian book fair that would be replicated around the world; the precursor of all rare book fairs as conducted by the trade today. Thomas had already begun to show his precociousness for rare book dealing, looking far and wide for books in the want list of collectors at affordable prices.

Lawrence Durrell's collecting focus was early Elizabethan texts, and Alan had been chiefly responsible for putting together this prize collection for his old boyhood friend. Once when Lawrence was travelling, his brother Gerald sold off some of Lawrence's books to build his own zoological library. When Lawrence came back and discovered this, he waited until Gerald went off on one of his expeditions and sold part of his zoological library. 'Happily,' Lawrence goes on to say in the festschrift, 'in each case the buyer was Alan, and in this way not a book was lost. He simply housed both collections until we each returned to base.'

He was born in 1911, and began his career as an antiquarian bookseller in 1927. He joined an old, large, well-known bookshop called Commins in Bournemouth, and was able to take over as its owner in 1936. He issued his first catalogue in 1957, and later sold the bookshop, and moved to London to become an independent antiquarian dealer. He rose quickly on the strength of the fine material he was able to offer to his customers, and was often 'a familiar figure at auctions with his large, luxuriating beard, a cape draped around him with large pockets to hold auction catalogues'.

When Christopher de Hamel was just a little boy in New Zealand, he wrote to several rare booksellers in England expressing his interest in buying illuminated medieval leaves – his budget, he added in passing, was an impressive £5. He notes, 'I still have those replies; some are quite properly dismissive, others politely condescending, but Alan Thomas sent a chatty letter explaining that I should not be discouraged even though five pounds would not go far.'

And the bookseller pointed out to de Hamel some small things he could still get for £5, and from thence went to the trouble to keep his young customer informed of things he could afford in that price range! Once in a burst of spending, de Hamel sent off £12, telling the bookseller it was 'practically all he possessed', and got a stunning manuscript leaf for it. That leaf today would be £800–£900. Thomas wrote a note to say he hoped de Hamel would not regret buying it since it was 'practically all he possessed'. De Hamel, as we know well, went on to make the study and sale of medieval manuscripts his life.

Here was an important bookseller dealing with some of the rarest and most expensive material, and he still took an interest in the collecting life of a boy who practically had no money to buy from him, but Alan didn't distinguish between his wealthy collectors and this impecunious customer. Brian Cron, a regular customer, had dropped in on him one day with no thought (or money) to buy manuscripts – he collected early printed books. This day, however, his eyes fell upon a little book in a slipcase that turned out to be not a printed book at all but a handwritten manuscript from 1480. He wanted it badly, even though he knew he could not afford it. But Alan further disappointed him – a German library had already shown interest in it, but if they were to pass on it, the bookseller would let him know in a week's time. He returned home and waited impatiently. When he did not hear from Alan, he went to see him again, and was told the Germans wanted more time. Instead, Alan showed him a larger manuscript which would cost twice more than the one Brian had been interested in. Alan said if the library bought the manuscript, he could have this one, which was even more stunning. 'But how?' wondered the collector to himself. He didn't have the money even for the first one. That's when Alan graciously offered to let him take any of these manuscripts in exchange for incunabula from Brian's collection. These were generous terms – Alan could so easily sell his beautiful and rare manuscript, while Brian's early printed books would probably stay longer on the shelf unsold. A few days later Alan himself came home, to personally convey that the German library wouldn't be buying it; he had brought along both manuscripts for Brian to choose from. Brian bought both, letting Alan pick the incunabulum he wanted from his collection. 'I am confident,' notes Brian, that 'the pleasure of the deal was equally divided between us.'

Alan Thomas obviously took satisfaction in supplying his customers with what they most desired, and thought of his own gain only later. Sotheby's renowned auctioneer Anthony Hobson tells us that a typical exchange between Alan and him before an auction began on the block was:

-Lot 2345. May I say 200 pounds to start this lot?
-Yes, sir.

The auctioneer goes on to say that he had always been grateful for Alan's almost daily participation in the Thomas Phillipps manuscripts sale (1965–77) because he bought the things others ignored or refused to touch: plain manuscripts without illumination, or beautiful Persian manuscripts that no one was focused on, busy as they were chasing European medieval manuscripts. Or even the Ethiopian, Coptic, and Armenian manuscripts that Alan pursued, knowing he was taking a risk but bravely bidding until he had secured it. But by zooming in on neglected lots, Hobson says, Alan also often got them for great prices.

Alan himself wrote well about antiquarian books and people, and his personal reminiscences of Solomon Pottesman, the exasperating but admirable scholar-collector of incunabula, in *The Book Collector* is now a classic.

Naturally, I wanted to find something of interest or significance connected to Alan G. Thomas. The first, as well as the easiest, thing to look for was a signed copy of the books he wrote. I got lucky, and found a copy of the festschrift that had not only been signed but also inscribed by Thomas to the renowned rare book librarian and collector, Decherd Turner. And laid into the copy, as a bonus, was a letter from Alan to Decherd! Later, I found a private press book that had come from his bookshop (*Bookman's Holiday*) with his invoice laid in. What more could I want?

TWO BIBLIOPHILE HEROES

CHRISTOPHER DE HAMEL AND SYDNEY C. COCKERELL

'Tea and Manuscripts'

Two of my greatest bibliophile heroes are Christopher de Hamel and Sydney C. Cockerell. Both knew and loved manuscripts intimately. Illuminated manuscripts were Cockerell's great love, while the whole field of palaeography is de Hamel's expertise. He is as fascinated with plain, unadorned manuscripts as he is with those that are richly illuminated. One operated as an amateur-connoisseur in the field, the other as a consummate professional. Cockerell became adept at identifying the work or signatures of scribes and illuminators from simply collecting and studying them on his own, while de Hamel made this his life's passion and work. De Hamel's hero is Cockerell, and it is quite easy to see why if de Hamel had lived before Cockerell, he would have been Cockerell's great hero as well. I wonder sometimes if Cockerell's spirit possessed de Hamel, who was once Sotheby's star auctioneer. With a middle-class salary Cockerell managed to acquire some choice illuminated manuscripts by keeping a sharp eye out for bargains, swapping with fellow collectors, foregoing luxuries, and stretching his funds to the maximum.

De Hamel came from a middle-class background too, and while still a young man, distinguished himself at Sotheby's with his scholarly catalogues and his supreme love and knowledge of manuscripts. He collected manuscripts on a modest scale, but with his wide and daily access to the best of the best manuscripts coming up for sale frequently at Sotheby's, and the manuscripts he consulted in libraries across Europe, he was given the privilege of handling them without having or needing to own them.

Sydney C. Cockerell's hero was William Morris. He had met Morris in 1886, and this eventually led to a close association with Morris and his private press. He began as the cataloguer of William Morris's library, and then became the secretary of the Kelmscott Press. Not wealthy like many of his acquaintances and friends, he nevertheless was the more fervent collector, leveraging his expertise and knowledge of illuminated manuscripts to secure the most expensive and beautiful books in an auction for the rich collectors he was bidding and buying for. How did it matter if he could not own these as long as he could handle them? When, in his 80s, Cockerell began selling off his manuscripts one by one, several dealers from around the world came hoping to buy a few. H.P. Kraus, the famous manuscript dealer from New York narrates this visit in his autobiography, *A Rare Book Saga* (Putnam,

1978), to show how, even ailing and bedridden, Cockerell was still adept at getting the prices he desired. Kraus entered the house and was led to Cockerell's bedroom where the crafty collector lay – and was instructed to go upstairs to where the manuscripts were held. Kraus selected the manuscripts he wanted to buy for his stock, and the negotiations began. After a lengthy session of hard bargaining, Cockerell at last smiled and agreed to all the prices Kraus had carefully and persistently negotiated for. Kraus left feeling pleased only to learn later that in a little book that Cockerell had with him by his side, and which he had been looking into now and then, were already noted all the prices the collector wanted for these manuscripts – and they were *exactly* the same prices Kraus had ended up offering him. It's difficult to slip anything past Kraus, a true giant in the rare book business as dealers and collectors had discovered, but Cockerell had managed it effortlessly, just lying in bed.

Of course, I desired something from the hand of Sydney Carlyle Cockerell. At Trindley and Everett, an antiquarian bookshop in Cecil Court, London, I found a book on calligraphic writing he had inscribed to his grandson. The really exciting thing about this copy was that laid in loosely in the book was a handwritten letter from Cockerell to his grandson, urging the boy to pay attention to calligraphy and lettering. Though a short letter, it was a fine example of Cockerell's handwriting. He was famous for a neat, tiny, humanistic script he had developed that was legible even when minuscule, and I had always been curious to see it. The letter was a perfect example of his strange but skilful manuscript hand.

For his Sanders lectures in bibliography, Christopher de Hamel spoke on Cockerell. Over the years he had been making many boxes of notes on his master, and had met many people who had known him. (These lectures were subsequently published in *The Book Collector*.) It was John Ruskin, de Hamel tells us, who first showed Cockerell about 80 medieval manuscripts from his collection in 1887. One can only imagine their effect on young Sydney. In 1892, the more significant event happened: William Morris invited him to catalogue his library of manuscripts and early printed books at his Kelmscott House in Hammersmith. It was the luckiest day of his life. He was often sent to auction houses in London as well as abroad to secure an illuminated manuscript or an early printed book for Morris. When the printer and proprietor of the Kelmscott Press died on 3 October 1896, Cockerell was at home and arranged the funeral. His next eighteen months was spent finishing up the business of the press, and winding up the shop.

And in 1898, at 30, he was without a job. He then found two part-time jobs, one as a private secretary where he could lounge around or pursue his interests, and the other, the real job he adored: assessing a large group of 210 medieval MS for collector Henry Yates Thompson that had been purchased from the Ashburnham collection. What a fantastic job he had, says de Hamel with some envy, for the next half a dozen years his routine was picking up a manuscript from Thompson's house, taking it home, and spending hours poring over the manuscript, and then cataloguing it. His fee? Five pounds for each catalogue entry.

In 1907, Cockerell married Florence Kingsford, the manuscript illuminator, and called her Kate. Being married now with a household to run, he told collector Harold Pierce, 'No more book buying'. He kept to it for a few months, but as de Hamel notes, 'addictive bibliomania' crept back in and, by 1917, he had bought 75 more manuscripts, and by 1925, they totalled a 100! De Hamel draws our attention to a note Cockerell made in his diary on 28 February 1901: 'Most beautiful morning – a sense of Spring in the air. Bought a 11th century fragment of a Lectionary at Sotheby's.'

'All successful book collectors,' de Hamel goes on to astutely observe, 'are obliged to spend beyond their income.' This is the nature it would seem of 'irrepressible bibliophily.'

Apparently, and surprisingly, for so meticulous a collector, Cockerell had made no catalogue of his manuscript collection; instead, he signed every manuscript he bought in ink with his name and date, as well as jotting notes on these medieval flyleaves! This is Cockerell's most endearing quality, says de Hamel, because he foliated the pages of manuscripts with his renowned hand of small, tightly packed but clear writing. He also had a habit of taking out damaged leaves, and rebinding the manuscript. Most of his manuscripts had a binder of great skill and beauty, Katharine Adams who had done several fine bindings for Hornby of the Ashendene Press. He called her Katie to distinguish it from Kate, his wife's name; having his manuscript bound by her was for him getting them 'Katied'. He wrote to Katie one day in 1924, saying he would like to one day get all her bindings in a row, and caress them as he recalled the 'pleasure each one has given me on its arrival, and whenever I have handled it since'.

Cockerell also delighted in sharing manuscripts, and gave away bifolium leaves to friends. People were invited home for 'Tea and Manuscripts' on Sunday afternoons when almond iced cake and tea was served on a long table, and if you passed well in the conversation that took place, you were invited to the room with the illuminated manuscripts. One visitor recalls how every room, including the bathroom, had memorabilia hanging on the walls related to Morris and Kelmscott. Ailing now, he took the ground floor bedroom and wondered if he would ever get the chance to go upstairs to his collection. At 84, he began selling some of them. J.R. Abbey bought a beautiful Florentine Psalter for £1,000. Cockerell wrote a note to Abbey saying he would not have parted with it for any price had it not been for how bedridden he was. In 1956, with the help of his neighbour, Brian Cron, he made a list of the manuscripts with the minimum price it should be sold for. Booksellers began arriving, from the UK, US, and Europe. A parade of booksellers came calling: Clifford Maggs, Quaritch, Pierre Beres, and of course Kraus who records in his autobiography how he arrived to find Cockerell 'supine and deathly pale'. Cockerell would also test all these supplicants – these buyers, with their knowledge of the manuscripts. He was impressed with Maggs, and also with Alan Thomas. 'I like him very much', he is said to have told Cron. John Fleming he did not like, and found ignorant of manuscripts.

Sydney Cockerell died at 94, on 1 May 1962. 'He was', concludes de Hamel, 'a marvellous collector...and my greatest hero.'

'The Descriptions Master'

When Christopher de Hamel turned 60, his friends and colleagues published a lavish festschrift for him. I found the tributes fascinating reading, and my admiration for de Hamel deepened. Titled *The Medieval Book: Glosses from Friends and Colleagues of Christopher de Hamel* (2010) the festschrift was a handsomely produced trade edition, printed in red and black with several colour plates. De Hamel had overseen manuscript cataloguing at Sotheby's from 1975 to 2000. Nicolas Barker, of *The Book Collector* says Christopher seems to have had a precocious taste for illuminated manuscripts. The encounter that would change everything for de Hamel, making him the star auctioneer and scholar that he is today, was a meeting with Anthony Hobson of Sotheby's sometime in the early 1970s. Hobson, a respected auctioneer himself, had been looking for someone to assist him with the gigantic Thomas Phillipps sale, perhaps the largest collection of vellum manuscripts then up for auction. He realized quickly that Christopher already had a wide and deep familiarity with manuscripts for a beginner, could read European languages, and had a superb eye for provenance, authorship, and other tell-tale signs in a manuscript that would reveal its origins and makings not visible to the rest of us. Since then, de Hamel has overseen many great manuscript sales, starting with that of Major J. R. Abbey. De Hamel himself believes that he has catalogued as many as ten thousand manuscripts while at Sotheby's. The way he wrote up entries also was so seductive to a dealer or a collector that they were willing to go past the estimate when bidding; a fine case in point is a manuscript from the John Carter Brown sale, when the legendary H.P. Kraus had come prepared for the estimate of £150,000–250,000 and ended up buying it for £700,000.

In 1984, he published his widely read and consulted book, *A History of Illuminated Manuscripts.* (The indefinite article a modest touch! points out Barker.) Two bestsellers followed, *Meetings with Remarkable Manuscripts*, and more recently, *The Posthumous Papers of the Manuscripts Club* (Allen Lane, 2022). In 2000, he became the Donnelly Fellow Librarian of Corpus Christi, Cambridge, and following that a year or so later, a member of the Roxburghe Club (what had taken him *this* long?). Between 2003 and 2004 he gave his now famous Sandars lecturers on Sydney Cockerell, 'a man after his own heart', comments Barker. In 2009, he was the Lyell Reader In Bibliography at Oxford. He is a collector, too, with a modest number of illuminated manuscripts and about five hundred fragments – both counts have probably tripled and quadrupled by now.

In the festschrift, one of de Hamel's colleagues, Diana Berry, recalls her first day at Sotheby's, when she felt such a sense of awe come over her thinking of all the gurus who had worked in this very office once: John Hayward, Tim Munby, John Carter, and Anthony Hobson. And now de Hamel. A haven of bibliophily and scholarship. The market for illuminated manuscripts took a turn up in the 1980s, nicely coinciding with Christopher's induction into Sotheby's. The big international manuscript dealers – Kraus, Quaritch, Breslauer, and Berenson – were all on top of their game and a new collecting public was forming. Christopher encouraged younger collectors to buy single leaves and fragments, an illuminated initial or a miniature or an early printed leaf, and made sure every catalogue began with a listing of single leaves and fragments. Berry talks of de Hamel's skill at catalogue entries, even adding a joke here and there, sure-footed about sniffing out the provenance of a manuscript, especially if the previous owner had been a woman, a nun, or a princess. This comes from hours and hours of looking at manuscripts, she says. Often, he was asked why he didn't take up an academic post, and his answer was always, 'Where else but at Sotheby's could I have so many manuscripts pass through my hands?'

At one Christmas gathering at Sotheby's, it was de Hamel's idea to assemble all their large medieval choir books, the Antiphoners, and have Schola Gregoriana, a group of talented nuns who read medieval plainsong to sing carols with them surrounded by candle light and illuminated books. His colleagues describe how much enjoyment they got out of the department under de Hamel, and his parties, many with medieval themes, including a board game he devised that collectors and dealers could play about selling and collecting illuminated manuscripts! James Stourton, a regular bidder in the saleroom, speaks of watching de Hamel quiver with excitement while turning the pages of a manuscript – it is a wonder to behold, he adds. He gladly had schoolchildren come and look at manuscripts, and once when he noticed a kid place his coffee cup next to a priceless Hebrew bible, de Hamel swiftly removed the cup saying, 'I'm not worried about the manuscript, but I didn't want you to spill your coffee.'

One of the most enticing essays in the festschrift is by Robert Weaver titled 'Floreat Vellomania' (a twist on Munby's well-known essay). Weaver was a collector of fragments of medieval manuscripts, in part thanks to de Hamel's encouragement. As a young collector, Weaver met de Hamel at his Sotheby's office on New Bond Street, to ask if it was possible to collect medieval fragments, and the palaeographer assured him that there was enough fine material to suit every collector's taste and purse. Weaver became quite adept at identifying which century a medieval leaf was possibly made in, and once chanced upon in a London bookshop two leaves for sale described as being from the fifteenth century. He felt they were closer to the twelfth century, but the bookseller was certain it was the fifteenth. With the permission of the bookseller, he took the leaves to Bond Street, and de Hamel confirmed they were twelfth century. The bookseller was so impressed, he gifted one of the leaves to this young vellomane.

After luxuriating in so much 'de Hameliana', I was keen to find something signed by him. It was easy enough to find a copy of one of (his many) books with his signature in it. It was only in 2019, that I found something more interesting. De Hamel had once given a lecture at the Rare Book School in Virginia titled 'Cutting Up Manuscripts for Pleasure and Profit'. It was later published as a pamphlet, inexpensively produced and priced (at $10, I think) but it had all but disappeared from the market. I had looked and looked year after year, even writing to the Rare Book School to see if they had a spare copy, but no luck. 'Christopher de Hamel' is one of my ABE Alert keywords, and it is quite usual for me to see almost on a daily basis email alerts for his scholarly books (which are constantly in print), but on that November morning in 2019, I received an alert for this scarce booklet, and without wasting a moment I bought it. I called the bookshop right after and asked whom it had been inscribed to. Sometimes such things turn out to be interesting association copies. 'It's to the biographer Donald Dickinson', was the answer. Not an association copy, but I was still very pleased: Dickinson, the biographer of bookman John Carter, is one of my favourite bibliophile writers.

Henri Schiller, a collector, after seeing the first catalogue de Hamel had worked on, told him: 'Mr. de Hamel, in one hundred years you will be sitting in heaven between the Bedford Master and the Boucicaut Master. Your name will be the Descriptions Master.'

'SHARPEN YOUR PENCIL'

H.P. KRAUS, MANUSCRIPT DEALER

The memoirs of rare book dealers have been some of my most favourite reading – indeed, I have preferred them to memoirs of collectors. Collectors immerse themselves in their subjects (their line or focus of collecting, that is) and frustratingly leave out details of their book transactions. Not so, fortunately, the dealers, who revel in how they acquired their stock, the negotiations, the prices paid, the collectors they served. Of the many modern memoirs of rare booksellers I have read, perhaps the most rousing is *A Rare Book Saga* by H.P. Kraus. If I have to rank the top six titles in the genre I would say after Kraus's account, I'd put Anthony Rota's *Books in the Blood: Memoirs of a Fourth Generation Bookseller*, David Magee's *Infinite Riches: Adventures of a Rare Book Dealer*, Leona Rostenberg and Madeleine Stern's *Old & Rare, Forty Years in the Book Business*, David Randall's *Dukedom Large Enough: Reminisces of a Rare Book Dealer* and Percy Muir's *Minding My Own Business, An Autobiography*. (And one honourable mention for an account that is not a memoir: *Rosenbach: A Biography* by John Fleming and Edwin Wolf.)

When Hans Kraus, a young rare bookseller from Europe, arrived in the United States in 1939, he was not known to the antiquarian trade. All he had carried with him was a suitcase full of his most precious stock, and a small amount of money. He would, in time, become a towering figure in the rare book trade, perhaps rivalled only by Bernard Quaritch, another giant of the trade, who had also left Germany for England. Kraus's inventory, almost at any given period of his bookshop's life, consisted of the most beautiful medieval illuminated manuscripts, and some remarkably rare incunabula. As a young bookseller in a new country, he was struggling until one day his fortunes changed. On an impulse he decided to pay a visit to a distinguished book collector, Lessing J. Rosenwald, packing his best books into the trunk of his car, and setting off with Hanni, his wife. Kraus felt sure Rosenwald would dismiss him, a nobody in the rare book business, having dealt with the top dealers in the world, but the wealthy collector welcomed him warmly. He left Hanni in the car, not wanting to give Rosenwald the impression that this was a social call. The dealer emptied his suitcase on to a table, and the collector began looking through them, with Kraus eagerly looking on. Rosenwald, notes Kraus, just had a smile on his face the whole time he was sorting – the bookseller saw the collector make two piles of the books, one bigger than the other. After a while, Kraus could not bear the suspense and asked which pile Rosenwald was considering buying.

The collector just carried on, this time re-examining the books. Finally, he pointed to the bigger pile and said,

'Figure out your price for these books. And sharpen your pencil!' He left the dealer alone, disappearing into the house. New to the language and the country, Kraus was puzzled by the 'pencil' remark, and only later figured out what the collector had meant: give me the best price you can. Rosenwald emerged from another part of the house, and asked for the price. Kraus took a deep breath and gave it to him: $4,500 (a huge sum in the '40s). Rosenwald silently walked out of the room, came back and handed him a cheque for the amount. This was the largest single sale Kraus had made since starting out as a rare bookseller. At the door, the dealer could not resist asking the collector about his reference to the phrase, 'sharpen your pencil'. Rosenwald laughed, and replied he had made more money by not knowing.

H.P. Kraus's account will serve as a sumptuously instructive and exciting panorama of high-stakes rare book dealing. He chronicles numerous rare book transactions in the book, many of them fabulous, highlighting his great successes as well as failures. We encounter other dealers and collectors, and the delicate, crafty negotiations that played out among them. He had courage and nerves of steel: at private sales and auctions, he paid enormously high prices to secure what he wanted without knowing who would buy them; he often did not have a committed buyer he was bidding for or even the prospect of interested clients he could then approach. He bought for stock, and very high-end material is seldom bought that way. Most dealers will drop out if the bid exceeds their set limit or the top price a client was willing to pay for it. Not Kraus. He didn't calculate how he'd do later on – whether he would be able to sell it at a decent profit or if he was going to be stuck with it for years – if he desired something, it went into his five-storeyed bookshop in Manhattan that had considerable staff and three manuscript experts. The firm of H.P. Kraus issued many excellently produced scholarly catalogues over the years, full of rarities and beauties. Two memorable auctions sales reveal Kraus's attitude as a dealer, his emotions, convictions, and technique. For sale at a London auction was one of the loveliest illuminated manuscripts produced in England: the *St. Albans Apocalypse* (a thirteenth-century manuscript). The English, Kraus points out, did not excel at frescoes or altar pieces, but were unsurpassed in manuscript painting and illumination – to have in your possession a manuscript written and illuminated by the monks of St. Albans Abbey was as good as owning a cathedral.

Kraus wanted it badly. William Glazier, a collector, called about it before Kraus left for London. He was interested in bidding for it – how much did Kraus think it would go for? £45,000, replied Kraus without hesitation. Glazier said Kraus could bid up to £32, 000 for him with 10 per cent added as the fee. The dealer agreed but was inwardly sceptical of this low bid; he had already estimated it would go higher. At the auction, Kraus was tense, nearly close to bursting, as he waited for the St. Albans lot to come up. Meanwhile, other manuscripts came and went, and Kraus bid and won many of them, and lost some, too. Finally, the moment arrived. And the bidding quickly crossed the £32,000 mark set by his client for the St.Albans manuscript. At one point it stood at £40,000 with Kraus as the highest bidder. There was finally a pause in bidding. Kraus felt he had won. But then in a low whisper from the room: £60,000. Raised by £20,000 – when that happens, it is done to finish any competition and intimidate the underbidder into giving up. Kraus shouted: £65,000! And it was over. Kraus had just paid the highest price ever paid for a book, translating to $182,000. He hurried out of the room and called Glazier, in all good faith, to offer it to him first (at what price Kraus does not reveal) but Glazier turned it down saying, 'too rich for my blood', which the dealer expected. On the other hand, Kraus was euphoric he had secured it. For now, he did not worry about when it would sell and who would buy it. It would remain in his keeping until then, for him to enjoy privately. Another famous manuscript on auction was the St. Blasien Psalter. Kraus was secretly willing to go up to £120,000 to get it, but told his wife, Hanni, he would stop at £40,000. The reason for this little dissembling was because the firm of H.P. Kraus now had many unsold manuscripts in the vault, but Kraus was still buying and paying high prices. Hanni was worried they would remain unsold. Even at £40,000, Hanni's first question was: 'Who would buy it from you?' K: 'I never think of that. The main thing is that I like it.' When that limit had been reached, Kraus continued bidding, competing with German buyers. Hanni kicked him three times under foot, but he went on. He had already gone much above the limit he had set for himself. At £62,000 it was his. As Hanni sighed with relief that it was over, he stayed to buy more at the auction, saying, 'Why rest on your laurels?' Hanni proved to be right. It sat with Kraus for 12 years before it sold to a German collector, for only 20 per cent more. When an expensive book sells many years after its purchase, it has to sell for at least twice or thrice more than the hammer price for a decent profit. He took a loss here. But Kraus emphasizes that he did not feel bad at all – such occasional losses is why he does not have to feel lousy about making a huge profit on something else. Besides, it had been his to enjoy for a dozen years.

One instance of the kind of sweet, high profit Kraus is referring to was possibly the day a lower-end dealer with no experience in selling manuscripts or rare books showed Kraus a manuscript for appraisal. Apparently, some customer had walked in with this manuscript wanting to know what it might be worth. Kraus was astonished looking at the item: it was one of the most beautiful Carolingian manuscripts he had seen, with many illuminated initials, and rare. The bookseller asked Kraus 'How much do you think it might be?' And the rare book dealer honestly answered: 'Many thousands of dollars,' but without putting an exact price on it. Kraus, now hot on the hunt, urged the bookseller to somehow keep the manuscript from going back to the client, instructing him to offer his customer whatever he wanted for it. When Kraus next visited him, the bookseller had successfully got the client to part with it. On the spot Kraus offered him $10,000, knowing full well that a small time dealer like this seldom saw such high profits. The seller, even though he may have suspected or felt it was worth much more, eagerly took the cheque, and gave Kraus the manuscript. For Kraus's part, he did not care what the bookseller paid the client to buy the book – he may have given him just $1,000, but what interests Kraus is what he could sell it for in turn. If the bookseller just made $9,000 more, he deserved it. Kraus was delighted with his coup, showing it off to colleagues and friends, and it soon got sold – and the price Kraus put on it and got? $175,000.

In 1959, Kraus wanted to lay his hands on a great collection from Merton, an English collector, rich in manuscripts and letters. But Bernard Breslauer, a famous manuscript dealer in London, beat him to it. Kraus accepted it, saying: 'Everyone cannot be everywhere' or 'You can't be everywhere at the same time.' A year later he had a chance to be in London, and invited Breslauer to dinner at the Ritz. The English dealer was still riding high from having swooped down on the collection. 'The catalogue is almost finished,' he told Kraus who then expressed a wish to see the books, hoping secretly to at least buy some of them from Breslauer. 'Of course, but let me warn you, nothing is for sale.' Kraus was surprised that after so many years of dealing with Breslauer, he would cut him out, and got up in some displeasure saying, 'If I want to see beautiful old books that I can't buy, I'll go to the British Museum.' The London dealer then insisted Kraus come with him, and after they had spent some time looking at the books, Breslauer signalled he was not averse to selling. (In fact, he had already sold some rare Anglo-Saxon manuscripts to Maggs, the bookshop, and the Robinsons – and Kraus the very next day went round there and promptly bought it off them!) Kraus realized Breslauer would not sell before some tedious bargaining had ensued, and finally Kraus left with some of the best things in the collection. Now, Kraus did not know what Breslauer paid for the books but he was more than willing to pay the prices Breslauer asked, fully realizing the London dealer was making a nice profit from it. After all, if *he* had been given the first offer or had been present at the auction, he could have had the books at lower prices, and could now have been in a position to *sell* them *to* Breslauer for a handsome profit. But this is how it works – we are accustomed to dealers selling to collectors, knowing they are making a nice profit from it, but booksellers buy from other booksellers, too, paying marked up prices. Kraus said he was not concerned what the other dealer had paid for it – he could have paid $10 or $10,000; what mattered to him is that he, Kraus, got it for the price he wanted to pay, and in turn sold it at the price that brought him his own profit from the deal.

The collector that Kraus respected and admired the most among his customers was Martin Bodmer, who was known in the rare book trade as the Prince of Bibliophiles. Shy, affectionate, and eminent, Bodmer applied his great wealth judiciously to collecting. Kraus goes as far as saying that Bodmer had gathered the finest rare book collection anyone could manage in one's lifetime. He had the one virtue most collector's lack: patience. 'He could say no and mean it.' That helped him to wait for the right copy, the right book, at the right price. Bodmer drove a hard bargain, and though rich, did not mind asking for a discount, pleading poverty. A classic example is Bodmer buying from Rosenbach *The Canterbury Tales* in a monastic binding for $46,000 when in the catalogue it was priced $85,000.

Another instance of Bodmer's discipline and focus experienced by Kraus was when he took a trip all the way to Geneva from New York, carrying the best things he had saved up to show his favourite customer. He had been invited to see Bodmer's collection and took this chance to sell some books that he felt sure Bodmer would want. The taxi dropped him off slightly away from the right address, and the dealer was left carrying a heavy valise full of books. On the way, as Kraus trudged along, he ran into another man also carrying a heavy book in a parcel. This turned out to be Bodmer. 'I must buy this book,' Bodmer told him; it had come from London on approval, and he had just collected it from the post office to examine it. Kraus asked him what the book was, but Bodmer would not say. Kraus said he had brought books to show him. Bodmer shook his head; said no, and explained. Because he had to buy this book, he was not going to buy anything else now. Kraus had to return to New York with his valise full of those heavy precious volumes. That was Bodmer: setting himself limits, and never being tempted to even take a look!

'Sometimes the best sales are those that don't materialize,' adds Kraus – something good came of the trip, after all: before departing, an idea flashed in Kraus's mind – he could not sell, but he could buy from Bodmer. Kraus asked him if he there was anything he wished to sell. The collector was not known to sell things out of his collection, but since he wanted money for this book in a large parcel, he agreed to look around and produced a small manuscript with exquisite miniatures as something he didn't mind letting go of. Kraus, fairly knowledgeable with manuscripts, could not identify it as anything important or valuable; it seemed average, except the miniatures seemed brilliant. A German hand. Bodmer wanted $23,000 for it. Kraus felt it was high for such an average manuscript, but paid it because he could not resist the fine illuminated miniatures in it. Besides, he felt the collector was pricing it higher so he could finance the book he was buying. When he brought it back, and had it examined by an expert, it turned out to be a notable manuscript, one of few signed by the Flemish illuminator, Simon Bening. Kraus was able to sell it for a considerable profit. Bodmer seemed to have missed seeing its significance. Lucky for Kraus, manuscripts were not Bodmer's field, books were. The reverse, too, happened. One time Kraus sold Bodmer a manuscript with superb illumination and miniatures for $12,000. Kraus turned a quick profit with it, having bought it casually in Milan for $3,000. Later, an art scholar published a monograph on it, pointing to the miniatures as being the work of a high Renaissance master. Kraus bitterly regretted selling it so quickly and for so little. It was the Michilino Book of Hours. However, he became determined to buy it back from Bodmer, and plotted ways to persuade Bodmer to sell it back to him. It was customary for Kraus to see Bodmer at least once a year to sell books, and each year from then on, Kraus would make offers for this Book of Hours, upping the offer every time, with

Bodmer turning it down always. It became an obsession with Kraus to get it back. At last, after 13 years, Bodmer sold it back to him for a fat profit. The whole affair had Kraus wondering why wealthy collectors such as Bodmer sell their books, the ones they coveted so much? After all, the money did not mean much to them, they could always buy what they wanted. Some reasons he hazards are: that their tastes change, or they become impulsive, or they just want to be validated in the eyes of their family and friends that they had bought well and demonstrate to them that they were not fools to pay so much. Kraus was able to sell this manuscript to the Morgan Library for an equally handsome profit.

But the greatest book Kraus bought from Bodmer was the *Luxembourg Psalter*, with its great miniatures, from the atelier of Jean Pucelle, the greatest miniature painter of the fourteenth century. Many years later, the time came for Bodmer to give up his collection, and this time he opened his library to Kraus to make purchases. Yet, when the time came to part with them, he protested at the things Kraus had picked out, saying 'you are denuding me, Kraus', to which Kraus replied, 'and you are succeeding in making me broke'. But in the end, Bodmer let Kraus take the books he wanted. Among these were the four Shakespeare folios and some quartos. Folios are moderately rare but could be got for a price, notes Kraus, but those fragile quartos were true rarities. Even second editions were rare; here was a first. Since the quartos were small, he decided to send them by airmail after carefully packing them, noting with pride that though he had not been doing any packing for the last 30 years, he had done a professional job. He insured them for $200,000. A fortnight later they had still not arrived in the US. Kraus looked at the postal slip – had he forgotten to ask the clerk at the Swiss post office to send it by airmail? If so, it would take several weeks to arrive and was vulnerable to mishaps. And then he noticed to further dismay, the insurance would cover only $50,000. If lost or damaged, it would be a huge loss to take. The kind of loss that would sink most booksellers. After a couple of months, Kraus gave up on them, feeling furious with himself. Then one afternoon when he was taking a nap, he was awoken by his staff on the phone to hear: 'They have arrived.' Who had arrived? He was not expecting any customers. 'The Shakespeares are here!' He ran down to the shop and kissed the books. After this, he almost did not want to sell them.

The next near-mishap had to do with the Constance Missal, then (incorrectly) thought to be a book printed before the Gutenberg Bible; nevertheless, it is a scarce and desirable incunabulum – only three copies were known to exist. Kraus heard that a monastery in Europe had a copy they wished to sell to raise money to build a hospital. Kraus flew there and after a protracted and tricky negotiation with the monks, secured it. But how to transport the book? Kraus and his associate decided they would not risk shipping it, and carried it with them, keeping it between the car seat, not wanting to lose sight of it. To celebrate, they had dinner and drinks and when they left, a waiter came running after them saying, 'Signor you left this.' It was the Constance Missal, wrapped in old newspaper. That night Kraus slept with it under his pillow.

Then there was one last transaction – or rather a non-transaction – where a wily, astute collector got the better of Kraus. Chester Beatty was known for his vast and splendid collection of beautiful manuscripts gathered from the west and the east (his collection of Persian manuscripts was unrivalled). Kraus had constantly made enquiries over the years if Beatty would sell the duplicates in his collection or perhaps things he did not want to keep anymore, but the collector didn't give him a single signal that he was open to selling. When he turned 80, the manuscript collector invited Kraus to visit him in Ireland. Even Kraus was agog looking at the collection, and after careful inspection picked 77 manuscripts offering £230,000 for the lot, plus he would make it £300,000 if he could take two other highly sought-after manuscripts, provided Beatty was willing to let them go.

'You give me great pleasure with these figures, Kraus,' said the collector at last. 'They are three times what I paid; I always thought I had paid too much. This pleases me indeed.'

Happy that the deal was concluded so quickly, Kraus asked when he could take the manuscripts.

'Oh, I'm not selling,' said Beatty, his expression changing.

Kraus was shocked.

'I am an old man, what could I do with the money?'

Kraus felt he had basically been brought all the way to give a free appraisal.

There are so many giants in the rare book trade, past and present, and Kraus had distinguished himself as a dealer in manuscripts of great beauty and rarity.

AFTERWORD

(Or What Happened at the End)

Quite fantastically, the most beautiful book in my possession is something I happened to entirely chance on. And not so surprisingly, it is also the most ruinously expensive book I've ever bought. It is a nineteenth century printed Book of Hours acquired at the 62nd New York Antiquarian Book Fair in April 2022 from a noted French manuscript dealer. I had had no intention of stopping by Ariane Adeline's booth, Livres Anciens, that April afternoon, and was rushing through the aisle to find another dealer when from the corner of my eye I caught sight of a book in her glass case; the display had the book opened to a beautiful full-page miniature in gold and colours. The little gallery lights had caught the gold nicely, and I was captivated.

I immediately asked to see it, and as I turned page after page, I found all ninety pages in it to be fully and highly illuminated – numerous decorations around the margins, several historiated initials, four half page miniatures and one full page miniature as a frontispiece done on gold grounds. The text had been printed letterpress, while the decorations and illustrations had been first engraved, then printed in black and white, and finally the colours and gold had been expertly filled in by hand. Now, I've seen numerous copies of such nineteenth century Book of Hours but they are mostly amateurish with gold paint for illumination, and the decorations confined mostly to the margins, with thickly applied colours.

What I was seeing here was something entirely different: for illumination actual gold leaf had been used, and the lovely historiated initials and miniatures had all been faithfully copied from actual illuminated manuscripts from the Bibliothèque Du Roi in Paris, and delicately hand-coloured. And the result is a modern Book of Hours that is as beautiful as a medieval illuminated manuscript.

In the few minutes or so that I had handled the book, I had also recognized whose work this was: Aline Guilbert, a popular illuminator who owned a workshop in Paris in the 1840s, that produced a series of hand-coloured, gilded Book of Hours. This one from 1843, *Livres d'Heures ou Offices de l'Eglise illustrés d'après les Manuscrits de la Bibliothèque du Roi,* had been her most successful, her great masterpiece. I already owned three Book of Hours from the hand of Mlle A. Guilbert (as she liked to call herself) and while they were all enchanting, this copy was special, one of a kind, sensitively hand-coloured and gilded by Aline herself for the family of Jean-François Champollion, the Egyptologist who deciphered the Rosetta Stone.

No expense had been sparred by Champollion who had

commissioned Guilbert to illuminate this Book of Hours as a wedding gift to his nephew, and the results show: burnished gold leaf, multiple colours masterfully filled in by hand, beautiful paper, and a fine, signed binding. In the market there are always three or four copies of the first (1843) and second (1872) edition of *Livres d'Heures ou Offices de l'Eglise Illustrés.* Most of the copies are usually hand-coloured, and there are a few without hand-colouring, left entirely in black and white. The hand-coloured and gilded copies of the first edition are pleasing, *but in none of them is the illumination in gold leaf*, while the colours are done in a heavy-handed way.

This copy with the Champollion provenance, with its lavish use of actual burnished gold leaf awash with hand-colouring, could only be the hand of Mlle A. Guilbert herself. This copy had been further personalized with two added manuscript pages – entirely hand lettered and decorated by the Champollion family's illustrator, Jules Feuquières; one of them is a charming ink drawing, highlighted in colour, with two hieroglyphic cartouches in honour of the two newly-weds, and a reference to the importance of Egyptian studies for the Champollion-Figeac family.

I asked Ariane, the dealer, for the price, bracing for the blow. While it did not break the four-figure ceiling I had set for myself, it came very close to breaching that barrier. I swallowed, and paid. I simply knew that I could never hope to see again a finer example of modern illumination than this exquisitely illumined copy.

I've outlined this purchase, this acquisition, with its

absolute beauty (and absolute price) because it provided an answer to something I had been wondering about in relation to my collecting: what next? I would make this major acquisition, this cornerstone in my collection of nineteenth century illumination, the last substantial acquisition. Henceforth, all purchases will be modest ones, acquired not for their beauty or rarity but for their utility and pleasure. Finding something that could not be topped came as a relief, because the next quarry would have to have been original medieval or renaissance illuminated manuscripts which, even at their cheapest, can be had only for something in the six or seven figure range. And I couldn't have gone there.

I had come to this rare book fair to mostly just look around, and perhaps make one alluring purchase: a little Persian manuscript from the late eighteenth century that I had had my eye on for several months. A Dutch antiquarian dealer had previously listed it in his stock for $950, but had dropped the price at the fair. The moment I touched the Persian, the owner was by my side in a flash: 'Shall I tell you what I paid for it?' he asked. And seeing how uncertain I looked, added: 'And you can have it for that price. No profit for me.' I nodded. 'I paid 600 euros for it at an auction, and I can let it go for that. I just want to be rid of it.'

Since he was in such a deal-making mood, I felt encouraged and offered to take it off his hands right away for €500. He hesitated perhaps for a second or two, and said, 'It's yours. I'm finished with it.' And thrust it into my hands. I was elated. I had studied it for long, while it had sat in his stock, with several photos of the manuscript displayed on his website. It had five hand-painted miniatures, with several pages of calligraphic script in gold ink.

I didn't expect to make a better find than this Persian treasure, and was headed towards the fair's exit, cutting across aisles, when I chanced on the Aline Guilbert Book of Hours. (On a more personal level, the biggest highlight at the fair for me were not the purchases – as satisfactory as they were – but it was finally having an opportunity to meet a bibliophile hero of mine: the scholar and bookdealer Sandra Hindman at her 'Les Enluminures' booth. Ms Hindman is the finest dealer of illuminated manuscripts today, and I have long been a fan of her work in this area. She was kind enough to sign one of her books to me with a warm and generous inscription that filled me with delight: '*For Pradeep: who loves medieval manuscripts too! (like I do).*' Sandra Hindman.)

Being transfixed with the Guilbert-Champollion Livre d'Heures and resolving, in spite of its price, to buy it then and there gave me another kind of pleasure, too: the realization that I did, after all, possess a sense of the '*fingerspitzengefühl*', which is a kind of bibliophilic ESP (extra sensory perception). Literally it means 'finger tips feeling', but in the rare book world *fingerspitzengefühl* is, as antiquarian dealer Leona Rostenberger characterized it, 'a tingling of the fingertips becomes an electrical current of suspense, excitement, recognition... Whenever or wherever it occurs, it is an experience that makes the rare book business a hymn to joy.'

In other words, a sixth sense for rare and fine books, the eye for that rarity that counts, the instinct to know with just a glance or a brief examination that the book in your hand, this particular copy you are handling, is important or special. What you do with it and how you act on it, is secondary. You may walk away from it or tell another collector about it, or – if you know what's good for you – you'll quickly negotiate a purchase. I've had *fingerspitzengefühl* happen to me several times in the course of collecting but more often spotting a sleeper or a hidden rarity online than in person! And knowing instinctively from my collecting experience that the copy I was looking at was eminently collectable, eminently gettable. Typically, we are talking about a copy or edition that is not listed or described in a bibliography but something unknown, some special attribute in this copy that sets it apart. In the case of this Book of Hours, even without knowing its provenance – that it was a copy illuminated for an illustrious French family by a renowned illuminator – I knew I was looking at something extraordinary where nineteenth century colour and illumination were concerned.

Many rare book dealers rely on this developed instinct, the *fingerspitzengefühl*, to make their finds. The instincts of collectors are similarly honed, and this is one of the rewards of collecting in depth. It's not so much about recognizing a book you've just run into as being extraordinary but knowing *how* extraordinary. Because I had seen numerous examples of nineteenth century illumination, I could quickly recognize that this copy at the fair was unlike anything else in its field, enabling me to see why the high asking price was fair, accurate, fitting.

There's an element of mystery to *fingerspitzengefühl* as well: one could even say it is about the book finding *you*, and not the other way around! In an antiquarian book fair with thousands of rare and beautiful books it is not hard for me to believe that I was led to this book.

Acquiring this exquisite Book of Hours also made up for the loss of not having won that other beautiful nineteenth century Book of Hours at Ader auctions, *Recueil de Prières*, just the year before (referenced in the chapter 'Illuminated in Gold and Colours') I had not expected to see another work of modern illumination in that class, but while *Livres d'Heures ou Offices de l'Eglise illustrés* may not surpass *Recueil de Prières*, it is a sumptuous replacement. Which is why collectors should cultivate patience (a lesson I am still learning) and put their faith in the rare book market.

You remember that rarity I spoke of at the beginning – the deluxe issue on Imperial Japan paper of *Gossip About Book Collecting*? And how I finally found a copy of this scarce edition (one of only 29 copies) after years of looking – well, just a few months after that, another copy in even finer condition of the Japan paper issue came on the market for an even fairer price! Well, the rare book market giveth and taketh away and giveth again, that's how it has always been; but in the grip of pursuit, lost in the rare book chase, collectors sometimes forget how the market is always looping, replenishing, offering, beckoning.

You may recall how I had earlier bemoaned my bad luck at never being able to locate and acquire a medieval manuscript leaf with an illuminated historiated initial in my price range? I was frequently the underbidder at several auctions for a lot containing a leaf with a historiated initial. Then in May 2022, I had unexpected luck. While leisurely browsing on *via*Libri for an underpriced historiated initial that was also illuminated (there are countless historiated initials in manuscripts and books that are in sepia or only hand-coloured but not gilded), it occurred to me that all my keyword searches had been in English – what if I entered the same keyword searches (historiated, hand-illuminated, etc.) in French German, and Italian?

While I had no immediate success, I did come across one exciting entry after I had scrolled through several pages of listings: buried in layers of AbeBooks listings was an antiphonary leaf from an Italian choir book from 1490 containing a large historiated initial that seemed to be on sale from the famous German auction house, Ketterer Kunst. The one photo posted of the leaf showed an attractive initial done in blue, pink and white on gold grounds. It looked like the listing had been languishing there for a while, and it was entirely possible that it had already sold, especially considering how reasonably priced it was – $800 – when it should have been at least twice that.

Too impatient and excited to email Ketterer Kunst, I phoned their auction house in Hamburg, and was informed that the leaf was still available. It had not sold at a previous auction, the lot having been passed on, and it was – unusually – one of those leaves they had decided to sell than bring it up for auction again. After they sent me additional photos of the leaf, I could see why it had been passed on: the face of the divine figure inside had been slightly rubbed and some of the leafy decoration in the scroll work extending out of the initial was again rubbed off.

But it was still a splendid example, a 19 x 14 inches vellum leaf with a historiated initial of four inches in burnished gold with its marginal decoration of acanthus leaves still bright and arresting. And thanks to its little flaws, I could afford it. It's not uncommon for manuscript leaves as old as this to have faces slightly rubbed away – they say that this may have been the result of its medieval users or owners repeatedly kissing the figures of saints, angels and gods in devotion.

I didn't dare ask anyone at the auction house why it had been priced so absurdly low just in case they suddenly felt inclined to raise it – this genuine fifteenth century leaf with a large historiated initial on gold grounds was a fabulous find. Good old-fashioned collector's luck? I guess I'll never really know. But this is what I mean when I say the market is always beckoning, teasing and seducing.

I'd said at the beginning how I had been a happy bibliophile simply content to just keep reading, sceptical as I was that book collecting would appeal to me. Then I saw my first fine press book, and though it cost more than anything I dreamed a book could cost, I wanted to possess it desperately. And then I was off, chasing them. This happened again when I saw an illuminated manuscript leaf for sale. I felt a sharp desire to own it, so that I could spend more time with it, to lose myself again and again in its shimmering beauty. I finally understood then that there is in the world a class of books and manuscripts that you can do more with than just read them; you can pursue them because they are elusive, you can draw them closer to yourself, you can revel in their craftmanship, and you can have a deeper physical, bibliographical engagement with them.

Looking back, I'm so glad I took the plunge and threw myself into collecting; and to everyone who loves and cares for books, I want to say – don't miss out on the many layered, intoxicating pleasures of book collecting. It is, as I discovered, the next level in a bibliophile's relationship to books. The intimacy you experience with books when you go from being a bibliophile to a book collector is heady and gratifying.

The book collecting game is not just afoot, it's at your fingertips – online! What are you waiting for? The lure of the rare book hunt, the thrill of the chase, the irrepressible glee of bargain finds, the satisfaction of acquisition, the joy of possession and the scholarly rewards of bibliographical connoisseurship, all beckon.

ACKNOWLEDGEMENTS

My gratitude and thanks to Judith Kavin Howard and Kater Crafts Bookbinders for graciously giving me permission to reproduce an illustration from the miniature book *You Can Judge A Book By Its Cover*: the wood engraving of 'A Happy Collector' by John DePol, which adorns the cover of this memoir. My sincere thanks also to fine press printer Robert LoMascolo for printing the letterpress keepsake that accompanies the special edition of this book.

My thanks also to the printers, booksellers, fellow collectors and bibliophiles who have been generous with their time and support. In particular, I wish to thank Rollin Milroy, Jerry Kelly, Jason Dewinetz, Bill Woodbridge, Frederic Shearer, Phil Bishop, Tim Hawley, Nick Basbanes, Bibi Mohamed, James Fergusson, the late Jerry Morris (who is missed), Krishna Gowda, V.R. Ferose, and Suresh Menon.

At Hachette India, my deepest thanks to Thomas Abraham, Poulomi Chatterjee, Sonali Jindal, Priya Singh, Parul Sharma, and everyone at the publishing house, along with Shiny Das, who not only made this book possible but turned it into such a fine edition. Much thanks especially to Bhavi Mehta for the beautiful bibliophile cover.

Lastly, I am ever so grateful to all those collectors, dealers, auctioneers, and bibliophile-writers from the past and the present who wrote – and continue to write and talk – about the rare book world, be it a memoir or a biography or a podcast. They have supplied me – and every collector for whom such things constitute some of their favourite reading – with hours and hours of bibliophilic pleasure, instruction and delight.

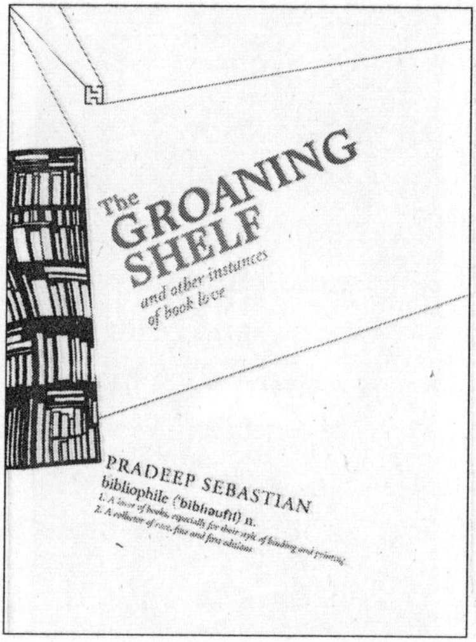

The Groaning Shelf and Other Instances of Book Love

1. A lover of books.
2. A collector of books.

Notes from a bibliophile on the romance of book collecting, the beauty of dust jackets, the lure of rare and first editions, the thrill of browsing in second-hand bookshops, the bibliomania of book thieves, movies about books, the inner life of a reader, and of course, favourites.

The delightful genre of Books About Books which looks at the book as physical object, as a crafted work of art where its bibliographical aspects – binding, typography, edition, condition, rarity – matter as much as the literary content inside, has seldom been explored in Indian writing with the cultic devotion displayed over these little essays that capture the drama of bookish obsession, the joys and snares of the bookish life, and the gentle madness that is book love.

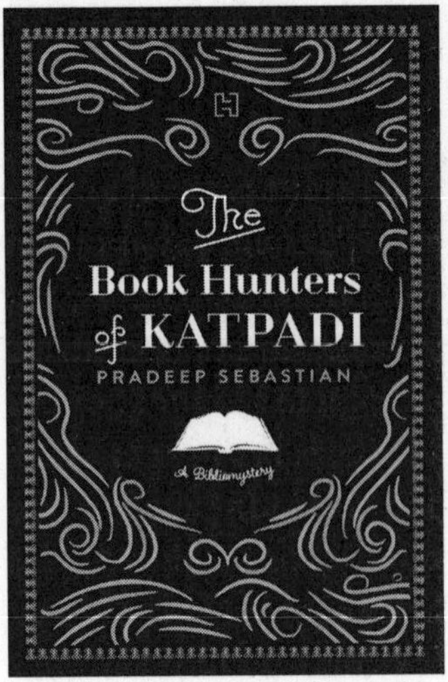

The Book Hunters of Katpadi: A Bibliomystery

Neelambari Adigal and her young associate, Kayal, together run Biblio, a one-of-a-kind store of rare books in Chennai, specializing in modern Indian first editions. The lives of these passionate bookwomen revolve around curious browsers, eccentric book collectors, private-press printers and the occasional thrill of unexpected discoveries of the antiquarian kind.

On a book-collecting trip to Ooty, Kayal stumbles upon an incendiary manuscript, long thought to be a myth, purportedly authored by explorer and translator Sir Richard Francis Burton. Almost simultaneously, a cache of priceless editions that looks like it could be from the 300-year-old library of one of the greatest book collectors the world has ever known, turns up at the bookshop. When it falls upon the two women to authenticate their finds, Neela and Kayal discover, quite suddenly, that their lives are more full of bibliographic intrigue than they could ever have imagined.

India's first-ever bibliomystery, *The Book Hunters of Katpadi* is the book every lover of the written word has been waiting for. In the tradition of the greatest in the genre, it holds within its pages adventure, action, suspense – and the sheer thrill of close encounters with prized print-on-paper.